WHERE *the* RIVER FLOWS

WHERE *the* RIVER FLOWS

A MEMOIR

rachel havekost

dedication

for us, and the river we braved together.
I'm happy to have gotten wet with you.

disclaimer + content warnings.

Darling Reader,

This book contains explicit content, including mention of suicide, self-harm, Eating Disorders, sexual assault, death, and developmental trauma.

There will not be trigger warnings throughout the book, so I invite you to take the words slowly and honor your feelings and body as you move through its pages. Take your time, drink water, and rest.

Names, dates, dialogue, and other details of this book have been modified to honor anonymity. Remember, this is a memoir—the nature of its writing is that it is remembered, and like all stories, it is not universal as it is not written in anything but our minds the moment it occurs. I have done my best to recall the truths as I once lived them, knowing that all our memories are colored by our unique senses, feelings, and context that delicately weave each moment together and make a memory.

I, Rachel Havekost, the author of this book, am not nor do I claim to be a licensed medical health professional. This book is not intended to serve as a how-to, roadmap, guidebook, or instruction manual for healing or recovery. Its sole function is to put language to my experiences in hopes of building honest, thought-provoking conversation around topics that are often branded taboo, shameful, or stigmatized.

You are not alone.

hotlines.

If you are having suicidal thoughts, seeking crisis support, or need a safe place to talk, please use any of the immediate resources below. It's ok and beautiful to ask for help, and you deserve support.

I have included some book recommendations at the end of this book if you are interested in learning more about mental health.

National Suicide Hotline: 1-800-273-8255
The Trevor Project: 1-866-488-7386.
Trans Lifeline: 877-565-8860
GLBT National Hotline: 888-843-4564
National Coalition of Anti-Violence Programs: 212-714-1141 (English and Spanish)
GLBT National Youth Talkline: 800-246-7743
DeHQ: LGBTQ Helpline for South Asians: 908-367-3374
Crisis Textline: text "HOME" to 741741
Online Crisis Chat: https://suicidepreventionlifeline.org/chat/

(list last updated May 15,2021)

a musical note to reader

An invitation (should you choose to accept it):

I have made a playlist:
"Where the River Flows,"
on Spotify
of songs I loved
and music I listened to

the very words
and melodies
that held me in the moments you're about to read.
ordered and numbered to flow from the beginning of chapter one,
to the last words in this book.

So maybe, if you can and wish to float alongside me
with these little love notes of song,

you'll find yourself in the pages
and you'll hear me in the music
so we can meet somewhere in the middle

while we float
while we flow.

Pausing the music as you rest your eyes
and picking up with me where you left off
until we find the end
together.

table of contents

prologue

When I started writing this book, I wanted it to be important. I wanted it to have meaning. I wanted it to accurately represent the truth I held in my heart the day I started writing.

And with each passing day that I wrote, I learned something new, and suddenly the words I'd written days before meant nothing.

I started over and over again, hoping each time I would have the final wisdom I sought to fill in its pages.

In February of 2021, I spent four days straight in bed. I couldn't stop crying. I hyperventilated during most cries. I clenched my fists. I fell to the floor. I clutched my belly. I choked. I felt my chest turn cold. And I wept. I wept and I wept.

And when I came to, I realized how despite the immense growth I have witnessed in myself—not just this year, but over the course of the last decade in therapy and service to mental health advocacy—that I am still the same insecure thirteen-year-old girl, fearing loneliness, starving to be seen, accepted, and loved.

I still know nothing.

And so, I share this book with you, not because it holds the wisdom or lessons that might heal you. Not because it carries the cure for what hurts you or hurts inside of you.

I share this book with you, because it is how I continue to show up for my life. It is how I stay courageous and loud in the face of my self-doubt and fear. It is how I wade deeper into the river of my life and flow.

I hope you will wade with me, here in the water. I hope you will dip your toes in the cold, frosty wetness. I hope you will let yourself stop fighting the current and come with me to the place where we know nothing together.

Where the river flows.

*if you are floating alongside,
you may now press, "play."*

part one
flooding.

I thought
if I wore my guilt on my sleeve
like they told me to do
with my heart

you'd see
how sorry
I was.

I didn't know
you just wanted
my heart.

one.

FORK IN THE RIVER

"I think we're moving on separate tracks," he said.

I was two glasses into my nightly bottle of Sauvignon Blanc, so my courage to speak my mind was open.

"You *think* we're going on separate tracks, or you *want* to go on separate tracks?" I challenged him.

"I want to."

"Are you saying you want a divorce?"

His vagueness irritated me. *Just come out and say it.* I thought. *Don't make me do it. Don't draw this out any longer. Say it.*

I wanted him to say yes. I wanted the endless crying and confusion and nights apart to end. I wanted a clear answer so I could move on in

1

some direction—any direction—and find relief from the torment of not knowing if I'd still be married to my husband in the coming weeks.

We'd been living in the not-knowing for months. Questioning our marriage, re-hashing our relationship, attempting to be decisive yet open to the possibilities of the future.

After months of therapy and trial separations, we found ourselves living in my brother-in-law's basement in the mountains of Central Washington.

We had been staying there for almost a month—a halfway-home as we navigated the recent COVID-19 outbreak, our lack of income, lack of housing, and of course, the ever-present elephant in the room: our marriage.

In the first week of May, the deadline for us to leave his brother's home was upon us: they had renters coming that weekend and we needed to figure out where we were going to live. We were running out of time—in more ways than one.

We were struggling to agree on where to live. Josh had an RV, and while he would have been perfectly fine living there, I couldn't see how an even smaller space would support us in the rekindling of our marriage. I think we spent more time that month arguing about what state to live in than we did about our love for each other. The real fear of not having a home or work became our priority, and our ability to focus on our actual relationship was stifled.

We bounced around the possibility that maybe we wouldn't live together—that perhaps the real trajectory we were heading down was towards divorce (though neither of us uttered that word).

We talked honestly—and carefully—about living together *not* as partners, living together *as* partners, and living apart. The conversation turned into an assignment, and on the morning of May 8 (I'll never forget the date), we drew out tables and charts complete with a legend and color-coordinated boxes. We reviewed all our options privately, rating the future of our marriage with colored markers.

When we presented our findings and unique charts to one another, I looked down at my journal and laughed.

"What?" Josh asked.

"I just can't believe this is what we're doing. We're making a chart to decide if we should stay married or not. How did we get here?"

He buried his head in his hands, the way he had countless times in the months before, and wept.

I wanted to cry, but I couldn't. I'd never seen Josh cry or feel so much as he did that winter, and every fiber of my being felt responsible for his hurt. My instinct then, as it always was when it came to his heart, was to take care of him. We did this well for each other—taking care. When I hurt, Josh's world stopped. And when he hurt, so did mine. We found ourselves this way so much and so well, that oftentimes we forgot ourselves in the caretaking.

For years, Josh took care of us. While I retreated into my dark places and became a shell of myself, he carved out a place in his heart to create space for mine so that we both could survive.

And now that he was hurting so gravely, and at the hands of my own doing, I felt it was my turn. As he held his head in his palms in tears the way he had so many times in the months before, I took care of us. I hollowed inside, leaving any semblance of emotion outside of my body, and I automated my words to sound helpful and good.

"It's gonna to be ok. We'll get through this. It's gonna to be ok."

And as he sobbed, I sat in silence. Not letting myself feel an ounce of the hurt that wanted to flood me. Not feeling the mourning and grief that would pour over me, flooding my body with doubt, anger, and despair in the year to come. Hoping, in my hurt and childlike way, that if I was good enough in this moment, I could protect us both from the pain that was coming.

Josh asked for some time alone that afternoon. I gave him the space, and as soon as it felt appropriate, I started drinking.

As the day turned into night, we found ourselves back in the living room, our charts and markers still sprawled on the coffee table where we'd left them.

I sat curled across from him in an old tweed armchair. The night was coming, and only a little remaining daylight crept in through the small windows. A vintage lamp in the corner of the room dimly lit the space, coloring everything with a sickly yellow. Josh sat across from me on the plaid couch: his legs open, hands and fingers facing one another— maybe even touching like he was in thought—I'm not sure.

I looked at him sternly, but with desperation. *Please just tell me the truth.* I thought.

"Are you saying you want a divorce?" I repeated.

He paused—long enough for me to feel the empty space and dissonance in his throat, not long enough for me to take back the question I so regretted asking.

He didn't look at me when he answered. I sensed his shame, and in many ways, his own disbelief at what came out when he opened his mouth.

"Yes."

This moment—this pause that came between his "yes," and my reply—was eternal.

I didn't move from my chair. I was shocked, but not surprised. As the pieces of what his "yes" meant formed together to make a complete image in my mind, I used every tool in my arsenal to keep myself grounded in the present moment.

"Ok," I said. "Ok. We can do this. We'll get through this. Ok."

I repeated this through bursts of tears. I would weep, then recover rapidly with words of encouragement.

"We'll get through this," I nodded vigorously. "We can do this."

"I used to think feeling sad meant I was making the wrong decision," he said. "I know I'm not making the wrong decision, but it still feels really sad."

4

"It's ok, we can do this," I repeated.

I clutched my wine glass, scanning the carpet, as if looking for some sign written in the fibers. I rocked back and forth in my chair, repeating the words "we can do this," hoping that maybe I might start to believe them too.

I felt my body stiffen. My heart doing all it could to soften. I couldn't let this be a moment where we turned away from each other—I had to keep us in compassion, even in this wreckage—I had to keep us safe.

We sat there, across from each other like this, for several minutes. My body frozen, my feelings dangling above me and bubbling below me, and the forced encouragement looping in the background.

We didn't process more after this. He asked me if I wanted him to sleep in the RV that night, and I said yes.

When he left the basement, I fell to the carpet I once scanned, as if I'd marked a spot as my landing ground. As if I'd needed to know the earth would be there when I'd inevitably fall.

I smacked the ground with my palms. Kneeling on the carpet, I curled my fingers into the fibers and wailed.

Just as quickly as the sobbing came, it went. I was in shock, and I knew from experience that there was nothing I could do to prevent the denial and fury that would soon come.

I sat there, on the floor, face covered in snot and tears, and I wondered what I was supposed to do next.

What the fuck am I supposed to do now?

I couldn't call anyone. Who would I call, and what would I say? *My husband just asked me for a divorce, without really asking?*

I wasn't even sure it was real. *Was he sure? Was this it? Did I corner him?* How could I possibly tell someone what was happening when I didn't fully understand it myself? Was this really *the* conversation? The last and final one? The one where he really means it, and I really let him?

I poured myself more wine. I put peanut M&Ms and a plain, untoasted piece of bread in a bowl, laughing through my tears at how quickly my Eating Disorder swept in to "take care" of me.

I finally moved my way to the bed—the bed where we once lay our heads together at night, falling asleep hoping the next day would be better. The bed where just the night before, we'd fallen asleep and said, "I love you," before clicking out the lights.

As I drifted off to sleep, it crossed my mind that it would be the first of many nights that I'd sleep alone. That I would likely never share a bed with my husband ever again. That the last time we would ever kiss had already passed without either of us knowing it.

In an instant, the way we once were was ripped away. Like a small and inconceivable death, we were no longer us.

He was gone, and so were we.

two.

FERRIES

I spent the next two weeks drunk, binge-eating, and imagining myself dead.

Just a few days after what I now call "That Day in May," I packed up what I owned and moved into an Airbnb, alone.

With COVID still being a brand-new disease, travel was restricted, and most hotels and Airbnb's were temporarily shut down. In "normal" circumstances (what even is a normal circumstance with divorce?) I would have gone straight to live with one of my parents (who were divorced and lived on the other side of the state), but with so many still unknowns about COVID and its transmission, it seemed too risky.

The Airbnb we found was just a mile down the road from his brother's. I rented it out for a month, which I hoped would give me

7

enough time to figure out what I was going to do, where I would live, and how I would put the puzzle pieces of my life together.

Josh helped me move my things into the condo, which reminded me of a 2005 Ikea display room. Once my bags were all inside, he stood, awkwardly, tentatively, and sadly at the doorway. He patted his legs and reached out his arms as if to say, *this is normally when I hug or kiss you goodbye, but I can't do that anymore.* Then he said, "Bye Rach," and started to cry. "If you need anything, you can call me, ok?" He ran his hands through his hair and turned to face the door.

"I don't think I should call you while I cope with this," I blurted, fighting back the flood I felt coming.

It wasn't what I wanted. But I knew that if I let him *soothe* me for the *loss* of him, I would never let him go.

He cried. I cried. Him standing in the doorway, me footsteps away by the couch, crying together but apart, and feeling the empty space between us like a dangerous river of lava, daring us to cross and test its bubbling toxicity.

We danced around the painful end, trying to be kind, trying to be careful, and trying to say goodbye without really saying goodbye.

We hugged, sort of.

Suddenly, we no longer knew how to touch each other. After ten years of knowing better than anyone how to touch and be touched, of holding and caressing, of kissing and enveloping ourselves into one another's arms and bodies, our fingertips became foreign, and our bodies knew nothing of how to be in contact.

I stood in the living room and watched him leave. His face red and eyes flooded. He stumbled out of the door, halfway stopping to look back and say goodbye, halfway paralyzed with how to do it without hurting me—without hurting him, without hurting us.

"Bye Rach, call me if you need a ride to the grocery store, or something."

"Ok."

The moment the door shut behind him, I wailed. I was certain he could hear me, but I didn't care. I paced the room, unable to stop myself from what I can only describe as burning from the inside out. I extended my arms out to my sides, not knowing what was going on in my body or outside of it, but unable to stop it from happening.

I ran to the window and pressed my hands against the glass like a five-year-old. I could see his RV still parked in the lot. I wanted to watch him go, as if to torture myself somehow. As if I was some helpless girl in a dramatic film. As if by playing out this role, I could hold on to the fantasy that in the end, he comes running back up the stairwell, and we are together again.

The RV rumbled. I watched the exhaust pipe smoke and the taillights turn on. It sat there for minutes, running but not moving, and I knew that meant he was sitting at the wheel, his head in his hands, wailing too. Maybe I was wrong. But I knew him and I knew us and I knew this movie scene too well—*our* movie scene—the one we'd played in other versions and other ways over the months as we unraveled, and our mutual sorrow almost stung more than the ending of our love.

When he finally drove away, I crumbled again. This time inward, this time into a small little ball on the floor—or on the couch, or under the kitchen table. I don't know. I can't remember.

How could I cut a cord so tethered, a love so embedded? How could someone, who days ago would walk in and out of rooms as my husband, now walk out of this room as not my husband? As not my lover? As simply someone I once knew?

And who would *he* be now, to me, now that he wasn't *Josh?* Now that he wasn't tethered to me, and I to him? And who would I be?

I couldn't wrap my head around what was happening. It was if I'd been pushed backwards into a rushing river, and without any knowledge of where I was going or why, I had to somehow build a boat beneath my body or I would drown.

While scrambling to find the pieces for my vessel, I tried to make sense of why I was pushed—or how I fell—and if the bank I'd been thrown from was really as bad as it seemed.

I thought if I could *make sense* of everything—if I could *understand* the problem—then I could accept the solution. That if I knew *why*, then the outcome would make sense and I could make peace with it. *Sense-making*, I later called it, was how my mind coped with the not-knowing, and how I kept myself out of acceptance and in resistance for so many months.

I scoured through everything I knew about relationships, psychology, communication, intimacy, and love. I questioned if our entire relationship was real or if I'd simply imagined it.

Had I been blind all this time? Was the person he was now the real him, and I'd just been with some stranger for ten years? Or was it me who changed? I had no idea.

I felt like I knew nothing anymore. Like everything I'd ever learned didn't matter, because it didn't work. We weren't going to be together. *So what was it for?*

What were the painful therapy sessions and arguments and tears for? So we could eventually leave each other? Is that what we did it for? For aloneness? For independence and "freedom"? Is that what we both craved?

My anger seethed and boiled beneath my skin, but I didn't recognize it. I had no idea that the incessant sense-making was a way for me to fill in the empty spaces between my rage and the uncertainty: a paint-by-numbers of the anger I felt so viscerally but was clueless to cope with.

I hoped that I could find answers so that I wouldn't have to feel angry.

If I could understand *why*, I wouldn't have to hate the person I'd loved for so many years.

If I could understand *why*, I wouldn't have to hate myself for the destruction I'd caused.

If I could understand *why*, I could leave the marriage with grace, gratitude, and understanding. I could make a quiet exit, a silent goodbye, and like all the other times in my life, stay as nice, kind, and small as possible.

When I couldn't answer the relentless "whys" and my inability to express any shred of anger towards Josh turned into more shut-downs and blackouts on the Airbnb couch, I took the anger and directed it in the only way I knew how: inward.

The sense-making had turned me away from the world and inside of myself, where the only answers I came up with for "why" and "how" and "what" were: *because of me, because I am worthless, and because I am mentally unstable.*

I wrote hate letters to myself in my diary. I stared at myself in the mirror and slapped my face for the first time in years. I called myself an idiot, and repeated "I want to die" many times. I lay in bed crying with a pillow over my face, hoping it would smother me.

I didn't want to wake up in the mornings. I wanted to sleep until… until nothingness.

I was so angry. I wanted to wash it away. Drink it away. Eat it away. Wash it away. Sleep it away. Numb it. Kill it. I hated the reality I was in and I didn't want it to be mine. I wanted it to go away before it was real. Before I had to accept it.

After two weeks of being in the Airbnb and a deep slide into a depression so severe that I grew fearful of my own thoughts, I asked my mom if I could stay with her until my eventual move to Los Angeles. I'd decided to go somewhere brand new—somewhere warm, somewhere where nobody knew me and I knew nobody, so I could at least feel free from the constant reminders of *him* in the smell of a pine tree or the cold, salty Pacific North West air.

Within a few days, I packed up my belongings, and with Josh's help, made the seven-hour drive from the mountains of Central Washington to the cluster of San Juan Islands off the coast of the North Western part of the state. We still had some boxes at his parents' home, which was on a neighboring island to where my mom lived, so we agreed he would drop me at the ferry dock, head to his parent's house, collect whatever I might need for…I guess my life, and meet up one last time before we said a final goodbye.

One night after dinner, my mom and I took a walk together on the empty island road. As the sun set behind the evergreen trees and the air grew cold and moist, I tried to explain to her (and I suppose, myself) how or why Josh and I had gotten here.

She couldn't make sense of it—the same way I couldn't, the same way he couldn't, the same way I imagined our friends and family wouldn't when we eventually told them.

We loved each other so much—so how come we were getting a divorce? What could have possibly gone wrong?

There was no concrete event, no singular point of suffering, no lack of love or care, no apparent trauma or gradual growing apart.

Only sudden misunderstanding, gut-wrenching gridlock, and a love strong enough to keep us trying.

"We spent so much time talking *about* our relationship that we weren't actually *relating* anymore," I told her.

She stopped mid-walk and looked at me, as if she understood for the first time what it must have been like for us to be in our relationship.

"I guess I always just saw you two as being so good at communicating, and you guys always talked about how much you worked on that kind of stuff."

"We were," I said. "And we did. That isn't untrue. But I think we became so focused on keeping our relationship alive that we weren't just letting it live."

She sighed, a heavy sigh that my mother made when she understood logically, but really couldn't understand in her heart.

For the first time, I felt myself in her sigh, and we related. She didn't try to fix or change anything in the silence as we walked back home, and

I didn't try to prove to her that I had done the right thing. We both knew, quietly, that this was something I would wrestle with for years to come, and neither of us had the wisdom or tools to prepare for it.

A few days later, Josh and I met one last time to exchange our few boxes and say our last goodbyes before I moved to California.

We met at the ferry dock that joined the two islands we were staying on—literal and figurative safe homes separated by a body of water that we once looked out on together from our own home, and one that now represented road trips and family vacations we would never have again.

He picked me up at the dock, and we drove to a park nearby that had a nice walking trail. Ironically, the park was dedicated to his great-great uncle, and there was a statue that had been left in his honor. We walked the loop and found the statue, where his name—our name—was carved into the stony structure. I took a picture. I'm not sure why. It was my name too, but it wasn't my family anymore. What memory would this photo hold?

We laughed and played on the trail, trying to make the most of the time. What else were we to do? There was nothing left to talk about.

There were moments I thought Josh was second-guessing his decision. The day before we met at the ferry dock, we video chatted to go through the boxes at his parent's house so he'd know what to bring for me. He pulled out old letters and my childhood photos and held them to the camera, and with his hands to his face to cover his tears, asked, "Do you want these, Rach?" As I bubbled inside, seeing my husband-not-husband cry over photos of little me, I said, "No, Josh, it's ok, we can do those another time."

"I'm sorry Rach. I'm trying, I really am."

How could he be so sad, yet so sure?

We finished our loop around the park in time to catch my ferry back.

He walked me to the ferry-dock building, and because of COVID, it was completely empty. We hugged and cried for a while. It felt like an hour passed, but it didn't feel long enough.

I tried to be good. I tried to believe it was real. I tried to make sure I said everything I wanted, and to say it with courage, gratitude, and love.

"I'm so sad and so sorry that this is where we ended up. But I'm so grateful to have spent so many good years with you and to have you as a partner. You are such a good man, and I learned so much from you. I care about you so much, and I really want you to be happy."

He started to cry harder. I think I probably did too. We sat there, unmarried but married, in love but out of love. Waiting for the ferry to carry me away. As I watched it approach, I felt panic rise in my belly. This was it—this was our sinking, this was the final moment, the end, the death and true goodbye. This is where we take our last breaths together. As the ferry came closer, I inhaled our last moments as husband and wife.

"Last call for walk on passengers heading to Lopez Island."

We stood up and had one final hug, sobbing as we did. His jacket smothered in my snot, my hair dampened by his tears, we melted into each other one last time, cradling our sorries and holding our whole world together for one last moment.

I watched him walk away, like I'd always done. I watched him go, waiting for him to turn back at the exit, like he'd always done. Savoring every last second of him, *with* him, and him of me, with me. Like we'd always done. As he approached the exit door, he turned around and gave me one final wave. His face wrought with sadness, guilt, and grief. I waved back, choking under my mask, and did my best to show him I would be alright.

I cried the whole way up the ferry ramp, and I didn't care who noticed. When I found a seat on the boat, I grew numb. I think I'd felt all my feelings. Or I couldn't feel them anymore. I'm not sure. But I put my whole body and heart on pause and left them there in the ferry terminal. I couldn't bear to bring the hurt any further. I wanted to make it go away—the hurt. I wanted to change the outcome. I wanted to choose a new ending. I wanted to eradicate the grief that I knew lay

14

before me. I hoped that maybe, if I found some way to make sense of what had happened, if I could understand what I'd done wrong, if I could understand *why* we had gotten here, that maybe I could stop it. Maybe I could fix it. Maybe I could prevent the tidal wave from coming, and I'd never have to drown again.

three.

VENICE

Come June, I'd settled at a co-living space in Venice, CA—a housing option for singles and misfits, living together but not living together in a modern dorm designed for adults. We were all hoping to get a fresh start. Hoping to find some sense of independence and hoping to do so in a city and place and time where nobody knew us, and we knew nobody.

"Do you need help with that?" A girl with long red hair asked. Her expression said, *I'm asking to be polite, but I really hate socializing,* and she didn't seem to bother to hide it.

"No, it's ok, I've been on a plane for a couple hours so it's my exercise of the day."

I smiled. My hope was that I'd befriend the people here. That—like my application had said—I was excited at the prospect of living with others, and that community was one of my values and something I cherished.

> "Great, Rachel! We are excited to welcome you to the Penmar community. Here are our COVID guidelines and regulations, since we are a co-living space, we are doing our best to maintain a cleanliness regimen and sanitization process, and all social events are cancelled until further notice. Welcome to Los Angeles!"

My Uber dropped me off outside my building, a brand new three-story complex just one block off Lincoln Ave, which as I later learned was the best spot to catch the best crime on the Citizens App.

"Man running naked with Axe caught on fire!" Jared, the twenty-three-year-old soon-to-be Million-Dollar-Listing realtor would cry, twerking in the kitchen while sending the fastest selfies on Snapchat I'd ever seen.

Jared, Alana the red-haired writer, and Zia, an Australian actress who taught me to say "cunt" without giggling, would quickly become my gloriously twisted Penmar family. We'd spend many nights twerking, checking Citizens App, feeding Jared snacks while he self-quarantined after a positive COVID test, and bothering our neighbors with our loud and inappropriate fake sex sounds.

It was like being in college all over again.

I lugged my suitcase up the three flights of stairs and flung it into my bedroom. The room was well lit, and just big enough for the wooden bedframe and mattress that came with the space. I had a good-sized closet and private bathroom, and while it was no studio apartment, it was my own.

For the next few months, I focused on finding freelance writing work to pay the bills and focused on therapy to manage my grief. I started to

18

build what I hoped might be a new life. I tried to make the streets of Venice my own, with long, masked walks and socially distanced trips to the beach. I danced in the night with my housemates and drank wine on the rooftop. I cried, and they let me.

And it was in the walls of my small room on the third floor of Penmar Ave that I started to unpack my life.

Unpacking bags, unpacking old parts of self, and unpacking years of my life—hiding and burying the unfathomable grief while desperately trying to pull my past apart to find answers to the questions that kept coming. The puzzles that carved crooked holes inside of me and begged me to solve them. The *how did I get here* and *what did I do?* and *what does he feel* and the never-ending hopeful, *is he really sure?*

In one of our last conversations during those final days in Leavenworth, Josh sat on the couch of my Airbnb with his heads in his hands, crying. He told me how guilty he felt—how scared he was that the hurt he was causing me might be a hurt from which I would never recover. I wondered the same thing, but I assured him it wasn't his fault. I didn't want him to feel guilty for the pain he caused me, just as much as he didn't want to cause me pain in the first place.

And while his guilt for being the one to make the final decision in our divorce told me of his love—I wondered if it was all he felt.

Did he also feel grief?

Did he also feel loss?

Did he miss me?

Or was all his guilt and pain actually tethered to the possibility that by hurting me, he wasn't the good guy he'd longed to be all along?

I wondered if I even got to know those things. If I ever would. If that *knowing*—the *knowing* I had once always had access to over a cup of coffee or simple conversation with my husband —if that *knowing* no longer belonged to me.

Josh so desperately wanted for us to be friends post-divorce. He was already talking about and prepared to move straight from marriage to friendship without skipping a beat. I had no idea how to even fathom that leap, let alone make sense of the fact that by doing so we were actually leaping *from* husband and wife, a true and tangible departure from the label and identity I'd known for so many years.

More questions kept coming, and my mind became consumed with the sense-making.

Sense-making was all I had. It kept me rooted in some kind of possibility, some kind of hope—that if maybe I could *make-sense,* if I could just understand the *why* and the *how,* then I could move forward: I would be able to see a path to friendship, I could remedy my wrongs and shortcomings, I could maybe find love again, I could heal from this hurt, I could move on, move forward, move.

When I couldn't make-sense in the sense-making, when questions turned into more questions, and the answers to those questions hurt too much to accept, I'd check out.

I'd turn to wine to stop my brain from thinking. I'd turn to food to stop my body from feeling.

I'd relinquish, thinking *if I can't make sense of this, then it's because there's no answer: no way out. So what's the point? Who cares? I might as well just eat, and eat, and eat, and check out of my life. Check out of coping. Check out of feeling. It's too fucking hard to feel this anyway.*

I was still very much in denial, and as the anger started to seep in and the sense-making couldn't solve the riddle of my anger, I grew clueless with how to cope.

I never got angry growing up. I didn't feel allowed to. We weren't an angry household. We shoved everything deep into little pockets of our subconscious, saving angry thoughts and feelings for our diaries or letters to one another. Fights were rare and far too scary to commit to, so we edged on anger, teetering near it but never allowing ourselves to fall in.

It was a falsely safe way to live, and I never learned to be angry.

Still, in the weeks after I left Leavenworth, and as time passed in my new home in Venice, I could feel that I was angry.

I started to feel angry with Josh. Angry that he hadn't given me enough time to remedy the damage he told me I'd done. Angry that he'd pulled my Eating Disorder into the story of our unraveling. Angry that he couldn't forgive me or accept my apologies. Angry that he seemed so ready and hellbent on a friendship, and angry that it seemed so easy for him to just bounce from husband to friend without feeling any loss of me.

Angry, that maybe he was right, and that my Eating Disorder and mental health had distracted me so gravely that I became an absent, distant, and neglectful lover.

We tried to keep communication open after I moved to LA, but it became impossible without mediation. I told our therapist that I wanted to have a conversation with him about my anger. That if we were to have any hope of friendship, I would need the chance to express how I was feeling. That if some kind of relationship were to evolve, *this part would have to make sense.*

Josh agreed to a mediated session.

"Hey Josh," I muttered through the screen.

"Hey Rach." From the minute the conversation started, I could feel his energy through the video. He was sad, holding back tears, lonely, and seemed distraught.

When Ama had us say why we wanted to talk, I said it was to express my anger. He said it was to discuss how we can take the next steps to having a relationship.

Then, she gave each of us "the floor" to say what we wanted. She reminded us that what we were saying was meant to come from a place of "kind, true, and necessary." In my private session with her the day before, I had told her I didn't know how I was supposed to express anger under the umbrella of "kind." She said that it was kind to express my truth and to share my feelings. I tried to believe her, but still couldn't really grasp what that meant, or how.

So, in our joint session, when she repeated that mantra, I was anxious that as I dove into my anger-list—the one I'd pre-written and clutched in my hands for the inevitable moments I would dissociate or forget my words—Josh would interpret everything I said as not following her rules "kind, true, and necessary," and would use this as permission to not actually hear me.

This was my fear—that my anger would be dismissed, misunderstood, and unheard. Invisible, not warranted, or irrational. That anger—unlike what Ama told me—couldn't possibly ever come in a kind package, and if I couldn't wrap my head around this new idea, then my husband and king of logic certainly wouldn't. Especially if it was directed towards him.

This next part is long.

It is, verbatim, copied and pasted from the document I used to express my anger.

I include it here, both as a way to commemorate that moment, and because it wasn't perfect. Because I didn't get it "right." Because in spite of my fear and self-doubt, I let myself get angry. And because in the moment, all I believed was that I needed to communicate *all of this* to him, or I would never be able to fully exist as me in any kind of relationship with him. The fear I felt about not being fully seen, even in my exit, lives and breathes in these words. And I want you to feel what he must have felt—to know what it might have been like to receive all of this. Because—as I said before—this isn't about blame. It's not that he was right or I was right. It never was, and it never will be. And yet, while steeped in denial and teetering the edge of fury, I wanted it to be about rightness. I wanted there to be blame. I wanted my anger to be justification for my innocence, because I couldn't bear the truth that perhaps the damage I had done *really did* warrant such a severing as divorce.

Thanks for agreeing to talk to me. So, I've been focusing on processing my unresolved feelings, questions, and anger. I noticed in the last couple weeks how much anger I was feeling and have been working through the patterns in which I don't allow myself to feel or express my anger, but rather bypass it and move straight to compassion.

In the last month or so, at least in our conversations, I haven't allowed myself the space to outwardly express or feel anger, which is something I rarely have done in my life or our relationship. In a lot of ways that has left me feeling unresolved in this chapter ending, and I realized I needed to honor those feelings, process them and understand them, and then express them to you, because they are a real and valid part of my reaction to you wanting a divorce, and I have the right to say them, and I think you deserve to know how I fully feel.

If I don't do this with you, I will hold on to it, shove it away, or turn it inwards, and that will only hurt me. I also want you to know how I feel, so that you can know the breadth of what I felt and feel, rather than trying to guess or interpret it.

I hope that when this conversation is over, you have a better understanding of how I feel about this, that I have spoken my truth and let myself express anger which is a part of my healing process, and that we are closer to understanding how we might fit into each other's lives in the future.

I know you really want us to have a friendship or relationship after marriage, and while I hope that I can get there, I know that without this part—without resolving this hurt, I cannot see a clear path for having any relationship moving forward. I will just hold this anger and it will turn into resentment. If what you truly want is a relationship with me, I hope you'll give me space to express my anger so we can continue to know each other—because to me that is included in a relationship, not excluded.

I'm angry because for so many years in our relationship, I had patience with you while I asked you to change or adapt to meet my needs. While I learned my own boundaries and needs and asked for them, and while you learned to navigate them.

You learned to validate me, to listen, to offer support rather than fixing or helping, to lift me up in public, and to be my safe haven in the face of triggering situations. This took YEARS for you and me to learn together, so the fact that you only gave me six months to learn with you what you are discovering are core needs in our relationship makes me feel angry.

I'm angry because I feel like you wanted our relationship to be fun and easy, and that your expectation that this is how relationships or life is supposed to be allowed you to bypass the reality of life, which is that hardship happens. This year has been incredibly difficult for you personally, and just because nothing you've experienced is classified as a mental health issue doesn't mean your individual conflict or challenges aren't also a contributor to the challenges in our marriage. You often said to me that my mental illness was a cause for you to think you couldn't do this anymore or be in this relationship anymore—and I get that.

But to deny that you never had your own anxieties, insecurities, identity issues, self-doubt, or sadness is unfair and denies the reality which is that all humans suffer. And to think you'll leave this relationship and find another one or find a life without any suffering infuriates me, because I think it's a poor excuse to throw in the towel when things got hard for us.

I'm angry because I thought we were committed to this relationship for life. I didn't want a divorce. Yes, it was hard and painful, but I thought we were committed to trying to find a way through, not out. In life, people change, values change, and relationships change. To expect us to stay the same for 70 years of marriage is unreasonable. Yes, this patch has been rough, and yes, we are learning we have some different values or interests, and yes, our sex life was bad and yes there were things that weren't working, but we committed to life together. We didn't commit to only the good times—I thought we were committed to growing through all of it, to facing the challenges, to adapting, and to building together.

I'm angry because you have told me that when I'm depressed or anxious or in my Eating Disorder you're not attracted to me —but for me to tell you that when you're not confident or insecure or unsure about what to do with your life that I'm not attracted to you is hurtful, I call hypocrisy. Just because your insecurities or anxieties aren't classified under the social construct of "mental illness" doesn't mean that I don't experience your mental and emotional challenges as impacting me and our relationship the same way you experience mine.

And maybe mine are more severe, but why do you think I spend so much time working on them? I wanted you to get out of your funk so that you could be the man I know you are inside, the same way you would always say, "I want you to see yourself how I've always seen you." You don't get to say that to me and not allow me to say it to you. We both want each other to be healthy and happy. Period. You were not happy. I was not happy. But I don't believe we were the sole or primary cause of our unhappiness. I believe we both had and still have personal work to be done, and much of that is our own to carry, and much of it is at the brunt of our instability and lack of safety and security and community. We were under so much external stress, but I don't think you gave us the chance to remedy that first.

I'm angry because I don't think you gave us or me a fair chance. I feel like you ignored or refused to acknowledge the multiple external factors that were adding stress to our relationship—lack of stability in housing, lack of security in money or job, lack of certainty around our future, lack of community and friendship proximity, lack of a place or space to nurture and call a home together, lack of routine or structure, lack of hobbies or personal interests, lack of mutual experiences or routine...these are all basic needs of individual humans and humans in partnership, and we quickly lost ALL of those in the course of a year, and never had the chance to rebuild them when we came back from our travels.

I feel angry because you made this decision unilaterally. There was no conversation or joint decision making unlike almost every other decision in our marriage. You just decided on your own. And even then—you didn't come out and tell me. You didn't sit me down to have a thoughtful, respectful conversation. You didn't offer me reasons or insight into your decision. You didn't give me or our relationship the respect it deserved in telling me you wanted a divorce. You didn't even say it outright. I felt completely blindsided, disrespected, betrayed, and undervalued in your delivery.

When I was done, I was out of breath, burning from the inside, and afraid to meet his gaze.

My palms were sweating as I lifted my eyes to the screen. The man I saw was not my husband. It was Josh—yes, but it wasn't the man I'd known for ten years.

What happened after felt so blurry. It stirred up immense anxiety and reinforced every fear I had about what might happen if I actually voiced my anger, thoughts, and reality out loud.

He became defensive, mad, and stubborn. His face looked pixelated to me, and I wondered if I was starting to see stars in my dizzy state, or if the connection was simply faulty.

"This is not what I expected. My highest value is joy, and you just don't want me to have that. It's like you want me to suffer. Do you even care about my feelings? You're still not taking responsibility. I didn't show up to this call to be a punching bag."

I did my best to stay present and grounded. I grabbed the crystal I'd placed by my side and rubbed it to stay in the moment. I focused on listening to him and nodding, without apologizing, without explaining, without backtracking.

I started to weave in and out of the present moment, my dizziness rising and the blackness clouding my head. The more I tried to hear and validate his perspective, the more dismissed, invisible, and scared I became.

"Look, I'm open to explaining my position, telling you my perspective, or answering questions, but I don't want to hear yours. I don't want anything to do with your anger."

I looked to Ama for support, but she instead validated his boundary.

"Ok, well, then I think I'm done here," I said firmly.

When the call ended, Ama asked to follow up with both of us individually.

"I feel like I was left to my own devices in the face of a fucking master manipulator," I told her.

"I felt cornered, trapped, and like there was really nowhere for me to move or go in the conversation unless I buckled, apologized, reverted my statement, or stayed silent. I didn't do that, which I'm proud of, but what happened is literally what I was terrified would happen.

Did he just gaslight me? I honestly don't know because I can't tell whether the physical and emotional reaction I had was because of what was going on in the moment, or if it was triggering some old shit. So I'm asking you, was he gaslighting me? Or was I not kind and true?

I'm so confused. I don't understand what just happened. And I didn't even recognize him, Ama. That's not the man I've known for ten years. Was that the real him and I've just been unable to see him this whole time? Has he been tricking me for a decade? Or did he become somebody else? Because that man in that conversation, that man did not love me or like me. He wanted nothing to do with me. And I don't know that man."

Josh used to love me more than anyone in the universe, I thought. *I used to be the safest place in the world for him. He used to be mine. How did we go from each other's safe, loving cradles to a dangerous, unfamiliar cave?*

Ama validated my feelings and reminded me that while Josh may not have heard or honored my anger the way I wanted or hoped he would, he did not gaslight me, and I had not been unkind or untrue. We were both just still incredibly hurt, and the things we could not understand, forgive, or make sense of were gripping us so tightly that we'd locked ourselves in a fit of finger-pointing, and while neither one of us wanted to admit it, we were hoping the other would take the blame for our unraveling.

We didn't speak for weeks. I couldn't look at him. I couldn't hear his voice. I couldn't make sense of how we'd grown so cold in one another's presence. I couldn't, until a year later, understand that the anger I felt really *was* warranted, and that by choosing to ignore it, I'd find myself channeling it in the same place I'd directed it for my entire life.

I started to turn inward. If I couldn't make sense of Josh—if I couldn't understand why he no longer was the man I once knew, or rather, why he no longer saw me as the love he once wanted—I would find the answers myself.

I called on everything I'd learned in seventeen years of therapy and my psychology graduate studies. I made diagrams of my family systems and drew lines between my childhood attachment styles and correlating adult relationships. I carved traumatic memories into rubber stamps and made craft books full of past stories so I wouldn't forget what was then, and what was now. I attempted to reconcile the unfathomable space I was in using the only construct I felt I had any control over: harnessing the past, trapping the glaring red flags, and rectifying a new me so powerful I could never miss the signs of danger again.

This was not a seamless process, and while I naively believed that catapulting myself into a historical research project of my own life would save me from suffering, I could not keep Grief's lurking limbs from crawling to the surface.

Grief, I learned, doesn't care how hard you attempt to understand her. She doesn't care if you are already depressed or suffer from suicidal ideation. She doesn't wait for you to be ready, and the longer you defer her presence, the heavier her weight becomes.

If you asked my housemates what it was like living with me during that year, they'd likely share stories of the nights we read tarot cards by candlelight, the moment I discovered that they *could* hear me when I cried in the shower, and the time I flushed an entire loaf of cinnamon bread down the toilet because I was in the middle of a month-long binge, and in my drunken state, that seemed like the only way to truly get rid of the temptation.

When I picture myself moving through the year, I visualize myself holding two, equally heavy platters in outstretched arms. Walking a tightrope over a raging gorge, wobbling in a wind that pierced my ears and made it impossible to hear. I imagine I've walked out onto the line, holding these two platters beside me, as if carrying them to some final destination where I hoped to one day present them at the feet of some great master:

"I've done it, you see? I've walked the line, I've braved the storm, and I kept the trays afloat the entire time. I managed it all, I held it all, and I did not look back."

I imagine, that sitting upon each of these platters were two separate, but wholly connected things: *Grief* and *Understanding*.

And as I walked across the raging water below, and my arms grew tired from the weight of them both, I could not put either one down in order to support the other. As Grief grew too heavy, so too did Understanding. As Understanding's weight pulled me down, Grief fell with her.

The more I came to make sense of my past—parts of childhood I did not have, the lack of true identity-development in adolescence, a college experience full of depression, anxiety, and hospitalization, a decade-long battle with an Eating Disorder, the lack of healthy relationships with men and sexual trauma, the not knowing my worth enough to say "no" or set boundaries or stand up for myself, and a radical inability to self-regulate that rendered me both dependent on and resentful of the important people in my life, *the more I grieved.*

The more I grieved the loss of a man so loving, of a history full of laughter and warmth, of the safety and security of a partner, of the families and gatherings we'd no longer have, of the friends and homes and experiences we shared, of the future we'd planned together and the stories we said we'd tell our grandkids, and the loss of someone who when it all got too scary could love, care for, and know me, *the more I understood.*

But as I walked this tightrope, I did not see the depth of Understanding to my left, nor did I see Grief's constant presence to my right. I simply saw the gaping nothingness ahead, heard the terrifying rumble of the deadly waters below, and felt the increasing weight of the platters I carried.

There were many times over the course of the year that I was certain I'd moved through the grief.

I fully believed I'd felt and expressed each phase, and come out the other side thinking, o*k, I can do this. I can do this. I'll survive this.*

It's not that I didn't move through the phases of grief—it's that I *did:* over and over and over.

I did feel shock and denial. I did feel anger. I did feel sorrow, hope, acceptance. I did make meaning and start to put the pieces of my life—one without Josh—back together.

And just as quickly as I'd put them together, denial would strike, or anger would flood me all over again.

After weeks of what felt like normalcy—in the midst of total abnormal COVID times in the LA summer of 2020—I found myself folding my clothes, humming to a song on my speakers, imagining a life where I was okay. I picked up a shirt of his—a large tie-dye shirt we'd bought just before the motorcycle trip that catapulted our unraveling a year before—and in an instant I was crumbled on the floor of my closet in tears. I held the shirt to my drooling mouth, snot covering the neck of the tee as I did everything I could to find his scent in the fabric.

Was this part of the grief, or understanding? I wondered.

Is this a moment or reconciliation, or have I returned right back to doubt and denial's cruel and confusing arms?

Was the hopelessness I felt one that all those who've lost endure, or was it the familiar loss of will to live I'd felt so many times before?

Or was it both, and did the simple carrying of both make it all so muddy and dark, that there was no point in trying to separate the two?

Did I grieve in order to find hope for living, or did I find hope for living in order to grieve?

I think this not-knowing is why I couldn't bear to choose one over the other: Grief nor Understanding.

And as much as I thought about dying during those summer months in LA, the fear of actual death kept me clinging onto both platters. I was too afraid that if I let one go—if I put Grief down for a moment or let Understanding take rest—the sheer imbalance would throw me from the tightrope, and I would die.

I wanted to live. And, I wanted to die.

I spent many, many nights falling asleep at night thinking, *you probably won't make it that long anyway*, or *you might as well be dead*. Many mornings, the first thought in my head would be, *I hate myself.*

It was not the first time in my life I'd felt the odd duality of suicide, and it wouldn't be the last.

The idea of dying had become a relief, and one that offered its services to me when life became altogether too much: a sensory overload of desperation, loss, worthlessness, or trauma. When the how-will-I-survive-this had no answer, and when the belief that I was alone in trying to survive it consumed me.

In these days and weeks of the all-too-muchness, I felt diffuse.

Can I ever rest or settle into who I am?

Can I ever know that I am real? That this is me, and not some version of me? That I am her—the girl I see in the mirror? The person I am becoming or once was?

Am I always shedding?

Or is nothing ever new?

I tried to write, and spent countless hours staring at my computer, the nothingness lasting for what felt like years in the space between my fingertips and the blank pages.

Though this was the first time during a bout of deep depression where I finally believed I wasn't completely alone, I still struggled to actually ask for help and reach out to trusted others when I needed it.

Instead, I soothed with old familiars: food, alcohol, attention from men, shopping, and incessant productivity.

I'd convince myself I'd healed from the grief—again—and flood my senses with Hinge matches and attention from men.

I'd then swiftly meet Grief face-to-face again, now shrouded with an added layer of shame for how it might look to my future ex-yet-still-legal-husband if he knew I sought the male gaze and intimacy while still grieving our marriage.

I drank wine on weeknights, justifying my behavior and steadily earlier start time to my housemates and myself with, "Well, it's COVID, everybody is drinking more." I'd end my nights with thirty-dollar Grub Hub delivery orders, waking up to ice cream stains in my bedsheets.

Most days, I did not recognize myself in the mirror. I was a shell of myself, drowning in my own cyclical turnstile of my Eating Disorder, self-hatred, and longing for love.

And through it all, when I'd run out of steam, when I'd stop and slow down, I'd be faced with the pain of what was still in front of me: the loss of my husband, the loss of our life together, and the loss of a reality that was so mine, so ours, for so long.

As much as I wanted to understand it all—as much as I sense-made and tried to make sense of the nonsensical—I couldn't.

Every ounce of worth I'd learned to create for myself in the last decade of therapy crumbled underneath me. I was—just as I'd once believed—a worthless piece of shit, who no one would ever love again. I was too sick, too mentally unstable, and clearly impossible to love. At least, to love enough to *stay* with.

As I spiraled deeper and deeper into a depression, as the binges became more intense and the purges returned for the first time in years, as the urges to die grew stronger and when I curled myself in a ball on the shower floor, banging my fists against my belly like I'd first done seventeen years before, I started to believe that what Josh had said to me in our last few days together in Leavenworth might be true:

"It's like there are three people in our marriage. You, me, and your Eating Disorder. And sometimes I think you love her more than me."

Was all of this unraveling because of her, my Eating Disorder, and my commitment to her?

Was it our fault, *hers and mine?* Did we do this?

Did we do all that we could for so many years to find the one thing we both craved—love—then *use the very same tools* to lose it in the end?

part two
floating back.

The entrance to my Eating Disorder was like choosing a slide at the pool.

For a moment in time, I lost sight of who I was. Standing at the top of the waterpark, I looked around searching for where to go. Wondering how to get back to the safety of the shallow end and cool relief from the burning sun.

But I was young and hadn't learned how to get down safely. I didn't know if I should choose the fast or slow slide, the straight or twisty, the covered or exposed.

Do I ask for help deciding? Do I call down to my parents for support? Do I follow all the other kids and pick their slide? Do I stay here and wait till dark, so no one can see me? Do I choose the slide that seems the most used? The least? The shiniest? The one with all the decorations and bright lights? Do I jump? Take the ladder back down? How do I get back to earth so I can find my footing?

In the end, I chose a slide.

Once I placed my hands on the edges of her mouth, once I felt the cold, slippery static of her seat under mine, I had tasted her comfort and trusted her. I met the water's surface on her back, safely and securely. And passersby seemed unphased, even celebratory of my speedy return.

And each time I found myself back at the top of the waterpark— lost, uprooted, and scared—I chose her to take me back down. I loved my slide. She knew me. She knew the curve of my bum and how fast I liked to go. She knew which time of day I liked to slide and what temperature I liked the water.

Even though all the other routes remained open—she became the most familiar. She became so familiar that I didn't notice the scratches I'd endure from her chipped paint. She became so familiar that I didn't realize how far she placed me from the other children when she spat me into the water. She became so familiar, that I didn't care when people started to suggest I try a sturdier slide, because they were scared the next time I used mine it would collapse underneath me, and I might not recover.

I believed my slide gave me superpowers. I believe I'd found a secret passage. I believed I could ride her forever, and that as long as I had her, I'd always have a safe path home.

four.

POOCH

I was never thin growing up. I also wasn't fat.

I was small and soft, and my belly protruded outwards in Buddha fashion. My bum was round and large, and my shoulders sloped narrowly. I had very little muscle tone, and though I participated in sports, I was hardly athletic. I remember from an early age noticing the difference between my body and the bodies of other girls. I'd stand in the locker room at gym time, staring as they removed their shirts, wondering how their stomachs looked so hard and flat. Questioning my own body and feeling that mine was somehow wrong in comparison.

I spent the summer between my freshman and sophomore year of high school dieting to no avail. I couldn't seem to shed the belly fat I so desperately despised. I just wanted to be thin like my friends. I wanted a flat stomach like the rest of the girls at school. *What was so wrong with my body that it couldn't take the shape and form of everyone I saw around me?*

I was certain that the shape of my belly was preventing me from finding love. That the boys at my school didn't want a round stomach, and that unless I looked like my friends or the girls I saw on TV, they'd find me disgusting.

One day in summer, right before my sophomore year of high school, I was at my friend's condo laying by the pool. We were catching the last few rays of Seattle sun and gossiping about the boys we couldn't wait to see come September. Her younger brother came to sit with us, and within moments of arriving he pointed at my stomach, and with a snickering grin said, "nice pooch."

I was mortified. *He saw it.* It wasn't in my head. The pooch wasn't some dysmorphic thing I'd imagined—it was real, and just as I feared, it was disgusting.

Weeks later after school began, I found out that Adrian, a guy I'd become romantically involved with, told his buddies that, "One day Rachel will grow out of her baby fat." I sickly took this as a compliment. That he'd seen the potential in my body, hiding under all this baby fat I too was convinced didn't belong.

The boys in my high school were always rating our bodies. Who had the nicest butt. The best abs. The prettiest eyes. We were like show dogs to them, parading in circles around the common area of our school, waiting to be selected and rated, hoping to go home with a ribbon.

I went harder on my diets and started cutting out food groups. I stopped drinking soda, reduced breakfast to a single grapefruit, and increased the times I went running each week.

When cabbage soup and "Slim 'N Six" DVDs didn't give me the slim-'n-six-pack I wanted, I started to grow frustrated with my body. I started to think something was inherently wrong with it—my other friends were able to work out and get fit, why wasn't I? What was so wrong with me?

My breasts hadn't yet developed, and I'd only had one period, so I was also convinced my body was somehow behind, somehow not advanced, not ever designed to be fully woman or fully beautiful. I was a pudgy adolescent, doomed to be small, soft, and round unless I found the secret that I was certain everyone but me possessed.

In November of my sophomore year, I took a road trip with Adrian. He was two years older than me, half Italian, and wildly romantic. I loved how intense and passionate he was, and when we were together, I felt like I was the only person in the world.

I wasn't, though, the only person in *his* world. Earlier that fall, he'd gone back and forth between offering me his affection and promising himself to another girl at school. The two of us finally caught on to what he was doing, and we confronted him about it. When faced with a decision, he chose neither of us, and I was crushed.

Still, weeks later when we tiptoed around the idea of hanging out together, I wanted his attention. I wanted his approval—to hear him tell me things about my body and her potential for sexiness. I wanted him to choose me.

We drove up to Vancouver, BC together—a three-hour road trip and border crossing away. The drive was quiet. We didn't have much to talk about, and I realized the majority of our time spent together had consisted of making out in stairwells or skinny dipping in the Puget Sound. *Did we even like each other?* I wondered.

Hours later, we finally arrived in the small town I wanted to take him to—the town my cousins grew up in and one that had nostalgic significance to me. I had hoped that maybe we could sneak into my cousin's house (who wasn't home), and have sex there—my first time, and in a place I felt safe. A very naïve and teenage fantasy, but it was my hope.

After walking along the pier in silence for what felt like hours, we stood awkwardly facing each other, his hands in his pockets, mine wrapped around my waist to keep me warm from the cold sea breeze.

"Should we just go?" He asked, not even looking at me.

"Sure, I guess."

Was I that boring? I thought. *He ended up choosing me, and still, I wasn't appealing enough, entertaining enough, or beautiful enough to hold his interest?*

We drove home in silence. We never talked about the trip, and we stopped seeing each other after that.

Years later, after my Eating Disorder became more apparent and visible to him and some of my peers, he asked me, "Did this happen because of me?"

I was flabbergasted by this question. While the timing made it seem that way, I didn't make any links or connection between him and my Eating Disorder. I didn't want to give him that much power—*how could his rejection, after all, be at all linked to my Eating Disorder? What could that moment possibly have stirred in me? What final straw could it have broken, and did it?*

I didn't make any connections between him, the feeling of not-enoughness, the longing for male approval or desire, and my Eating Disorder for years. Nor did I draw any conclusions about where my father fit in, nor the patriarchal, misogynistic conditioning that extended far beyond my nuclear family.

Conclusions and connections weren't of any interest to me at fifteen—my consciousness only knew one thing: I just wanted to be thin.

And so, in the days after our miserably awkward trip to Vancouver, I sat in the loft of our family home in Seattle and typed "Pro-Anorexia Website" into the desktop search bar. I found a blog on LiveJournal (which in those days was of the original social media fabric alongside Myspace and Xanga).

I scrolled the pages for wisdom. Countless photos of hip bones and ribs lined the pages. At the time, I found these photos alarming and somewhat disturbing. *Who would want to look like that?* I remember thinking.

Still, if these girls managed to get their bodies to such a frail and fragile state, they must have the secret I would need to finally achieve my ideal body.

As I scrolled the pages of LiveJournal, I learned little by little just how powerful I could become over my body.

I read entry after entry of daily caloric intakes—girls who were tracking their food to the half calorie, documenting their mileage and sit-ups to the decimal, and measuring every last inch of their bodies.

This was not a system, it was a way of life, and I wanted in.

And so, as if signing up for some new religion or entering into some cult, I indoctrinated myself as a member—I was and would be, Anorexic.

I carried shame around this decision for a long time. As if in the choosing, I wasn't qualified for actual sickness. That because I *chose* Anorexia, it was not a disease I fell ill to. That because I decided to stop eating, it was my fault, my responsibility, and a disgrace to the *real* people suffering from Eating Disorders that I even considered myself to be one of them.

So even in my illness, I allowed myself to believe I wasn't ill. I convinced myself it was temporary—a two-week free trial that I would cancel before getting charged. I would use and absorb the skills of Anorexic-others, then get out as soon as I'd reached my ideal weight.

This, I later learned, was a lie my Eating Disorder would tell me for the rest of my life.

She was never interested in offering me a free trial. And I didn't choose her. She was carved in me long before I sat down at my family computer. Because—as I refused to believe for years—she wasn't just about my body.

For the next two weeks, I followed a new ritual.

Every morning I would sneak into my parent's bathroom to use their scale. I'd wait until I could hear the sound of my mom in the kitchen downstairs. I'd be ready in my towel, hovering at the top of the staircase until I knew I had my moment. I'd rush, as quietly as possible, into their bathroom.

I remember often peering into their closet, imagining which of my mother's clothes I could sift through. I'd see my dad's slippers on the floor, filled with holes but never going to waste for his love of them. If I had enough time, I'd stick my face into my mother's magnifying mirror, just to get a closer glimpse at the hairs in my bushy brows.

Most of the time, my heart would be racing, as the fear of being caught trumped any closet-curiosity.

The ritual was:

Tap the scale and wait for "00".

Silently place the towel on the ground.

Step, with as little sound as possible, on the scale.

Hold your breath.

Pray.

For the first month or so, nine out of ten times my ritual was a success. I was losing weight rapidly, and the dropping numbers on the scale reinforced my daily starvation.

Most days I ate nothing except the dinner my parents prepared me. After school I'd run for thirty minutes on the treadmill—if it wasn't thirty minutes it didn't count, and if it was less than three miles it didn't either.

At lunch I'd find ways out of seeing friends. The only escape I can truly recall is pretending to sleep on the common room couches.

"I'm just so tired today!" I'd lie.

Beyond that, I truthfully cannot remember where I'd go. I have visualized every room and corner in my high school, scanning for memories of my lunchtime hideaways. I have no idea where I went.

I don't remember buying lunch and tossing some of the food to make it look as though I had eaten. We had no cafeteria, and most students went off campus for lunch. So did I just stay on campus? What did I do during that forty-five-minute period every single day? Surely after weeks of refusing to go get food with friends someone would have said something. *So where did I go?*

And how did nobody notice?

Looking back, this has always been something that astonished me. I was visibly losing weight, and rapidly. But nobody at school said a word. Eventually my family stepped in, but not a single teacher or classmate ever said something to me.

I don't think back on this as if it was the school's fault or as though my friends should have intervened. I think back on this and I'm reminded of how little we knew about Eating Disorders, let alone mental health, as a culture.

I certainly didn't have any understanding of the disease, and I was living with it.

Mental health was for psychologists, therapists, and the *mentally ill*—not for mainstream media or those who were generally functioning. Instagram, TikTok, Twitter, Facebook, and mainstream social media was non-existent, and the plethora of vulnerability and information we have at our fingertips now was nowhere when I was in high school. I lived, as I imagine many people did, in secret—keeping my thoughts, fears, and shame hidden in the pages of my diary or trapped in the subconscious fabric of my every unconscious behavior.

If you had asked me then (and I'm pretty sure my eventual doctor and therapist did) *why* I wanted to starve myself, I would have responded, "I just want to be thin."

At the time, and for years and years to come, I believed that was true. I really believed that my Eating Disorder had nothing to do with control, anxiety, self-worth, or any of the "hocus pocus" therapists tried to shove down my throat. I thought I was unique in this way—like an unsolvable puzzle.

I am, quite possibly, the only case they've ever seen that is purely about being thin! I'm not mentally ill or psychologically sick, I just want to lose weight and I've found the secret!

I used to mock the runners at Greenlake on my way to school. Sitting in the front seat of my dad's SUV, likely freezing and begging him to turn the heat on but only met with, "There's no sense in turning it on until the car engine gets to this marker," pointing at the engine thermometer on the dash. *I know,* I'd think, *so what's the harm in letting me turn the dial up just to let me feel like it's coming?*

National Public Radio (NPR) would hum in the background. I despised the radio in the AM and wished we could listen to music or something other than *This American Life.* Swirling my Yoplait around with my spoon to make it seem like I was eating breakfast, I'd stare out the window through the Seattle rain and watch the runners huffing around the lake before beginning their day. *Fools.* I'd think. *You're doing this the hard way.*

I assumed every runner was on the same mission as me, and that the only reason someone would wake up before 7:00am to run was to lose weight and be thin.

The track in my head became so repetitive, and the pattern I followed each day became more ingrained.

By December of 2005, only a couple months after reading the Pro-Anorexia post I'd found on LiveJournal, I had grown so thin I could see my bones. I thought to myself, *this is probably good enough,* and started to look for ways I could maintain my new body. I desperately didn't want to gain weight and had become afraid to eat, but I knew if I kept up what I was doing, I would continue to drop in size, which I didn't want either.

I sat down once again at our family desktop and returned to the Pro-Anorexia website. I typed in my question and posted it to the forum, awaiting Pro-Advice from Pro-Anorexics.

"I've gotten to my ideal weight. How do I maintain it?"

"If you want to stay the same weight, you're not really Anorexic."

What?

I was dumbfounded by this response.

Why am I not really Anorexic?

Do I think I'm Anorexic?

Does this response deny a reality I had chosen?

Was I glad to be renounced of a title I never subscribed to? Or was this proof that, even in my illness, *I wasn't sick enough to be ill?*

As winter came, my family started to notice the change in my appearance. My hair was thinning, my face was gaunt, and I wasn't trying very hard to hide my body. I wanted to be seen. I wanted people to recognize my thinness. It made me feel powerful. Like I could do anything.

On days where I ate so little that I saw stars upon standing, I believed I had accomplished the impossible, and I went to bed proud of the growls in my belly.

There was so much woven into the pleasure I gained from not eating. I don't think I was conscious of it at the time, but there was something about the secrecy and discipline that delighted me.

Hiding became a game I could play—a divine mastery of sorts, where I had ultimate power, ultimate privacy, and ultimate wisdom. I hid everything. Especially from my parents, *especially* from my mother.

After my morning weigh-in ritual, I'd wait for my mother to return upstairs so I could take her place in the kitchen and fake my breakfast. I created masterpieces in the kitchen, shaking cereal boxes to make it sound like I was pouring bran flakes in a bowl, opening the fridge and cupboards to give the illusion of milking and spooning my cereal. I'd leave tiny traces of cereal crumbs and a lick of milk in the bottom of the bowl, topping it off with a moist spoon to create the perfect "just eaten" breakfast dish.

It was a rush.

To know I had fooled my mom and that I had a secret of my own made me feel utterly powerful. As long as I could keep this from her, I could have something all to myself. As long as I held the secrets of my fast-track to thinness, I could have a superpower nobody else could. I was special, powerful, and impenetrable.

This is what my young mind believed. Now, seeing the words "superpower" and "thin" to describe what I wanted tells me so much about the naïve framework I was living from. How could I know that the power I sought was because I felt so powerless at home? How could I know the longing I felt to be seen was so normal, so basic that it was ok for me to simply ask for love and affection? How could I know that my desire to be thin was not actually my own, but one twisted into my young brain by the media, and reinforced daily when friends said, "I hate my thighs" or my mom said, "If you eat too much one day, just have one less piece of toast at breakfast the next day to compensate"?

Nobody taught me anything different—nobody taught me anything. I was, like many teenagers of my generation, reared to succeed, perform, and excel academically, cultured to attract, impress, and adhere to the male gaze. Education, social systems, and western culture didn't focus on my mental or emotional wellbeing—it focused on my brain as a machine for producing excellence, and my body as a vehicle for male desire and pleasure.

And my parents weren't taught anything different either. Nor were the parents of my peers. So, I, like many others, was raised in a web of misinformation about what it means to be human; conditioned by systems designed to keep us hungry, unsatisfied, and insecure.

I didn't know any of this at the age of fifteen. My mother and father didn't either. We just operated how we thought we were supposed to, and we did that together for the next seventeen years. Trying, as best as we all could, to live within this web, to follow the rules, and to maintain the structure and conditioning we'd all lived with for generations.

Growing up in this web was like living in a home full of whispers.

My family never spoke about anything. I didn't know my father had a drinking problem until his drinking problem ended my parent's marriage when I was twenty-two. I didn't know my parents even had relationship problems until I knew he had a drinking problem. If my mother and father argued, I never saw it, and they never told us.

Secrecy was our currency, silence our forte. And I excelled at this in my Eating Disorder. It was one thing I learned well, and a skill I readily adopted to maintain her firm grip.

I think the secrecy created an undercurrent of anxiety for my entire family. Or maybe, the anxiety of my entire family is what bore the secrecy.

I later learned that my father's emotional absence was in part what hurt my mother in their marriage, and I can imagine her longing to know him is what fueled her intense longing to know me. She wanted so badly for her and me to be close, and for me to tell her the ins and outs of my life as a young girl.

I longed for privacy, as most teenagers do. And I found her attempts to know me intrusive. She wanted to know my every move, and once she knew, she'd criticize or ridicule it for not being the right one.

My mother had poor boundaries and little impulse control, and would often say things like, "I know I shouldn't say this to you, but…" or "You told me not to tell you these things, but I feel compelled to tell you…"

She made me feel as though what she believed was so righteous and so true, that my needs and feelings would bow and change in the presence of her words.

I often felt as though I had no choices around her—even if I was given the option to choose, I was met with, "Are you sure that's what you want to do?" or some other doubtful statement that rendered me confused, lost, and small.

So, when my Eating Disorder unfolded, naturally, my mother became hyperaware, hyper-involved, and incredibly dismayed by the not-knowing. She'd watch me so closely—at night if she heard me in the kitchen, she'd scurry down the stairs, just to see what I was doing. In the mornings as she caught on to my routine, she'd start questioning what I'd eaten for breakfast. At one point, she read my diary.

Still, I didn't think my Eating Disorder was about control. I didn't think it was about my mother. I didn't think it was about the boy who made me feel not-enough or my father who was missing from the entire picture. And years later when therapists hypothesized it was, I still denied any connection between my Eating Disorder and anything deeper or more complex than "I want to be thin."

For many years I felt shame that I believed my Eating Disorder was all about my body. I wasn't a good enough Anorexic in the eyes of the Eating Disorder communities I interacted with online, and I wasn't a traumatized enough client with a good enough reason to have an Eating Disorder in the eyes of my therapists. I was never good enough, anywhere, to anyone.

I just want to be thin, I thought. And I did. There wasn't a shred of falsity there. *Whatever unlocked secret or trauma my therapists suspected isn't there. They won't find anything. I just want to be thin.*

I don't judge or shame my younger self: I did the best I could with what I knew and believed, and I really believed that being thin would make me happy. It was simple to me.

Now, I know it wasn't so simple. And it certainly wasn't simple in the years to come.

There was nothing simple about the damage I did to my body by starving myself for years on end.

There was nothing simple about the belief that I was doomed to be broken and alone for life.

There was nothing simple about the endless relationships I lost because I prioritized my Eating Disorder.

There was nothing simple about the dangerous, risky positions I found myself in because of how much I wanted approval, acceptance, and desire from men.

There was nothing simple about seventeen years of therapy, treatment, and hospitalization.

Simple doesn't even begin to accurately describe what it was like for my parents to watch me lose interest in living.

It was never as simple as, "I just want to be thin."

five.

RUTHLESS RUSS

I sat in silence my whole first therapy session—feet dangling off the couch, arms crossed, eyes rolled. I was halfway through the tenth grade and about to turn fifteen—something I was more interested in discussing than my deepest, darkest secrets. I remember feeling cold. Not because it was winter, which it was. But because I was always cold then.

I was there against my will—my mom had expressed concern about my eating habits (or lack thereof), and quickly intervened.

Russ's office was as cliché as a therapist's office gets: adorned with framed diplomas, an ostentatious bookshelf cluttered with psychobabble, a brown leather couch, and Russ.

I remember his teeth; they were so long and white, and he had a funny way of keeping his upper lip constantly curled so they were always in view.

I spent many sessions with Russ like this. Defiant, cold, stubborn. I wouldn't let him permeate the fortress I had built.

Why would my mom, or any doctor, think that a fifteen-year-old girl with Anorexia would want to talk to a forty-five-year-old man about why she hated her body?

I had an entire team working for me (though in my mind they were against me). Between appointments at The Children's Hospital, my primary care doctor's office, and the church where I met my nutritionist (which I found bizarre considering we weren't religious, and I hadn't set foot in a church since my childhood friend Ophelia took me to Sunday school to paint murals of Adam and Eve. Even as a seven-year-old, I instantly knew that church and Christianity was not for me, and I swore off religion altogether).

I hated my mom for taking me there. I hated The Children's Hospital where I attended my doctor's appointments for mocking my tinkering adolescence, and the way I felt so powerless and naked in their child-sized hospital gowns.

I hated my doctor for being thin, and for the way her razor-sharp knees pointed through her sheer black stockings. I hated my nutritionist for knowing less than me about food. I hated her haircut and her stupid scarves that she wore indoors.

Everything enraged me. Everyone was against me. And I refused to let my guard down. This was how I kept my power, and I wasn't giving it away to anyone.

Especially Russ.

Russ tried. He tried so hard. He leaned into me and stayed curious. He tilted his head and asked questions. He really wanted to know me— he wanted to let me be seen and understood.

His curiosity was foreign and alarming, and I interpreted his interest as manipulation. I assumed his questions were interrogations. I believed he was out to get me—on some mission from my mother to control, stifle, and shame me.

It's not that I didn't want to be seen or understood.

I desperately wanted to be known. I craved total acceptance.

But at the age of fifteen, I didn't know how to share myself with anyone. Not *really*—not in the ways I know now as a thirty-two-year-old woman. Not with vulnerability and honesty. Not with boundaries and clear communication. Not with reciprocity and balance. And *especially* not with men.

I assumed—unconsciously—that to be known I would have to simply make myself attractive enough, visible enough, or enticing enough that someone (or some man) would be so drawn to me that the allure of *me* alone would call for knowingness.

Mystery, illusion, and drawing in the gaze of others became my method of harnessing the very interest and curiosity Russ so readily showed me, and that I so quickly turned away because I'd done nothing to earn it and therefore, must be a cover for some hidden agenda.

Ironically, it was the reinforcement my Eating Disorder needed to assure me time and time again, that if I wanted to be seen—if I wanted to be known, I would need to be sick.

What started as a longing to be loved and seen for my physical beauty digressed into the warped belief that the illness itself was what drew the attention I so craved. I towed the line between longing for perfection and longing for pity. Using my body as a signaling flag, oscillating between peacocking in times where I felt beautiful, and waving distress calls in the depths of my sickness.

I never used my words, and I didn't know how to. I used my body.

So, in therapy, when Russ and all future therapists would ask me how I was, or what I felt, or what I was thinking, I froze. I did not know what it meant to put words to feelings. I did not know that my thoughts were "normal" or common, or even safe. I was certain the thoughts in my head were only in *my* head, and that if I spoke them out loud, the world would know how sick, twisted, and completely fucked up I really was.

I couldn't let anyone know I was bad. I couldn't let my therapists know. I needed to be *good*. I needed to be good at home. I needed to be good at school. I needed to be good to my friends, I needed to be good at therapy and at everything. I needed to be good at *life*, and I needed to be a good *person*.

I pressed on like this for most of high school: defiant to my therapist's support, furious with my mother for controlling me, and convinced that if they just *let me be*, I would be fine. All I wanted was to reach my ideal weight, stop restricting, manage my intake, and be "normal." It wasn't a big deal, and they were making it one.

Of course, I was wrong.

It was a big deal, and I needed help. But I didn't want to change, nor did I see why it was important that I do so. I was trapped in a narrow view where all I could see was potential for beauty, potential for power, and potential for total acceptance. And as much as I know now that my mother's attempts to help me came from a place of love and care, her way of communicating that to me was flawed, and the message I received was, *you're bad, you're making a mistake, and I need to fix it for you before you fuck your life up more.*

She never said those words to me, but she also didn't say, "I love you so much, and I can see that you're really struggling. I know I might not be who you want to talk to about this, and I want you to know that no matter what, I love you forever."

I'm not even sure if that would have changed anything.

My therapist asked me this year, "If you could say something to your younger self—when your Eating Disorder started, what would you say?"

I laughed, and paused to think about it.

"God, I don't know. The first thing I thought when you asked me that was, she probably won't even listen to me. Fourteen-year-olds want power, control, and agency. Developmentally, that's pretty normal. They feel like they're already adults, and they want to feel like they are smart enough to make big decisions on their own. So, I think it would be naive to assume I'd even have any influence with some wisdom or future-self message.

"So, I guess what I would tell her is, 'in life, you will make lots of choices in order to feel loved, accepted, and like you belong. Some of those choices will bring you joy, and some will bring you suffering. I want you to know that no matter what, you cannot make the wrong choice, you will always be loved, and you will always belong. You are the maker of your life, and no matter what you do, or what you choose, and how it unfolds, you belong."

Even though I have fantasized about what my mom could have said or should have done, I really don't know that there is or was any better or right way for her to handle my Eating Disorder. She handled it the way she knew how to with the tools she had available.

So while my mother's panic grew and her attempts to intervene grew more controlling and laced with her own anxiety, so did my anger.

For most of high school and early college years, my mother was so, *so* worried about me. And she had no idea what to do. And I'm sure suggesting to her that she even *entertain* the idea of adopting the thought, "Ok Rachel, I trust you, do what you need to," while watching me starve myself, would have been laughable.

How is a parent supposed to watch a child hurt themselves? That makes no sense.

I don't think there's any right answer here. Because while my mother did everything in her power to stop my Eating Disorder, my father simultaneously did nothing. And his physical and emotional absence (while less concrete or apparent to me as a teen and for the years that followed) was likely just as unhelpful as her overbearing concern.

Which would have been preferable? Two parents giving their child total trust and support? Or two parents giving them concern and intervention? Or something in the middle, where both are on the same page, with a balance of supportive trust and an adult hand that knows when to intervene because their child is, after all, still a child?

As far as I was aware, my father didn't even *know* I had an Eating Disorder. My brother certainly didn't. If they did, it was never spoken about. Only in the dark corners of my therapist's office or in the silence of the dreaded car rides with my mother to the doctor's office was it known. Even then, we didn't *speak* about it.

Just as I wondered for years after beginning therapy as an adult if more trust and space from my mother would have helped, I too wondered if attention or concern from my father would have softened me.

Was it their so distant ways of parenting me that kept me in this vicious cycle? Where I longed so desperately for control and privacy over my life, yet longed for the love, attention, and care from others? Is this in part why now, as an adult, I remain so closed off and scared of intimacy, yet do all that I can to attract it? Am I in this push and pull now, just as I was then, forever running back and forth between my mother and father?

I asked myself this question, and so many others after I started therapy much later in life. After I *chose* to go, because I finally wanted help freeing myself from the viscous cycle I'd fallen into.

I also wondered, and still do, why I—the patient/client/human receiving help—was never included in my own recovery process. It was as if the moment I walked into Russ's office as a fifteen-year-old, I became enrolled into a new kind of secrecy. While the therapy room had more dialogue and language to describe my mental illness than the outside world, there was still so much I wasn't allowed to know. That even in the place I was meant to feel the safest, I was left in the dark.

Neither Russ, my doctor, nor nutritionist provided me with a diagnosis when I first started therapy. For years and years after that, not a single professional I saw gave me a clear run-down of their medical analysis, plan, or protocol.

Nobody ever said to me, "Rachel, do you know why you are here? You have been diagnosed with XYZ, and here is how we are going to treat you. Do you have any questions about the diagnosis, plan, or team that's assigned to support you?"

To this day, I cannot tell you what is on my medical record. No therapist has *ever* told me, or even asked if I wanted to know.

A few weeks after beginning therapy with Russ, I sat in my doctor's office, this time my legs dangling off the side of the leather medical bed, the sound of parchment paper crinkling under my bum as I waved my feet back and forth. Staring at the fish tank in the room, thinking how lovely it must be to be a goldfish. Aching to be away from the grip of my mother's watchful eye. Painfully aware that my Eating Disorder was killing her, but unphased by the reality that it was also killing me.

"Ok Rachel—hi mom! How are we?"

"Fine," my mom lied. Acting as emotionally distraught as possible, putting on a pity-show for my doctor, as if to say, "Please help me, can't you see how hard this is for me?" *We get it, mom, this is hard for YOU. My Eating Disorder is so, very hard for YOU.*

"Alright mom," (the doctor addressed my mother as "mom," as if to keep her soft in her role as mom and clearly communicate the power dynamics in the room) *What a load of crap,* I thought.

"So, mom, Rachel needs to reach this weight in two weeks. Ok?"

My mother nodded and choked back tears. The doctor put her hand on my mother's shoulder, consoling her.

I sat there, wondering if anyone would console me. Waiting for the doctor to turn to me and say something—anything.

This was my appointment, right?

I sat there, the invisible patient, watching them comfort each other and sadly discuss my body and my treatment. I made a mini orchestra with the parchment paper below my bum, hoping the sounds of the still-here-girl quartette might alert them to my existence.

I may as well have been a fish in the fish tank.

We left the doctor's office, and I almost laughed as we walked out.

Why did I even need to be at that appointment? It clearly wasn't for me or my wellbeing. It was in service of my mother, her anxiety, and a prescription focused on fixing the "problem" so that SHE could sleep better at night. What a fucking joke.

Why didn't my doctor turn to me and say, "This must be so hard for you"? Why didn't she take *my* shoulder and say, "This is what we believe you are struggling with, let's talk about it together"? Why was I not included in my own doctor's appointment, and why didn't I hear, "What questions do you have about your body, your mind, or the support we are offering you"?

How did my recovery become about mother?

I was furious. I remember leaving the doctor's office and stomping my way to the car, announcing to my mother, and whoever else was in the parking lot, "If I have to gain weight, then I'm gonna have fun doing it."

I angrily popped open the hatchback trunk of her purple hatchback and grabbed a bag of cheddar popcorn from the groceries. I was starving, and *this was going to be fun, god damnit.*

As I shoved the popcorn in my mouth on the way home, my mother looked at me in terror from the driver's seat. At one point she said, "Don't eat the whole bag, you'll make yourself sick."

My heart sank. My throat clenched so tight I thought I might suffocate. *I can't do anything right*, I thought. *What do you want from me?* I held back tears, holding the open bag in my lap and staring, frozen, out the window.

If I eat one more bite, she'll take the bag from me. If I put the bag away, she'll have won. It's either lose all my power and freedom at the hands of her fury, or succumb to her influence and give it away of my own free will. Which

is the better option? Hold my ground and have my freedom taken away? Or
hand away my freedom and keep some semblance of control?

I operated in this small, narrow lens for most of high school, and many years after. One in which I could never do anything right, where I had choices but no power, and where I had to—at all costs—be perfect. It was a small, small tunnel to crawl through, and the further I crawled into its narrow mouth, the tighter the space became, and the more careful I would have to be to not be touched or scathed by its edges.

Any attempts my mother made to help me only pushed me further down the tunnel. Any suggestions my therapist and doctors made to pull me out reinforced the idea that I couldn't be trusted. I wasn't paranoid—it wasn't that I thought my mom or my doctors were literally trying to hurt, harm, or control me—it was that somewhere in my subconscious lay the desire to have power over my life, and I believed that I should have the right to choose Anorexia if that was what I felt would give me said power.

I am outside of that tunnel now, and I can see so much that fifteen-year-old Rachel could not. I know now that there was so much more at play than just power and control. I know now that wanting to be thin and beautiful was not just about being thin and beautiful. I know now that my age, brain, and normal social development played a role in the conflict between me and my mother. That teenage years are all about finding one's sense of self and identity. That at fifteen-years-old, most decision-making and influence is peer-based, not authority-based.

I know that its normal and healthy at that age to exercise independence. And that my reluctance to recovering was probably (in part) a normative teenage urge to exercise that independence. That once I started binge-eating, it was another way to exercise that independence.

I know now that teenage years are a time of self-discovery and exploration, a time when we learn who we are, where we start to make sense of self, we start to form an identity—not necessarily the one we'll carry for life, but hopefully one that lends a good enough foundation from which to grow.

My Eating Disorder became my identity. I was her, and she was me. In times where I lost control within my Eating Disorder, I believed I was losing control over a part of my *self*. My identity. My who-I-was.

As time went on, the line between my Eating Disorder and my *self* became so blurred that I could not see my Eating Disorder as something separate from me. I lost touch of what it felt like or looked like to eat "normally." I didn't know what hunger felt like—because I *only* knew what hunger felt like. I didn't know what feeling satisfied felt like, because I only knew what full beyond physical comfort felt like. I had no idea what other people ate or didn't eat, how often or when, how much or in what combination. My body became such a confusing place to live inside, and I often didn't recognize it as my own.

Because the nature of my Eating Disorder was turbulent—because it was like holding onto a tornado, because it was the constant battle between restricting and bingeing and holding the rest of my life together in between—it became impossible to find any real grounding in my identity. Who I was *was* my Eating Disorder, and my Eating Disorder was a wild and unpredictable storm, so I was a storm too.

My sense of stability became rooted in my ability to keep myself in the eye of her. As long as I was in the center of the turmoil, holding the tornado from the mouth as I waved it overhead, I felt as though I had the power I often craved. It didn't occur to me to let the tornado go, or that the tornado itself was causing so much suffering. I held to it with all my might, unaware of the destruction it caused in its path.

six.

LULLABIES

By my senior year of high school, I had fallen deep into depression. I'd taken my weight-gain plight to an extreme, and after months of depriving myself of food, everything tasted so good, and I couldn't get enough. I started bingeing late at night when my family had gone to sleep, and like all other parts of my Eating Disorder, I had to keep this secret.

Quietly, I'd rummage through the cupboards and slip crackers in my pockets. I'd tiptoe to the freezer and take small spoonfuls of ice cream, hoping no one would notice how much of the cookie dough I'd taken. I'd take bites of leftovers, handfuls of cereal, and small bunches of everything I could find, hoping to leave enough that no one would notice, but take enough so that I could feel the fullness.

Many nights I'd lay in bed in pain. The pain of the binges was a physical reminder of my failure, and I hated feeling my belly so full.

On weekends when my mom would go out of town (she visited her parents in Florida often after my Bubbie had a stroke), my binges had space to grow. When dad was in charge, my brother and I knew all rules went out the window. This was when he swapped his 5:00pm Budweiser for vodka, and by 10:00pm he'd be passed out on the couch and we'd be able to do whatever we pleased.

One of these weekends, my dad made us a traditional dad-dinner (he was a phenomenal cook, and I missed out on many of my dad's good meals because of my Eating Disorder). We had steak and a sauteed rice dish—at least, my brother and my dad did. I'd adopted a new disordered behavior where I ate all my meals with baby utensils. (Yes, utensils meant for babies—the ones with soft plastic covers to protect baby's gums, and with tongs and spoon ladles the size of an adult thumb.)

I ate my steak with a tiny fork and plucked the peas from the bed of rice with a baby spoon. I had already binged that day at school, and I could barely swallow the beautifully cooked steak.

After dinner, I ran upstairs to take a shower. I couldn't bear the feeling in my belly any longer. I knew my dad wouldn't check on me the way my mom would—there was no fear of him pressing his ear to the bathroom door to hear if I was purging or not.

I stood in the shower, contorting my stomach and flexing my abdominals to try and pull the food up from my belly. I could never make myself throw up by putting my fingers down my throat—I was convinced my gag reflex just didn't work, and I'd found other ways to produce a purge. After vomiting what little steak I'd eaten and using my toes to push it down the drain, I started to sob.

I sat on the floor of my shower tub, the water splashing over my face and body, and wailed. I rocked back and forth, and as I did, I started to strike my fists against my stomach. I hit the belly I hated so much. The fullness that hurt so badly. The pressure that reminded me how much

I'd lost the control I'd so proudly harnessed just months before. I struck the place that made me so unlovable, the place that held the food I never wanted to eat, the place that reminded me when I sat down or zipped up my pants or ate that I was not the girl I wanted to be, and that just when I'd had a taste of her, she was taken away from me.

The purging didn't happen often, and that was the only time I hurt myself until later in college. But the binge-eating continued, and as hard as I tried to restrict and lose weight again, I'd lost all control and a new voice in my head had grown stronger than the one that helped me starve.

Just one cookie won't make you fat. Come on, you deserve it. It's ok, just one bite. You fat fuck. You've already gone this far, might as well eat the whole box. What's the point? You're already disgusting, might as well go all the way you fat piece of shit.

The voice in my head became so powerful. So strong. So loud, that she became all I could hear, and I lost the ability to be present in most places in my life. My grades started to dwindle, I stopped dressing myself in anything other than sweatpants, and my alcohol consumption at parties became less about having fun with my friends and more about disappearing to escape my own subconscious.

I was no longer seeing Russ or my team of doctors for my Eating Disorder. I had gained back the weight my doctor wanted me to, and more. My mother saw this as a sign of recovery, and her concern waned. And as her concern waned, my desire to return to a state of sickness increased. I needed to be sick so that I could get the care and concern I'd felt from her, even if I hated her strong grip. I needed to be sick so I could hear comments from my peers like, "You look so thin!" or "How did you lose so much weight!" and "Are you going to eat that?" I missed the attention. I missed the concern. I felt more invisible, less special, and like I had lost the secret power that had once made me so important.

I was certain that still, the only road back to love, the only path back to attention, the only way back to any sense of power or recognition of self, would be to crawl back into the narrow tunnel.

I believed this for years to come. And I shoved myself into that tunnel over and over and over. Hoping each time for a new outcome. Hoping each time, I'd come out on the other side, instead of being pulled out or scratched too badly to keep going.

I stayed this way, with eyes fixed and heart closed, mind focused and body constricted, hoping, believing, that one day by making myself so utterly small and invisible, that I would finally be seen.

In the summer after my senior year of high school, I really didn't love myself, and I was convinced my unlovability was tethered to my body.

So when a boy from school told me he liked me in a time and space when I felt so physically unworthy of his love, a small part of my heart cracked open to the possibility that it was really *me* he wanted.

I often wonder how I allowed my heart to open when I was filled with so much self-hatred. Maybe it was the longing for someone to fill the space I couldn't fill myself. Maybe it was a small glimpse into the inner knowing that I was perfectly lovable and wonderful just as I was. Maybe it was that I hated my body so much, that his affection towards me could only be linked to my actual self, and this reckoning was too real for me to ignore.

Maybe it was Lyle, I don't really know.

Lyle and I were classmates all through high school. We didn't share social circles, and while he spent his arts periods singing in the vocal choir, I was bearing my heart with the acting ensemble in the theater.

Our circles sometimes overlapped at parties, and with only eighty-some students in our grade, we certainly knew each other and had mutual classes over the years.

I first noticed Lyle—like *really* noticed him—when he was unavailable.

He had asked me to dinner in the fall of our senior year, and I think I said "no" in some awkward or roundabout way.

I'd had several love interests in high school after the boy who went to Vancouver with me, but I was always quickly turned off and sometimes repulsed once they expressed too much interest.

My only real high school boyfriend—the kind where I called him my boyfriend and he called me his girlfriend— lasted about a month, and after his nightly phone calls and gentle way of kissing me at school was altogether too unsettling, I broke up with him.

"I just can't imagine having sex with him," I remember telling my best friend. I was attracted to him until he was attracted to me—a classic pattern that followed me for years.

The fantasy in my head was one I'd played out over and over and over. I wanted to be chosen, to be selected, to be desired so badly that no obstacle—not a rejection, not a distance, not even an existing partner—would stand in the way of someone's undying affection for me.

Because without any obstacle, how could I know the love was real? Without a fight, how could I know a love for me wasn't simply convenient? Without true trial and tribulation—on either of our parts— how could I know that I'd truly *earned* any of it?

None of this was conscious behavior. I would have a regular ol' crush, become frustrated that I liked unavailable people, and sit with the longing to be chosen until I was either rejected (which spun me into a spiral of insecurity) or chosen (which led me to feel suddenly smothered and unsafe around so much attention).

I longed for devoted attention, desire, and affection because I was starved for it, and I pushed it away when it arrived because its presence was so unfamiliar that my body didn't recognize it as real.

The simple answer to this psychological puzzle is my relationship with my father. And while it is a somewhat one-dimensional revelation (and one I denied in the same way I denied how my Eating Disorder had something to do with my relationship to my mother), there is truth to it.

Because as I learned years later in therapy, our attachments to our primary caregivers do leave imprints. They matter. No matter how big or small the events of our childhood, the people who raise us are the ones who teach us—whether intentionally or vicariously—what it means to love, how to care for ourselves, and what to do when life gets hard.

When I was four or five years old, my dad would read me bedtime stories. I'd dress up in my favorite nightgown (usually a matching set to one of my American Girl dolls), curl up in my floral bedding, and pick my favorite Disney princess story for the night (usually *Beauty and the Beast*.)

My father has always been theatrical. A natural performer, brilliant musician, former dancer, and gifted creative, his bedtime stories were top tier and rich with dramatic storytelling and epic characters.

After finishing the story, I'd always ask him the same question: "Dad, how long does it take you to fall asleep at night?"

"Oh, five minutes, I'd say."

Five minutes!? I'd think. I knew it took me much longer than that—and no amount of *Delilah Warm 106.9* could soothe me to sleep that quickly.

"How?" I'd ask, genuinely desperate for my father's wisdom.

I wanted him to give me his secrets. His answers to living. I wanted him to teach me—to take me under his wing and offer me the guidance and wisdom I knew lived in him.

I loved him, and I trusted him. To me, he was the smartest, funniest, most creative man I knew.

I wanted so much for him to see me the way I saw him. I wanted him to tell me how smart, funny, and creative he thought I was. I wanted him to see *me*—to really see *who I was* and to help me identify her.

I sought his wisdom so that maybe he could see that I was a place to entrust his wisdom—that I was worthy of the knowledge he possessed, and that I was worth the secrets I was sure he had to life.

It was in small moments like these—curled in my bed, clothed in my white nightgown, talking about something mundane like how to fall asleep at night—that I looked to my father for his love, delight in me, and a little life lesson.

"How do you fall asleep in just five minutes dad?"

"Just stare at the doorknob until you fall asleep." He kissed me on the forehead, smiled, and left my bedroom.

As a four-year-old, I couldn't decipher whether this was literal advice or sarcasm. And so, I spent many nights staring at my doorknob, waiting for magic to happen.

I trusted my father deeply and took these small instructions seriously.

I trusted him on road trips when he'd tell my brother and me, "We're almost there, maybe ten more minutes." When an hour would pass, the anger and fury in me would boil, but I loved my father and couldn't get angry with him.

I trusted him when I'd get A's in school and he'd say, "Well an A is good, but a B is better because it shows you're learning." I didn't want to disappoint him, because I loved him—and took this to mean I wasn't learning like I was supposed to be.

I trusted him when he said, "Your mother is just being sensitive, and she'll get over it," when he, my brother and I formed our little rousing gang-ups poking fun at her insecurities.

I assumed he was all-knowing, wise, and right: we weren't being cruel, *she was just too sensitive.*

So when I was poked at by my friends, when they made jokes at my expense, and when it hurt me, I assumed I, too, was too sensitive.

So when I felt angry for being lied to or tricked, I kept my mouth shut because it wasn't worth losing the relationship by getting angry.

So when I did my best to please someone or make them proud, I expected it never to be "right" or enough—or possibly too much.

I wanted his pride. I wanted his affection. I wanted him to select me for his teachings, to pass on his wisdom, to sit me down and tell me what it meant to love and lose, what it meant to try and fail, how to cope with insecurity and brave the scary storms. How he mustered courage and what it was like when he fell in love with my mother.

I wanted him to choose me, because I felt at times that he never wanted me.

That perhaps, because I was conceived the night of their wedding, that maybe my birth was an accident, and my existence therefore not one he'd planned for. And maybe, even if that isn't entirely true, the simple knowing of this truth led me to believe I had to earn my right to be his daughter.

My father was not—and is not—a bad man. He raised me with the skills and resources he had and did the best he could based on his own upbringing.

I think a lot of people find out how their upbringing impacted them through therapy, and this newfound awareness can lead us to hate our parents or blame them. I certainly did this for a long time, and went from thinking my childhood was "perfect, happy, and normal," to thinking my parents were horrible people and emotionally abusive and toxic.

I know now, that while some of their behavior may have hurt me, and while there may have been times their lack of or mode of parenting could be labeled as "toxic" or emotionally unsupportive, that my parents parented me the way they did because of their own upbringing, cultural norms, and a lack of education for parents in general. This doesn't right a wrong or justify anything, nor am I suggesting that anyone who has experienced parental abuse of any kind should (or even could) simply excuse or forgive their parents because "they did the best they could." Everyone's circumstances are unique—and there is no right or wrong way to make sense of how our relationships with our parents impacted us. That is entirely up to the individual. Period. End of sentence.

In my case, I *did* blame my parents for many years once I learned about childhood development, attachment styles, and how much of my inner dialogue and self-worth stemmed from how they raised me or modeled what it meant to be a human.

There were points in my adult life I had conceded that I'd never have a relationship with one or both of them. It took me years to learn more about them and their upbringings to better understand their humanness—their natural adaptations to their own parents, communities, and life stories. It took more time to come to grips with the reality of generational trauma and its intersection with a poor education system that does not teach us how to bring a person into this world. That my mother's Jewish lineage and the ancestral trauma from the Holocaust, along with continued antisemitism for decades that followed, absolutely rendered a passing on of deep anxiety and overwhelming need to protect one's family at all costs. That the responsibility my father carried to parent his younger sisters while his own parents fought so ruthlessly robbed him of his own childhood or knowing that he was—just as I longed to know—special, loved, and cared for.

Once I'd learned these truths—then and only then could I acknowledge the way their parenting impacted me *without* creating good guys and bad guys, without drawing lines in the sand, and *with* room for relationships with them as autonomous adults that look, act, and feel different than they used to—as long as we were *both* willing to learn, change, and grow. Reconciliation is not one-sided and doesn't happen just because one party does the work.

My father learned from a young age that his needs were not a priority, and that love was something you just trusted existed without it having to be expressed, stated, or shown.

This is how he fathered me: without emotional expression, without statements of love and affection, without clear acts of love and compassion that a child could understand. And with the unmet need still full in his heart to be loved and taken care of too.

This doesn't mean he didn't love me, nor does it mean he never tried to express his care. He did. And still does. My father expressed his love through music and dance. Through smiles and play. With nonverbal expression, that while an integral part to attunement in childhood, was lacking in verbal, emotional, and cognitive connection.

And, as a young child without the emotional maturity or cognitive reasoning to know this truth, I interpreted his lack of clear, verbal, physical attention as a lack of love, and I learned to cope with this not knowing the only way I knew how.

I interpreted the lack of communication around his love and affection to mean that if someone loves me, I have to guess or assume it. If it's unclear that they care for me—or if they don't communicate it—I don't automatically assume this means they don't like me—I assume it means I have to work harder to get them to show it.

This has twisted itself into all kinds of problems romantically: if a guy I'm interested in shows me no signs of his own interest, I don't take that to mean he isn't interested. I take it to mean that he probably *is interested*, I just haven't captured his attention in the *right way* or *enough.* I then spiral into a set of behaviors that most would consider unhealthy: I find out what this person is interested in and I become interested in it. I find out how this person talks, and I talk this way. I mold myself so deeply to fit what I think they want, under the spell and fantasy that *this is how they will choose me.* When this works—which it sometimes does—I end up in relationships or brief encounters where I am masquerading as someone I'm not.

These relationships quickly dissolve, because as soon as I feel safe enough to show up as I really am, I'm usually rejected. For so long I thought this meant that who I really was simply wasn't lovable or desirable.

I have learned this is completely backwards: if I show up in a mask, and someone loves my mask, then the "real me" underneath is going to be a surprise. But if I show up as *me*, someone will love *me*. And then there is nothing to hide, reveal, or unleash.

This was not a truth I learned quickly. It was a truth I didn't have the chance to reconcile for decades—and even when opportunities presented themselves for me to learn another possibility, I was so ingrained in my way of understanding myself, men, and relationships, that the instances of potential cracks in the system looked more like anomalies than opportunities for something different.

I think this is why Lyle's affection befuddled me. I wasn't trying to be someone else with him—I was always me. In my hurt, in my silliness, in my expressiveness, in my sensitivity. And still, he seemed to like me.

And while there was still so much of the wanting to be chosen at play (he had a girlfriend when I first noticed him), there was a second piece that had been missing in my previous and fleeting partners: Lyle really *saw* me. And he liked me when I felt at my worst. When I felt disgusting in my body. When I felt unbeautiful. When I was depressed, anti-social, and self-loathing.

Was it he who was so different than all the other boys? Was I different in his presence? Or was it both? I wasn't sure.

There was, though, something different about Lyle. He was kind, attentive, and curious. He was, in some ways, hurting too—battling his own silent insecurities, questions, and doubt.

I had never felt so seen by a boy. He liked my heart *so much*. And he managed to hold it so tenderly, in a way I hadn't ever experienced.

In the summer of 2007, right before going to college, we dabbled in a gentle love. Our romance started out softly. Like a lullaby. We fell into each other clumsily and foolishly, like little children kicking a ball back and forth for the first time. Connected, curious, and a little fumbled.

We went on dates. I rode in his bright blue Volkswagen Golf (no shoes on the dash—Lyle loved cars and took as good care of them as he did of me). We sang Rascal Flatts at the top of our lungs. We danced. We drank red wine with friends and made out on sidewalks at midnight.

71

We held hands. We lay in bed, looking at each other silently, both too shy to make a move.

I was still a virgin. I don't know if Lyle was—I still don't. I never asked him. We didn't talk about sex, and we never made love. We never did anything besides kiss.

One day in late August, just a few weeks before we were meant to leave for college (him to California, me to New York), we were with some of his friends at a beachfront park for a little picnic. While we were there, one of his friends called me Lyle's girlfriend, and quickly, Lyle corrected him.

"Oh, we're not boyfriend and girlfriend."

I stayed silent and cocked a sheepish smile. I was hurt and a little confused, but mostly, didn't think I had the right to say anything. If Lyle didn't want me to be his girlfriend, that was the end of it. I had no say.

Later in the car, he looked at me and said, "I'm sorry if that was awkward before. It's just we're going to college and I don't think it's a good idea to do that having a girlfriend."

He was kind about it—Lyle was always kind.

I looked at him, hoping to see if I could find any sense of doubt or second-guessing in his face. His eyes were so blue. Looking at him, I couldn't help but feel safe in his gaze, like he was showing me his soul. And I could feel him—as if his soul was made of the ocean—it held the wisdom and depth that most of us will never see, and in the depths of its waters, life of the most unfathomable magic was born. He sparkled.

"I totally agree," I lied.

Lyle didn't make some kind of demand or rule that I believed I had to follow. He simply stated his very valid wish to go to college untethered, and I remained silent.

What I wanted to say in the car that day was,

I really like you and I feel like I'd either like us to be boyfriend and girlfriend or be nothing at all, because I have a massive crush on you.

72

What I didn't have the words for was,

That hurt my feelings. It made me feel like you don't really like me, and it made me feel super insecure.

What I regretted never saying for the years that came after his eventual death, but never found the courage to say, was,

I love you.

Instead, I folded myself up, stayed *good*, and hoped that if I followed the imaginary rules I'd taught myself about how to be with men, he'd one day finally pick me, and we would be together.

seven.

BREAKING WATER

I left for New York a few weeks later, and he for California. We stayed in touch over the fall, randomly calling each other late into our drunken college stupors, sending silly texts here and there.

Over Winter break we immediately connected and rekindled the same softness we'd had over the summer. This time, though, there was more uncertainty, less communication, and more unease. At least on my end.

I wasn't really sure if he still liked me. And when I felt he did, I wasn't sure if it would last. I assumed when we went back to school the same pattern would unfold: not his girlfriend, not my boyfriend, and not much conversation about it otherwise.

That summer in Seattle we stopped hanging out as much. I remember consciously making a decision to look elsewhere for male companionship, without ever explaining to him why, without having a conversation about my feelings (or his), without ever letting him know I was feeling terribly insecure because I loved him and had no idea what to do with that reality. Without ever asking, "Do you love me too?"

Sex became a hyper-focus of mine in my first year of college. While I wasn't the only virgin in my friend group, I desperately wanted to "lose it." I wanted to get it over with so I could "start having it."

Nobody had ever talked to me about sex. My mother is convinced she had a sex talk with me, but I have no memory of it. I had zero sex education in school—I'm not sure if I missed it because of the time in sixth and seventh grade when my family lived abroad in Belgium, and the international curriculum timeframe for sex-ed simply didn't match with US curriculum, or if it was just a massive lacking on the part of my high school education.

I really have no idea.

But I was never taught about sex. I didn't know a thing about my Vagina (I learned the actual names to the parts of my Vagina—and that the Vulva is actually the outside anatomy of the genitals, *not* the Vagina—when I was thirty-one years old).

I knew nothing about the reproductive system.

Safe sex? I knew about birth control and condoms, but not a clue about how to have a conversation with a partner about contraception, about Sexually Transmitted Infections (STIs), about testing, or that it was even okay to talk to a sexual partner about these things.

Forget about any sex education that honored or reflected the LGBQTI+ community—there was barely a safe space for those communities to be seen, let alone be represented in a sex education that didn't exist.

I learned about oral sex on an AOL instant messenger chat in the seventh grade from a French boy named Arturo, who asked me, "Have you ever given a BJ?" to which I immediately replied, "What's a BJ?" then subsequently googled the mystery abbreviation.

My best friend in the ninth grade taught me how to give oral sex. She taught me a special technique she used on her boyfriend.

"I learned it in Cosmo," she grinned. This was how I learned to "give head."

In the ninth grade, my girlfriends and I put frozen bananas in condoms to see if we could replicate a dildo to try and feel what it would be like to have sex. Fucking cold, I found out.

Everything I learned about sex was from my peers, and we taught each other about sex based on information we pulled from magazines, media, pornography, and the secrets we'd hear in the whispers of bathroom stalls about "what boys liked."

And so, my entire sex education was a peer-taught, collaborative gossip-based system oriented around pleasing, serving, and navigating a man's anatomy and sexual desire, omit of any understanding for my own anatomy, my own pleasure, nor the construct of a safe, open, and consensual space that exists between two partners in conversation around the act of sex.

I did experience pleasure and had a regular masturbation practice. I first discovered my clitoris in my parent's bathtub around age four, when the water pressure from the tub faucet hit my body in a way that made me feel all tingly.

Masturbating became a secret and very enjoyable thing for me from a very young age, but without any guidance or understanding of it, I came to believe it was a private, bad, and possibly shameful activity that I shouldn't tell anyone about.

For many years I used my imagination when I touched myself, until my next-door neighbor—the same one who took me to Sunday school all those years ago—showed me a porn website on my family desktop. It was 1999 and the internet was still new, and the website was like a clickbait shop for twelve-second clips of the most bizarre and obscure videos I'd ever seen.

We were both eleven when she showed me this website. At first, we'd look at it and laugh—watching videos that we thought were strange and certainly not meant to *really* turn anyone on.

The more I engaged with this website, the more I started to find videos that *actually* aroused me. And once I had my own laptop five years later, I was so familiar with the world of porn, that I no longer could achieve orgasm without the stimulation of an online video.

When I saw breasts and vaginas for the first time in these videos, I tingled the same way I had in the tub all those years ago. I was totally aroused.

I wasn't ashamed or confused by this—I just liked it.

The female body was glorious to me. And I fantasized about naked women often.

In high school, I felt the conflict of my sexuality. I was attracted to men and women, but I didn't really know where I fit when it came to my sexual identity.

Bisexuality was still (and truthfully, still is) written off as a "fake gay" or "gay in the closet" or "fetishization of gayness."

To this day, I don't feel like I fit into the Queer world. I don't feel fully recognized or accepted. By being somewhere on the spectrum, I feel like I just belong nowhere.

I never officially came out, because it felt like there was nowhere for me to come out from and nowhere for me to go to. I have remained fully steadfast in my sexuality and only halfway recognized, straddling the closet door, not belonging here and not belonging there.

Being bisexual (I don't even really like that word. The "bi" is still too binary, as if to say I'm half straight and half gay, fifty percent attracted to men and fifty percent attracted to women) for me is not an either or—it's a full-fledged, fluid experience of attraction to folks with the same genitals and different ones. One part of me doesn't turn off when the other is on, and it's not a binary system that flips back and forth.

I like men. I like women. I like non-binary and gender-fluid human beings. I like people.

I know this now. But feeling like my sexual identity was not even a real thing made it even more confusing when my sexual encounters with men were repeatedly one-sided, painful, and unpleasurable, and my sexual encounters with women were erotic, reciprocal, and free of expectations.

I started to wonder if something was wrong with me, or if I was just completely gay and not bisexual like I believed I was. *Am I all fucked up because of porn? Am I just not able to connect to my body because of shitty sex with shitty men? Am I just fucking gay? Or am I bisexual like I feel I am, and there's some truth to all of the weavings happening under the covers?*

There was no safe place for me to ask these questions. No community or group in school I could join to make sense of my sexuality. Even though I wanted to date and sleep with women, I had no idea where to start or how to meet other queer folks, and even if I had, I think the internalized fears and judgments I had about my sexual interest in women not being real or valid might have stopped me from even trying.

Porn, my friends, tabloids, and movies taught me that my pleasure didn't matter when it came to heterosexual intercourse, and that lesbian sex was—like all other things in sex—in service of the male gaze.

I continued to avoid real intimacy, and instead I focused on masturbation.

Still, self-pleasure for me became an act of dissociation. I did not use masturbation to connect with my body, senses, imagination, or pleasure: I used it to mentally check out, to latch on to the pleasure of complete strangers in a video, and to move further and further from any real sense of my own body and desire in sex.

79

I had no idea how to ask for what I wanted in sex, because I was both completely disconnected from my own sexual and sensual experience and under the impression that my job in sex was to please my partner.

This belief was reinforced for years once I *did* start to have sex with men.

When I slept with men who pushed my head down to their genitals.

When I slept with men who held my hair back and thrust themselves inside me so deep that I couldn't walk for days.

When I started to believe this was just normal sex, so I learned to leave my body while men bit, scratched, and bruised me during intercourse.

When I had the courage to say "no" to a man's advances, and their response was, "You're being such a tease."

When I had the courage to say, "Stop, you're hurting me," during sex, and after a few minutes passed, was met with, "So do you want to keep going?"

When I cried during sex because I couldn't breathe, and eventually lay flat on my stomach thinking, "I just have to wait until he's done."

I was a vehicle for their pleasure—nothing more than a walking sex object—a vacuum, a vessel, a void.

Sex became lifeless for me. A place I'd go when I longed for attention, and a place I'd disappear from on arrival because I was too scared to really be there.

Once I learned sex didn't have to be just about the other person, I was suddenly fearful of engaging with it. It was terrifying to recognize how many dangerous, risky, and truly harmful sexual experiences I'd endured. My mind didn't know it, but my body did—I regularly dissociated during sex, both with men I only met once, and sometimes with my husband when I said, "Yes" but I really wanted to say, "No."

This was why I often drank alcohol before sex. It allowed me to turn off my brain and stop thinking so much. It alleviated the fear I felt when entering into the sexual arena. It calmed my anxiety and panic associated with the sensation of being touched in certain places, and it stopped me from shutting down completely the moment a man looked at me with aroused eyes.

Still, as the years went on, I showed up for sex again and again. Always hopeful that *this time*, I would ask for my needs. *This time* we might go slow enough for me to become aroused. *This time* I would have the courage to say "No" or "Stop," and *we would*.

I wanted to mend my relationship to my sexual body. I wanted to experience pleasure and safety and play in sex. I wasn't interested in giving up on a life of sexual exploration and joy.

Once I started to try and meet my body in sex—once I started to make amends with my Vagina and care for my sexual self with care and love—I started to have to get really present during sex, and that was terrifying. I felt self-conscious, insecure, and unsure—my pleasure actually mattered, and I had no idea where to start or what to do.

Sex was so confusing that I chose not to even think about it, and I continued to engage with it as though it was a service I provided (to men) for most of my adult life.

I wonder, too, if this male-focused outlook on sex is also what led me to lose my virginity the way I did. Under the guise that sex was a task to perform, and my virginity subsequently a milestone towards said performance—a scene in some sick, twisted play, where a part of my body is used as a prop in service of the protagonist's final soliloquy. That the loss of my virginity was solely associated with male penetration, and that the oral sex and fingering I'd done with girls long before I had sex with a boy "didn't count" as "popping my cherry." That I never was—in my own mind and in the messages I received—an important player on the stage of sex.

And so that summer—my last summer with Lyle—I wanted to lose my virginity so badly that I didn't care who it was with, or where. I was playing my part in this show, and I was ready to deliver one hell of a performance.

One night that summer, I was at a party with a longtime friend from elementary school. From across the room, I saw a boy who looked familiar, and realized he was an old summer camp crush from lifetimes ago.

We talked for a while, drank for a while, and kissed for a while. After a couple hours, we went to my car where we had sex, and I "lost my virginity." I didn't tell him it was my first time. He didn't wear a condom, and I didn't object. It hurt, but I didn't say anything. I moaned and made the faces I'd seen in the porn videos, and I put on a good show.

The next day, I got a text from him.

"Hey, it hurts when I pee. Do you have an STD?"

I didn't say, "No, that was my first time having sex."

I just said, "No, I'm sorry!" As if it was still somehow my fault. I never heard from him again, and I was far too scared to ask my mom if I needed to go get tested. I ignored the message and moved on with my life.

A few weeks later, Lyle asked me to go to the beach with him and some friends. It was something we used to do often together but had tapered off of over the summer.

Truthfully, I'd been avoiding him, because I was under the impression he didn't want to have sex with me, and I was so focused on having sex that I decided it would be more efficient to do it elsewhere than have an honest conversation with him.

"Hey, what happened with us?" He asked genuinely as he drove us to the beach.

"What do you mean?" I asked innocently, knowing perfectly well what he meant.

"We haven't really hung out at all this summer."

"Oh, yeah. I've just been really busy."

We stayed fairly silent the rest of the drive. I turned up the radio. We sang a little Sean Kingston, rapped to a little T-Pain, and shared a few awkward smiles.

I still loved him. I really did.

In the deadly silence of our miscommunication I still loved him. I hoped he loved me too. I just didn't know how to tell him. I didn't know what to say. I was convinced he would freak out, shut down, or reject me.

At the beach, we sat around a bonfire with our friends. Someone told us they'd heard that a paddleboarder had gone missing earlier that day in the water, and we were all pretty spooked. Hovering around the fire, Lyle's arm around me, mine clasping my knees as I curled and retreated.

It was the last time I ever saw him.

eight.
DROWNING

Three weeks later, I was in Connecticut at a family member's Bar Mitzvah. I had gone up alone, as I was the only one from my immediate family living on the east coast.

Around 2:00am after a long night of an open bar and a lot of dancing with my vibrant, extended Jewish family, I got a phone call. It was two of my high school friends who were also in New York for college—and two of my friends who I wouldn't have expected to be spending time together.

"Hello?"

With no small talk or conversation, without a beat or pause between my answer and their next words, they said,

"Rachel, Lyle is dead."

My mind went blank. I knew two Lyle's—there were two Lyles in our grade. Surely it wasn't him. It couldn't be him—it *couldn't* be my Lyle.

"Which Lyle?" my heart was pounding. *Please don't say Rivers. Please don't say Rivers. Please don't—*

"Rivers."

No, no, not Lyle, no, this can't be real, this isn't real—

"Rachel? Are you there?"

I couldn't speak.

I wanted to choke but I couldn't swallow.

"I need to go. I need to go find my aunt and uncle."

"Ok, call us—" I hung up the phone, or maybe I just dropped it on the floor. I can't remember. My entire body felt flooded, and I couldn't think straight. It was as if my body had taken control and my mind was letting it—this was impossible to process, and it couldn't be true—it couldn't.

My aunt and uncle were in the same hotel as me, and I felt compelled to go find them, as if they might have some answer or news, like somehow, *they* might be able to confirm for me that no—Lyle wasn't dead, and this was all some big mistake, and I was just dreaming.

Despite there being a working elevator, I ran the four flights of stairs up to their room. I banged on the door, and my aunt answered.

"Rachel? Are you ok?"

"My friend just died," I panted.

I stood there, in their hotel doorway, frozen.

She looked at me with wide eyes and quickly ushered me in. She was a former psychologist, and I could sense her analytically empathic mind working to wake up and create space for me—both physically in her small hotel room and mentally in her half-sleeping state.

"Do you want to sit down?" She gestured to the edge of the bed where my uncle's feet poked out from under the floral bedding. I immediately regretted coming to their room.

What was I going to say? What would they?

"I'm ok," I said. Still frozen. "I'm going to try and sleep."

"Ok, if you need us, we're here," my aunt said, but I was already halfway out the door, galloping back down the stairs, racing to find some answer…my body running high on a mission to somehow escape the hotel maze, the unreal story, the nonstop track on repeat in my throat:

Lyle is dead.

I hadn't even bothered to close my hotel room door, and I nearly fell as I tumbled into my room. I collapsed on my bed, my face buried in my pillow, my heart pounding and my throat closing with every breath.

I was still drunk from the party and completely stoned from the afterparty. My mind was spinning. I couldn't think straight. *This can't be true. This has to be a dream.*

I turned on the TV, hoping to quiet my mind. The television didn't work, and I immediately felt rage flood my body.

I yelled at the television for being a "fucking idiot." I ravaged the mini-fridge for something to soothe me. I found a Toblerone, and cradled it between my lips, barely bothering to spit out the foil as I bit into the bar.

I wept in bursts. Wailing for a moment, then stopping abruptly. It felt like my mind was having repetitive false starts—I would feel suddenly full of sorrow and rage, then just as instantly my entire body would freeze up emotionless, as if I had emptied, as if I had lost my soul.

I eventually fell asleep and woke up with chocolate on my pillow and salt in my lips.

Lyle is dead.

These words haunted me—on repeat in my mind, whispering themselves in my ears like a deadly sin.

Lyle is dead.

I spent the next week in complete and utter denial.

Lyle had died in a boating accident, where his body had been thrown from the boat and he subsequently drowned. They couldn't find his body for a week.

The irony of our last encounter with the missing paddleboarder has not left me.

I spent every waking hour googling "Arizona lake death" and "Lake Powell news death" and, "freak boat accident Lyle Rivers." There was no news for days, and I wondered how tortured his family must feel in the not-knowing.

When they finally found his body, I knew it was real. The week of doubt, hope, and grieving limbo was over.

Lyle was dead.

My college roommates had no idea how to comfort me. My parents were thousands of miles away, and they didn't know how to soothe me.

In October, I flew home for his funeral. His father played the trumpet, and I wept as I wondered how he could muster enough breath in his mourning to play so beautifully for us. For his wife and daughter. For Lyle.

I avoided everyone at the funeral. I couldn't face his parents. Even though I'd been to his home many times for dinners and family gatherings, I couldn't bring myself to approach them. I couldn't face his friends—our friends—people we'd spent weekends with and taken camping trips with—friends we'd played music with and chanted New Year's countdowns with and watched sunsets with.

I couldn't face myself. I felt like I didn't belong there. Like I didn't deserve to grieve. Like I wasn't worthy of missing him. I wasn't good enough for him. I hadn't shown him that I loved him. I'd never *told* him I loved him, and this made me an unworthy griever.

My badness, my worthlessness, and my not-enoughness convinced me that I was not allowed to mourn his death. That my sorrow would be perceived as selfish and self-centered by those who did a better job of loving him. *What's she so sad about.* I imagined they all thought. *They weren't even that close.* I was certain they whispered. *She wasn't even his girlfriend.*

I grieved silently, and I spoke to no one about my sorrow. I did what I'd done countless times—I took on the guilt of what I hadn't done in our relationship, made his death about me, and believed that by ignoring the reality of what was happening, I was acting as a martyr. In reality, my guilt was only turning me inward in a time when it would have been kind, loving, and respectful to walk up to his parents and do the thing I didn't do, which is tell them how much their son meant to me and that I loved him.

But I didn't tell his parents this until ten years later, when I finally realized the damage my guilt had done, and when I realized it wasn't about me, but about him. About his death and gone-ness, and about telling the people close to him how important he was and *still is*, so that we could keep him alive with our still-existing and never-gone love for him.

I went back to New York after his funeral. As fall turned into winter, I retreated more and more into myself. My best friend and college roommate at the time had a new boyfriend, so she was rarely home. I spent many nights alone, drinking and watching YouTube videos of his choir performances.

I started self-harming to cope with the guilt. To cope with the pain—or lack of pain.

Some days when I felt no grief, guilt would seep in to say, *how are you not sad? You should be sad. You should be grieving. You should feel guilty. You fucked this up. You should be in pain.*

I used hairpins and paperclips to make scratches in my arms. And then I'd ridicule myself for not being a "good enough cutter." for being too afraid to draw real blood, to use a real razor. A few times, I *did* use a real razor blade, and it horrified me.

When I went home for winter break, I was massively depressed, hated myself, and convinced it should have been me who died instead of Lyle.

Most nights I'd go to parties with friends, drink until I blacked out, then drive home drunk in my truck, hoping it would crash. I became careless with my life—too drenched in self-loathing to stay alive, but too afraid of death to kill myself—hoping the universe would take care of dying for me at the hands of my reckless behavior.

By the time I had returned to school in January, I was in a state of desperation. My Eating Disorder had developed into constant binge-eating. My weight was at an all-time high. I was pouring vodka into soda cups and drinking during class. I slept until 4:00pm most weekends and faked doctor's notes to get out of class. I was a shell of myself, barely functioning, and riddled with a guilt that told me I was better off dead.

One night in December, while my roommate was at her boyfriend's apartment, I set myself up for my regular alone-time ritual: vodka, videos of Lyle, and writing.

I'd drink myself into a stupor and watch him sing songs like "No Air" and "Sun and the Moon." I'd sing with him, and cry over the adorable way he'd shake his hands to the rhythm while he sang. I'd write vicious letters to myself in my diary—words I wouldn't wish on anyone.

That night, I went into the bathroom of our dorm room and swallowed a bottle of over-the-counter pain pills. I don't even know if it would have been lethal. But my intention was to go away and never come back.

As soon as I did, I panicked. *What am I doing,* I thought. *I don't want to die.*

In my memory, I called my friend to come and help me, and in a seamless process she simply took me from the bathroom floor and into the taxi that ushered us to the emergency room.

I later learned—almost a decade later in an honest conversation where she opened up to me about her own fear and trauma around my attempt to end my life, that she had to break the bathroom door down where she found me.

She took me to the hospital where they admitted me and put me on an IV drip and charcoal shake. I vaguely remember answering a slew of psychological intake questions—shouting things at them like, "Yeah I'm fucking depressed. Yeah, I hate myself and cut myself. Uh huh, yeah I also have an Eating Disorder."

The ER seemed so dark. I don't know if it was, or if I was so messed up from the alcohol and pills that everything just looked twisted. As I faded into sleep, I could see the outline of my friend and doctors standing there, shadows hovering beside me, maybe murmuring something to me, maybe silent, I don't know.

I woke up confused, disoriented, and incredibly hungover. I blinked my eyes open, adjusting to the unnecessarily bright florescent lighting that seemed to blind me from every corner.

There was no real "initiation" or "welcome" to the hospital. This was not some beautiful arrival into a recovery center, and nobody gave me a tour or shook my hand or even asked my name.

Upon waking, I was slumped in a wheelchair with my belongings in a plastic bag on my lap. I was tucked away in some corner behind what appeared to be a front desk. I was alone and had no idea where I was or what I was doing there.

I think I got up out of the wheelchair, still in my hospital gown, and approached the desk. This part is still quite fuzzy—I imagine I was still coming off of my drunken stupor and whatever drugs they may have given me to sedate me.

Somewhere between waking up in the wheelchair and being fully conscious later in the day, I was assigned an escort and taken to my room.

I was on suicide watch, which meant I wasn't allowed to be alone. A nurse was by my side around the clock. When I showered, she was there. When I used the bathroom, she was there.

I would like to say she was kind, or at least showed some compassion for the fact that I had just attempted to take my life and was now suddenly in a foreign place with none of my belongings, no phone or internet access to contact a friend or family member, and zero privacy, but she was not kind, and showed no compassion.

I'm sure she had dealt with hundreds of difficult, angry, and far more volatile patients than me in the past, and her demeanor was likely a boundary she'd created for her to protect her own energy.

Honestly, I don't remember much about those three days. Though I journaled extensively to try and retain as much of the experience as possible, my actual memories are fragmented. Like small pictures or stories that enter my mind, the entire experience is made up of stills.

I can see myself in the shower room crying. I wasn't allowed to use the bathroom in my bedroom—I was required to use the suicide watch bathroom which was a single stall room with a curtain. This allowed the nurse—my escort—to stay in the room with me—I wasn't allowed to be behind any closed doors alone.

I remember Zeff. I remember his long black hair and the white ribbed tank he always wore. I remember him telling me about his bunny, and the ex-girlfriend he had who made him want to kill himself. I remember him doing pushups in the hallway and looking at me without breaking eye contact in a way that made me feel both uncomfortable and adored.

I remember thinking, *this is as good a time as any to try parting my hair on the opposite side.*

There was an arts therapy group I attended, where one of the men drew a picture of aliens. He said it was meant to be him, or something like that.

The dining hall was dark, and blue. There was a TV, which played *Law & Order* exclusively.

I have no eloquent way of describing the stale state of the New York City hospital. It was, as I imagined most psychiatric floors of a city hospital to be—white, sterile, cold, and towering above the surrounding buildings.

I shared a room with two other women—one who never moved from her bed, and another who frequently paced our room describing the brilliance of her son's classical piano skills back home in Germany. The woman across from me—the one who never moved—looked like what I imagine Dory from *Finding Nemo* would look like if she were a human. Her face perpetually dazed, her eyebrows fixed in an upward delusion. She'd sometimes murmur a word or two, and occasionally roll over in her bed, making brief, petrified eye contact with me as if to say, "Help me, I'm trapped in this body, they've taken my mind, and I may never be me again."

When I saw my psychologist, he told me I would have to call my parents for insurance purposes. I didn't want them to know I was there at all, and if it hadn't been for that, I don't think I would have called them.

Truthfully, I don't even know if it was me who called. It could have been the doctor. If I had a conversation with them, it's one I don't remember.

At some point, my college roommate came to visit me. She brought me a journal, and it was in those pages that I divulged the details of my roommate's German tales and the odd, lifelessness of the many people I interacted with. People who I imagined once had lives and families, childhoods and stories, who now appeared in the hallways and dining hall like ghosts, fragmented leftovers of who they once were, physically there, but entirely lost.

They had us all take meds—pretty much like what I had seen in movies. Like clockwork, we'd line up and take our paper cups of medication without question. Who knows what I was taking. I don't remember if they ever even told me.

I didn't learn much in my actual therapy sessions. What I learned there was far more embedded in the utter rock-bottomness of it. I witnessed a potential life that I knew did not belong to me—one filled with a sedated, soulless, teetering existence. I didn't ever want to return to that hospital—or any other—ever again.

I wondered if they made the experience so horrible on purpose: as if the treachery of being there alone was the medicine to never return.

A few weeks after I left the hospital, my mom came to visit me in the city. We never talked about the hospital. In fact, I didn't talk about the hospital to anyone for years, and a decade later when I finally told my brother about the experience, I learned my parents had never told him, and I wondered what other secrets our family had been harboring.

I remember us walking together through Central Park, my mother and me. We stood together at the top of the Belvedere Castle, overlooking the cloudy, crisp New York winter day.

"You know," she said to me, "if you need to take some time off school and come home for a bit, your father and I would be okay with that."

I looked at her in disbelief. My body filled with gratitude and relief flooded my face.

"Really?"

"Of course."

She hugged me, and I held back tears.

The thought of disappointing my parents was unfathomable. And it never occurred to me that I was allowed to ask for a break, no matter how much I was struggling. In my mind, I had no good reason to be struggling, I didn't deserve to ask for help, and surely my success in school far outweighed my wellbeing.

I needed this permission from my mother. I needed the approval from my father. I was too scared, too embarrassed, too ashamed to ask for the relief and rest I so desperately needed. My mother offering me rest was the most soothing medicine, and I fell into her arms and let her cradle me, the way I imagine she'd wished she could have for all those years.

nine.

BREATHE

A few weeks later, I organized my leave of absence with the school, and arranged to go back home at the end of the second semester.

I was perplexed to find out upon my return from the hospital that I was only required to have *one* counseling session to clear my return to classes.

I was just on suicide watch in a hospital, and you're going to sit with me for an hour and determine that, yes, I am fit to return to five days a week of class from nine to five? Without continued counseling? What the actual fuck?

Even *I* knew that was ludicrous, and I barely cut myself any slack or held an ounce of compassion for what I'd just experienced.

I was meant to complete my final semester, then take my leave at the end of spring.

I was a theater major at New York University (NYU), and my program was demanding. While most of my peers were in class a few hours each day for three days a week, I was in class from nine to five Monday through Friday, plus rehearsals in the evening for our performances.

I struggled to keep up that final semester, and while I managed to get through with good grades and my body intact, I was nowhere closer to a life of balance, peace, or joy.

When I returned home for the summer, I was relieved to know I wouldn't be returning to school in the fall. And, I was still incredibly depressed and in the belly of grief.

I continued to do what I knew how to in order to cope: drink, eat, and talk to nobody. I socialized and went to parties and hung out with friends. But I still didn't *talk* to anyone.

Who would understand? Who would know what to say? And who would care?

I was certain my existence was a burden. I had *no* reason to be depressed, *no* reason to be sad, *no* reason to have an Eating Disorder, *no* reason to exist, *no* reason for anything. I was a worthless shell of a human, and if someone really cared, they would notice my suffering, and come to my rescue.

This was entirely backwards, but it was the story I lived by. I fully believed that if I was worth existing, worth living, and worth being loved, then someone would sense my suffering and save me.

As I held firmly to the belief that I had no responsibility in my suffering, so too did I believe I had none in my recovery. And as I shamed myself into thinking it was my fault that I suffered, I shamed myself into thinking I should live alone with those consequences.

It was a cycle of thoughts and behaviors that left me internally tormented and externally stuck.

I spent most nights that summer drunk on my parents' couch, watching *Grey's Anatomy* reruns, and crying myself to sleep, my lips covered in breadcrumbs and my belly full of binge.

There were days when my mother would berate me for being depressed. She'd passively urge me to get a job, sending me emails and Facebook messages asking, "How many jobs have you applied for today?"

My father rarely spoke to me—not because he didn't care but because I don't think he knew how to.

My brother was still living at home, and I'd occasionally hang out with him and his high school friends in the basement, acting as the cool older sister.

Life was quite meaningless for me during that summer. And as my friends returned to their college towns and fall came, I was reminded of my failure, of my inability to function, and of the fact that I was a pathetic loser who couldn't even get through her second year of college.

In late August, I started my first blog. I called it "Lefron," which had become my alter-ego after a longstanding obsession with Zac Efron. I'd merged Le + Efron to make "Lefron," and gone so far as to change my email, Facebook name, and username for many websites to said penname. This was absolutely a joke, which became a theme within my writing and coping itself.

Humor and sarcasm were ways for me to deal with my self-loathing openly without having to *really* be vulnerable: it was a way for me to be honest and open a window into my world of despair without having to really deal with the intensity or truth of what lay beneath the surface.

Though I've released a lot of perfectionism in my life, it still takes every bone in my writer's body *not* to edit the excerpt from my decade-old blog that you're about to read (and I'm talking about grammar and punctuation—editing the content is not my concern here, I'm legitimately anxious you'll think less of my writing if you see the errors in my decade-old blog. And, this is an exercise in radical letting go, so here you are). Perhaps, even in this explanation alone, I've allowed my perfectionism to seep through, as if to say, "Dear reader, excuse the grammar and punctuation and writing, I was only twenty-one. Have mercy."

Welp, here goes. My first blog post read:

> As I begin my 5am shift this morning at a gym downtown, delivering the usual nod and grin to incoming members, packing lists start running through my head. (Per usual-when is a list not running through my head?) September approaches, and thus the giddy excitement of back-to-school shopping, the prospect of seeing old friends, and the hopes that maybe this year that boy will notice you quickly approach.
>
> Then a realization crosses my mind.
>
> How silly of me. I don't have to pack. I don't have to plan. I don't have to worry, dread, anticipate, dream horrible naked dreams…For the first time in 16 years I'm not going back to school. For the first time in 16 years my September brings no drastic change, no structured rubric.
>
> What will I do with my hands when they are so empty without No.2 pencils? What will strain my mind at 2 in the morning and later fill me with pride when I click "save"? However, will I survive a gradual transition from summer to fall, when most of my life school has so kindly made the flip for me?
>
> I've thought this over, I remind myself, this is what I want. I want no structure, no boundaries, no man to stick it to. I asked for this–I asked for complete unknowing; the horrifying idea that I have no idea where September will take me this time around.
>
> In the years past (while each different and unpredictable) I was assured the fact that September brought October, October Halloween, November Thanksgiving, December Christmas,

January New Year's... There was an endpoint for every month—a checkpoint reminding me that the next one was coming. A cycle, or train ride rather, that I rode in circles with different passengers through time. Now, I've gotten off the train—and while I know what stop I got off at, I have no idea what train I'm catching next.

As the months went on, I kept writing. I had no expectations for this writing, and it didn't bother me that the only people who read it were my kooky aunt and my mother's best friend. I wrote for me, and the fact that it was public was a byproduct of not thinking anyone would ever read it.

Shortly after I started writing, I started working. Slowly, I was finding my way off my parent's couch and taking steps towards some semblance of young adulthood.

I found a job at the front desk of a gym in downtown Seattle, and occasionally I'd babysit for my high school mentor's daughter at his home on Vashon Island.

These retreats to Vashon were always peaceful and a welcome getaway from the city. One morning after babysitting, I took a run along the Island's quiet backroad.

As I normally did that year, I listened to my curated "Lyle Playlist" while I ran. This made me feel connected to him—as if my runs would somehow keep him and I tethered together, and as though this meditative space between my feet, the pavement, and the outside air was where he lived, and I had access to him.

I was still looking for some sign or reason to live. Some invitation from the universe, some guiding light to point me in a direction and say, "Rachel, there is a reason to be here, and *this is it*."

As "No Air" started to play—one of the songs he sang and one I'd watched him perform in the YouTube videos I'd torture myself with all year in college—I noticed a hawk appear in the sky above me. My entire body flooded with chills. As I ran, the hawk flew beside me. It followed my path and kept my pace, as if it was keeping me company with every step I took.

I started to well up, and eventually, I burst into tears. As I ran, I kept checking to see if the hawk was still there. I started to laugh as I cried, and the sky seemed to crack open with my heart.

It was Lyle.

I had never experienced something like this before—I was a self-proclaimed atheist and didn't believe in any higher power or consciousness. I was vehemently convinced there was nothing outside of me or anyone else that could explain our existence, and that we were all just bodies moving through life, eventually to die.

In this moment, I felt something different. Even if it wasn't *really* Lyle—even if it was some coincidence or false meaning I drew from the song and the hawk and the sun, I felt a sensation in my body that told me to trust myself and allow the moment to be whatever it needed to be.

And it needed to be Lyle. It needed to be him flying beside me. It needed to be him giving me permission to be free. Free to live, free to let go, free to move on, free to breathe. Free to be, and to know he would always be there: in the wings of the birds above, in the earth beneath my feet, and in the beating of my heart.

As the song came to an end, the hawk disappeared. I stopped abruptly to scan the sky and look for its wings. I couldn't find it anywhere—just as suddenly as it appeared above me, it had vanished, and I wondered if I'd imagined it altogether.

That day, I decided to live.

I decided to live because Lyle couldn't. And if I could believe that it should have been *me* who died and not him because *he* was so worthy of living, then I could use that same logic to live on behalf of someone who deserved the life I was still blessed with.

I started to take care of myself, the way I would have imagined Lyle caring for himself. I fed my body well, and I moved it. I spent time with friends, and I made art. I went to work and started saving money to take a two-month backpacking trip through Asia with my cousin.

I wrote, and I imagined what I might want for my life. I imagined the future—something I hadn't thought about in years. I imagined the future, because for the first time in a long time, I had hope.

part three
floating.

"Your desire to be beautiful is ok,"
she whispered.

"Your *definition* of beauty
might need
a little tweaking."

ten.

SLIDING DOOR

By the age of twenty-one, I had come to accept and love many parts of my body for the first time in years. I was eating regular meals, exercising, and felt good about how I looked in my clothes (and naked).

I felt attractive, desirable, and beautiful.

I engaged with men the way I had previously engaged with food: their attention and presence soothed me, filled me, and made me feel less empty. I let them do what they wanted with and to me, because it instilled a sense of being wanted in a part of me that didn't yet know it felt unwanted.

I had no boundaries with men—I never said no, I didn't ask for what I wanted, and I assumed whatever they wanted was what was "right" and good. This played out in the types of dates we went on (shitty sports bars, whiskey in their living room, no date at all) to the sex (their pleasure first, only rough painful sex, no sleepovers).

These encounters made me feel powerful, desirable, and wanted. For a time. Until they left me feeling used, disrespected, and alone. These relationships were fleeting and always ended with me attempting to create something more than just a sexual relationship and getting shamed, shut down, or finding out the person I was sleeping with was really interested in someone else.

At the time, online dating hadn't shifted into the swiping world of Hinge and Tinder, and to meet someone online you had to fill out an intensive application and exposé—even if you were just in it to quit it.

I had an account on Match.com, where my profile read like most of my sarcastic and dry blog posts:

> Bangin' twenty-one-year-old with a fat booty and a quick wit. Wait—I meant twenty-one-year-old woman who can cook pancakes and wear an apron. I'm lost, how does this work?

> You won't find me in the kitchen unless you want burnt toast, but I'll happily pack a flask in my backpack when we go hiking together. Did you say naked drumming? That's great, I'm a nude guitar player so our band will certainly be famous.

> Please only match with me if your dog's name is Harry. Or it's hairy. I do not like bald dogs.

I matched with older men often. It was not rare for twenty-seven- to thirty-year-old men to reach out to me.

One night while spinning the wheel of Chatroulette in my parent's basement, attempting to soothe my boredom while feeding my insecurity, I heard the familiar "ding" of a new match on Match.

You've matched with Jake!

Who is this Jake creature? I wondered, gleefully.

I loved getting matches. It was a total high to get that notification—even if I had no interest in who I matched with, it was validation that I was desirable, and I craved the hit.

"Hey Rachel! I've seen you at the front desk of Allstar before, I work next door and work out in the morning sometimes. What's up?!"

Before responding, I analyzed every inch of his profile.

Age: 29
Height: 6'1"
Eyes: Blue
Pets: Yes, one dog
Job: Sales
Location: Seattle

So far, so good.

He barely had any photos of himself on his profile, but from the few he'd posted I could tell he was good-looking. He was super fit, covered in tattoos, and his sharp jaw and slick hairline told me he was either a total player or simply full of himself.

I kept reading.

Relationship history: Divorced.

Divorced? Yikes.

This seemed like a red flag to me (I was still under the impression that divorce was some kind of death-sentence or sign that you were damaged, bad at relationships, and shouldn't be trusted).

My gut said, "This guy is trouble," and I declined his invitation to hang out and went on with my life.

A few weeks later, I was working my regular 4:45am shift at the gym. I loved this job, because it was a rush to get a smile and hello from the early bird lifters every day, and it fueled my ego first thing in the morning.

One day, as I shoveled my Light N' Fit yogurt and muesli, Jake walked into the gym. I almost spat my yogurt on him. He was energetic, charming, and incredibly attractive.

This was the guy I turned down? Fuck I'm an idiot.

I was struck by his forwardness and lack of embarrassment by my initial rejection.

For the next two weeks, I observed him carefully. He'd pass the glass windows of the gym every morning at 7:00am sharp—and like clockwork, he'd turn towards the window and wave at me. His timeliness matched his character—he was clean cut, clean shaven, and his hair was always perfectly coifed into a neat triangle atop his head.

Every morning, when the sun was starting to rise and the streets of downtown started to wake up, I'd organize myself and prepare for his gaze. I'd stand alert, gently facing the doors, my hair perfectly curled and rested to one side of my neck so he could see my face. I'd look to the door (but not face it—I had to seem aloof and as though the timing was magically aligned).

On mornings when I'd miss his gaze—either because I was checking in another customer or couldn't hold my bladder any longer—I was devastated. It felt as though I'd missed a meal or lost all replenishing and nourishing feeling for the day. On these days, I'd make sure to stay late after my shift, working out and cruising the gym floor in hopes he'd take a lunch workout and we'd have our five seconds of eye contact and "what's up!" exchange.

I longed to take back my initial rejection. I wanted to be re-chosen by him. I wanted a do-over, because his lack of insecurity around me made me believe I must have not been that desirable in the first place, and my rejection had no impact on him whatsoever. I had no power and was not *really* desirable. I had made a mistake and should have said yes.

I had recently quit smoking, but I knew that every morning around 9:00am he would take a smoke break with his buddies. I picked up smoking again and started taking my ten-minute break right before him so that he might see me smoking and stop to talk with me.

I stopped drinking for a couple weeks to shed a few pounds—I wanted to be as physically attractive as possible, and the promise of being chosen was enough to harness the discipline of my Eating Disorder I had let go of for so long.

I was peacocking. Using my body as bait. Making myself as available as possible, camouflaging myself to mold to his interests, all in the hopes that he would want me badly enough to choose me again.

One morning, I was standing in the stoop where I took my morning cigarette. It was cold—and I held my arms around my body as my once snug pants sagged around my hips.

As I inhaled the smoke from my Marlboro Light, Jake walked by with his coworker. He stopped and looked at me.

"You smoke?" He asked.

"Yeah," I shakily said, doing my best to produce a flirty and seductive grin.

"Have you lost weight?"

"I guess so," I replied, again trembling beneath a sheepish smile.

As he started to walk away, I blurted the words, "I changed my mind!"

I startled myself with this statement—though I'd practiced and rehearsed it in my head for days, I didn't think I'd find the courage or opportunity to ever say it.

He stopped and looked at me, puzzled but curious.

"About what?" He turned to face me and put his hands in his suit pockets. I could see his thigh muscles pressing through the fabric, and I felt instantly small, naive, and a little aroused.

"Your offer to go out. I thought about it and I changed my mind."
He laughed, in a chortled chuckle kind of way. In a way that said, *oh really? You've got to be kidding me.*

"Ok then, well, I'll text you sometime." He pulled out his flip phone, took down my number, and walked away.

I melted in my stoop. I don't know if it was the rushing high from the tobacco I so recently took up or the wave of hormones and adrenaline flooding through my body, but I was high.

It took weeks for him to text me. I'd see him still, every morning. But no text. I waited and wondered if he ever would. I wondered if he was punishing me, or even torturing me for my rejection. *I deserved it*— I thought—and I would wait.

Finally, a text came through.

"My place. 9:00pm. Don't eat before you come. Papi will be waiting."
What did that mean? Who was Papi? Don't eat? Why not? Immediately, I went to Wikipedia.

Papi is associated with…wait what is dominance? What is submissiveness? BDSM? What is this? Does he want to lock me in a cage? (This, I now know, is not the nature of BDSM, and some of the safest and healthiest sex happens in the kink community where communication, consent, and respect are of paramount importance. Wikipedia in 2010, of course, did not educate me on this, nor did any other forum or blog post I stumbled upon.)

I let the internet take me down a rabbit hole, and eventually I determined that this guy must want some type of leather-bonded sex relationship with me, in which I was his slave, good girl, and obedient, and he was completely in charge.

I desperately wanted his approval, so I went along and decided I would like this too. I would enjoy being submissive. I would like being told what to do, how to do it, and when to do it.

At 9:00pm, I arrived at his studio apartment, with no idea that this was potentially a risky first date. I had blinders on. I had never been taught about safe communication, consent, or even what an appropriate date looks like, even *if* both parties are simply seeking sex, even *if* both parties want to engage in BDSM or kink (which, when consensual, communicated about, and done with trust and safety, is perfectly healthy and ok). I didn't even know if BDSM was *actually* what he was interested in—I took one word, "Papi," and ran to the internet, too embarrassed to ask my potential sex partner what he meant. Too scared to ask what he liked. Too unaware that it was ok to tell him what I liked too.

It also didn't occur to me that our dramatic age gap created an immense power discrepancy: he was twenty-nine, and I was twenty-one. He absolutely was in a position of power, and he abused it, whether he was conscious of it or not.

The first time I went to his house, we drank whiskey with diet soda and listened to rap music on his television. He had a small first floor studio that I entered into through the sliding door facing the alley— never the front entrance, never in daylight. We talked casually—maybe about hikes, maybe about Eminem—I'm really not sure. We shared cigarettes on his apartment patio, and I pretended to like what he liked.

Our first night together colored all the rest. It started with rough oral sex, and quickly moved into rough intercourse. I was never touched, licked, or pleasured. It was always for him. His skin was completely shaven—from his ankles to his face. He was tattooed, with FTW sprawled across his chest. I didn't know what that meant until almost a decade later. I'd drive home, slightly drunk, slightly bruised, and with a swollen throat.

We'd text casually throughout the week—he'd give me a "green light" if I could come over that night, or a "red light" if he had to wake up early. He'd cancel frequently, and each time I'd be disappointed, as I'd plan my entire week around our evening together.

I thought what I was doing was empowering. I believed I was "getting mine," having fun, and stepping into my sexuality.

There was nothing about what happened to me in our nights together that was fun, "mine," or even remotely connected to *my* sexuality.

I rarely shared any of myself with him. Even in the giving of my body as a vehicle for his pleasure, I didn't *share* myself with him: I kept my sexual desires, my personal life, and emotions outside his small apartment. I assumed that if he wanted to know more about my insides, he would ask, and that if he didn't, my insides didn't belong in the story of whatever "this" was.

Some nights I'd show up in costume—a sexy schoolgirl or wearing a trench coat with nothing underneath. I did everything I could to please him. To keep him interested. To be wanted.

One day, out of the blue, he texted me during daylight—something he'd never done before.

"I just read your blog. Holy crap you're a great writer! You should come over tonight." I was shocked, but excited. *Did he want to get to know my insides? Did he like who I was inside? Was this the night he'd fall in love with me?*

He asked me to come over at 7:00pm—the earliest I'd ever gone to his place. It was still light out when I arrived, and the entire mood of our encounter had shifted. He pulled my blog up on his desktop computer—the same one he'd watched porn on while I sat on his lap, pretending to enjoy myself, just weeks before.

"This is awesome!" He announced. He was an incredibly enthusiastic man—everything was awesome, and he had a routinely optimistic outlook on just about everything.

"Thanks," I said shyly. Though my blog was incredibly vulnerable, raw, and full of stories about my mental health, I was not yet comfortable expressing or sharing these stories in person.

We shared our regular whiskey drinks and talked about me, for this first time in our two months of encounters. He suggested at one point we go get food, and we drove together in my truck to the Jack in the

112

Box up the hill. This was our first time doing anything together outside of his first-floor apartment.

After curly fries and a few more drinks, we had sex. He tried to please me for the first time—and when he did, I froze in the foreignness of it. He asked me to tell him what I liked and wanted, and I couldn't.

"I don't know," I tried to say in a sexy voice, "I like what you like."

I could feel him growing frustrated, and eventually he gave up and inserted himself in me. I was relieved, because at least the painful penetration was familiar. And in the relinquishing of my own desires, pleasure, and longing to be known, I was in the only place I'd ever been in sex: in this unfortunate familiarity where my brain felt safe, and I learned again that *this was how sex must be.*

When he finished, I expected him to offer for me to stay the night. He had, after all, invited me over earlier, wanted to learn about who I was, gone with me in my car to get a meal, and offered me attention and interest in my pleasure sexually. Surely, he would also ask me to stay the night.

But he didn't.

I drove home drunk, confused, and furious. I felt rejected, used, and abandoned.

Why did he show so much interest in me? Why would he pull my personal life into the mix if he didn't like me? Or was it just that after learning so much, he realized how undatable I really am, and that all I'm good for is the sex I so readily gave him? Hadn't I given him enough? Wasn't it now my turn? Isn't this how it works? Sex for love? My body in exchange for his heart?

I sent him a Facebook message the next day telling him exactly how I felt. It was the first time I had stood up for myself to any man, and the first time I had expressed anything to *him* that was remotely related to my needs, my feelings, and my interests.

I told him I felt used and taken advantage of. That he shouldn't have let me drive home drunk. That he made me think he liked me by reading my blog, and then made me feel terrible about myself for not asking me to stay over.

I wish I could find this message, but after tirelessly digging through my Facebook, Zuckerberg informs me Jake no longer has an account, so our messages have evaporated.

His response was cold and short. He told me I shouldn't have expected that from him, and it wasn't his responsibility to make me feel good. That we were always in a casual thing, and that my reaction was out of proportion.

Months later, I received a text from a number I didn't recognize.

"Hey, I just wanted to reach out and apologize for how I treated you. I hope you're doing good!"

I had a hunch it was him.

"Who is this?"

"Jake!"

I sat in the back of my dad's car, wondering for a few minutes if I should respond. By this time, I'd left my job at the downtown gym, and had started working as a server at restaurant. I was saving money for my backpacking trip to Asia and had started fresh in many ways over the summer.

Still, I did what I normally do in these scenarios: I skipped over my hurt, swallowed my anger, and moved straight to empathy and compassion. I forgave him, as if nothing had ever happened.

"No worries, thank you."

"Maybe we can go for a hike sometime!"

"Sure!"

I left it there, feeling surprised, bewildered, and a little delighted.

A few weeks later, a coworker of mine at the restaurant told me she needed some extra help at the gym she managed. It was the same branch of gyms I'd worked at before, and the location of this gym was just blocks from Jake's apartment. I knew he went to that gym sometimes, and quickly, fantasies of being chosen returned.

It was as if the experience shifted nothing in me, and my worth and desirability was still completely tethered to the potential of being chosen—again. *I could work at this location, and Jake and I could finally have a re-do at what was an initial hiccup in our love story.*

I let this delusion carry me all the way into decision-making, and I used this fantasy as fuel to accept the front desk job.

On my second day, a tall, rather fit guy waltzed into the gym and walked right past the front desk. He didn't check-in, or even bother to stop and try.

"Who the hell is that?" I asked my manager.

"Oh, that's Josh! He works at the front desk too, so he doesn't have to check-in."

What a douche, I thought.

I would soon discover that Josh was nothing short of a good man, and seven years later would be my husband.

eleven.

TOES IN THE WATER

This is the hardest part for me to write. The part I put off the longest. The part I avoided and convinced myself didn't belong, wasn't necessary, and wouldn't move this story along.

In many ways, that pushing away itself mirrors how I was towards the end of our marriage and how I ultimately pushed Josh away: I convinced myself it was obvious that I loved him, so apparent and so clear, that I didn't need to say it, didn't need to show it, and even *now* didn't need to include it in the story that so clearly begins and ends with our love.

I fell in love with Josh in a way that has often left me believing I will never love anyone the same way again.

The way I loved him made no sense to me. It was all encompassing. It was safe. It was full of warmth, affection, delight, and desire. He became the safest place for me to be, and with him, I was always home.

Josh understood me in a way nobody had before. It was as if he saw inside of me, and he saw the magic I'd buried away for so long. He wanted me to see the magic too, and he did everything in his power to pull it out of me so I could see what he saw.

Josh treasured me, and I treasured him. We held hands in public. We wrote each other love notes and left small gifts on each other's doorsteps. We showed interest in one another's hobbies and spent time with each other's friends and families thoughtfully and intentionally.

We blended so well into each other's lives. His friends became mine, and mine his. His older brother my new big bro, my little bro his new younger brother. Our parents loved us respectively and welcomed us into their homes.

Josh made me feel like I was the most vibrant, sexy, intelligent, funny woman in the world. And he made me feel *like* a woman—he empowered me to stand firm in my womanhood and made me feel like I was capable of anything, and that together, we were invincible.

Our friends saw this in us too. I became the go-to girlfriend for relationship advice, and the communication box and tools Josh and I worked so hard to build were like a treasure chest to my friend group.

I was proud of our relationship. I was proud to call Josh my partner. I admired him, respected him, and adored him.

I didn't feel this way off the bat—when I met him at the gym that winter, I wasn't interested in him. He represented, to me, all the men who'd previously disappointed me. He was tall, fit, charismatic, and exuded confidence. I was certain he was out for one thing only—sex, attention, and power.

So, it confused me when Josh asked me questions about myself during our work-shifts together. It befuddled me when he'd show interest in my writing and show up in the morning holding a coffee for me—with a little nonfat milk and one Splenda—something only someone who'd read my blog closely would know.

Josh mystified me. He was smart, curious, and warm. He looked at me when we spoke—like *really* looked at me in a way most people didn't. He looked at me as though he wanted to know me, and as though in some way, he already did.

We never stopped smiling. We laughed so much together during our shifts—poking fun at our insanely anal boss, laughing about the guy who would show up at 4:45am, who was perpetually angry that we wouldn't open the doors until the gym opened at 5:00am. He'd leave me long-winded notes in our community log—a book meant for daily shift updates about the flow of the day or logistics of the work, but a space he'd use to write humorous love notes and draw pictures of our future together—scribbles and doodles he knew would probably get him in trouble, but shamelessly put on the pages anyway because he knew I would read them.

Josh broke all the rules. He lived life as if it was his movie to direct, his book to write, his game to play. And play he did. This enticed me, because my whole life I'd been an avid rule-follower, constantly agonizing over the potential repercussions of doing the wrong thing, and play was a foreign, unfamiliar, and out-of-touch concept.

When we met, I was teetering the edge of my own rule-bound lifestyle, certain that my choice to take more time off of school to travel and break the traditional college-career-marriage-babies-retirement track was my own defiance against "the man," and I liked that he was interested in life outside the box too.

I think this is what intrigued me most about Josh. He didn't fit the mold of what I expected—or maybe stereotyped, or maybe had experienced—men to be. He was kind, empathetic, and interested in my life.

He was also strong, smart, and opinionated. And while his stubbornness about being "right" muddled opportunities for us to connect or repair in conflict at times, it was a quality in him that grounded me, kept me centered, and made me trust his unwavering certainty when at times I had none.

His curiosity for life and me, his willingness to hold space for my vulnerability and emotional world, and his real, genuine desire to know me and for no endgame or expectation of anything other than connection, was different.

And oh, how I loved the way he talked about life.

"I just want my life to be like one long documentary. Like a really good book. I want my life to be interesting."

When he said things like this to me, I felt myself fall more and more into him. Not in love, just into him. Like he was me and I was him. So much of the way he saw life was how I saw it too, and I'd never met anyone who thought so deeply about the world, human nature, or thoughts themselves the same way I did.

His mind was beautiful. Analytical. Thoughtful and philosophical.

We talked about life, meaning, purpose, travel, and passion. We shared the ways we were fed up with how life was *supposed* to be, and like a lover's tennis we'd rally back and forth, filling the court with lofty ideas of how we *wanted* life to be, serving our grand ideas and what-ifs and how we'd be able to break the mold and do things our way.

Josh would tell me his favorite quotes or recite lines he'd read in books, and he'd do so in a way that made me feel as though he'd pulled them from his rolodex of wisdom just for me.

He'd see some small thought of doubt or insecurity bubble in my throat, and intuitively, he'd take both of my shoulders gently in his hands, turn me towards him, and tip his head down to meet my gaze. It was as if he'd create a small safety circle for us, a place only we could go: a place he'd meet me to bring me back to earth.

He'd say something perfect: something certain, something true. His words would simmer through me and warm me. They seasoned my soul and added a flavor to my life that I would taste on my tongue for years to come.

One night just a few weeks after we met, we went out for a few beers and a game of pool—the perfect escape from the cold Seattle winter and a good reason for us to get some time alone. As we sat down for a pint between games, Josh asked me to tell me about my life. I panicked. No one had ever outright asked me about my *life* before. Without stopping to breathe, I recited my entire life story in under five minutes, nearly blacking out from the overwhelming vulnerability I felt from a simple exposition and play-by-play of my life.

"Are you ok?"

"Ya, I just sort of blacked out there. I don't normally talk about myself that much."

He laughed.

"You barely talked! That was like, the fastest life story I've ever heard. Rach, I love hearing you talk. I love the way your mind thinks. I love everything you have to say. You got some thick walls, and I'm gonna keep knocking on them until I kick them down."

I loved this about Josh. He wasn't afraid to try and see me. And he didn't stop trying, ever. When I'd shut down in conversations that scared me, when I'd dissociate in moments of anger, when I'd lose myself and leave my body while trying to express jealousy or fear, he'd keep trying.

On one of our shared morning shifts at the gym, I was simmering in anxiety, my mind rising dangerously close to the surface of my consciousness, about to leave my body the way I would sometimes when it all felt like too much.

I was anxious about something in the future—worried about what the hell I'd do when I got home from Asia without a job and without a plan. Panicked about making the wrong choice, picking the wrong hostel, going to the wrong city. Terrified, secretly, that if I left, I'd lose

121

Josh forever, and the safeness I felt with him was something I'd never feel again.

He noticed me there—far away and spiraling, and gently pulled me into the safety circle. Once I arrived, I could see nothing but me in him and him in me. He smiled when he knew I was there, as if he'd been waiting to greet me. He then said something I was certain he had concocted just for me. A medicine statement brewed with tenderness; healing words he'd delicately molded to replenish and fill me with their perfect wisdom:

"Rach, there is no right way, there is only the way you do it."

I exhaled, and it was as if I hadn't known how to breathe before that moment.

This became our motto, and as the years pressed on, we were committed to doing things the way we did them. We became unconcerned with doing life "the right way," and only concerned with doing life the way that filled our souls, gave us meaning, and enriched our worlds with color, texture, and flavor.

His blatant disregard for social norms and expectations was the invitation I had been seeking to step outside the box I'd kept myself in for so long. To step off the riverbank where I'd sat fearfully for years, afraid of what might happen if I actually got into the river and let the water take me.

Josh was wading in the raging river of life: curious, eager, and optimistic about what might happen if he leaned back and let the water take him. And when I met him, he stood there—beaming, confident, and hopeful in the frosty wetness, holding out his hand for me to join him.

The choice was so simple. I was decaying there, stagnant on the river's edge. My heart longing to see where the river flowed, my body paralyzed and frozen on the bank. My mind a mess of fury and fear as the world around me said, "Stay still," and my heart and soul whispered, "Jump."

Standing there, seeing him so ready to brave the current, and wanting me to brave it with him, I was fearless. Safe. Certain.

Without looking back, without looking down, without caring about the freezing cold or the sharpness of the rocks beneath my feet, I waded into the river with him. Eyes locked on his, mouth permanently pressed in a lover's grin, I reached my hand out to meet his.

He took it, firmly, rubbing his thumb in my palm the way he would for years to come when he'd hold my hand. He leaned down to meet my gaze, gently met his forehead with mine, and from his sweet and tender smile whispered, "It's just you and me."

We slowly turned to face the same direction, towards the river's end. Hand in hand, we leaned back, and let the water take us. Trusting, that no matter the current, no matter the weather, no matter the forks and turns and rocks that may come our way, it would always just be him and me.

twelve.
LOVE LETTERS

Josh and I did as much as we could *our way* in the first year of our relationship.

At the end of December, just a few days before my flight to Hong Kong, I had a going away party. Josh came, and we drank shitty liquor and bantered late into the night surrounded by some of my close friends and coworkers.

The next morning, we planned to meet at the breakfast spot next to the bar, pick up our respective vehicles (we were both proud anti-drunk-drivers), and say goodbye before I left for Asia.

Hungover, I sat with my hands tucked between my bum and the leather chair beneath me, sweating over my eggs benedict and waiting for Josh to arrive. I was excited to see him. I was always excited to see him. I was also perpetually scared. Scared this would be the time he'd say he no longer wanted to see me, scared he'd stop liking me, scared what I'd say (or wouldn't say), and what would happen after we said goodbye.

Would he want to talk to me while I was gone? Would we see each other when I got back? Does he actually like me, or is this just a convenient fling before I go to Asia?

My Blackberry dinged.

New Message from Joshy Poo:

"Almost there!"

I was always early. He was always late.

As my nerves intensified, I felt myself start to quiver and sweat the way I always would when I'd wait for him. The anticipation of his smell, the peering out the window hoping to catch him sauntering down the street with his joyful bounce, the waiting for him to come blazing through the door, entering into a room how he always did when he knew I was in it: eyes sparkling, mouth grinning; as if he'd come on stage to give me a one man show, a performance titled, "I love ya Rach, and boy am I happy as hell to see you."

As I looked down at the melting Hollandaise, I heard the jingle of the bells over the door, and I knew it was him. I looked up, and just as I imagined he would, he waltzed into the diner, eyes locked on mine, grinning from ear to ear.

He had a way of smiling when he saw me that felt all mine. He didn't smile for anyone or anything else like this. It was a smile made for me, born when I was born, and unbreakable when we were together. I saw the words "I love you," in that smile, long before he ever said them.

"Hey Rach! I don't have long, I have to go clean windows, but I wanted to see you, and give you this."

My heart sank. I wanted him to stay all day. I wanted him to stay the night before. I wanted him to crawl into my suitcase and come to Asia. I didn't want to say goodbye, and certainly not this fast.

126

"Oh, ok, no worries." I lied.

He handed me an envelope, and I laughed.

"What the hell is this?"

"Haha, um, yeah I didn't have a real envelope."

I looked down at the yellow envelope in my hands, covered in pictures of handymen giving thumbs up and the Midas logo plastered on the back. It was an envelope from a car repair company, and an envelope that likely had held some bill or follow up document from a servicing he'd done.

I later learned Josh was the king of holding onto papers and documents that were completely useless, but he beautifully recycled them into love notes or envelopes to hold his letters to me, and in some way, it made them more uniquely his, and that made it more uniquely ours.

The envelope was so full it wouldn't close, and I could see several pages of yellow composition paper folded up inside.

"I wrote you a letter. But don't read it until I'm gone." I could tell he was a little embarrassed, and I liked that. He was opening his heart to me, and I softened.

"Well, I hate this, but I gotta go."

We walked outside together, and we hugged. He held my shoulders and pulled me into our safe bubble, rubbing his hands up and down my arms as he looked at me.

"If you wanna write me while you're gone, that would be ok," he said.

"What, like pen pals?" I joked.

"Ya, you know. Or just photos of your butt and stuff," he joked. We laughed. I started to well up inside, but I couldn't let him see that. I hadn't known him very long, and I didn't want him to see how soft I'd become in his presence.

"Rach," he tilted his head down and met my eyes, which had fallen to the ground. I looked up. "Yeah?"

"My buddy told me a quote the other day I think you'd like. He said, 'The secret to life is to enjoy the passage of time.' So, when you're thinking about me and missing me and thinking, 'Gosh I should have stayed in Seattle with that hot guy from the gym and never come here at all,' just know that we are both passing time, and that just like you want me to enjoy it, I want you to, too."

I smiled. His sense of humor grounded me, and he had a knack of honoring my sensitivity while still delivering his own comedic way of coping with sad moments.

He hugged me, and I hugged him back. We kissed, and our faces melted into one. I felt his tongue in my teeth, his cheeks in my hands, his hands on my back and our bodies curling and folding into one another. We pressed ourselves together like a swirling whirlpool, barely breathing, tumbling and stirring our bodies under the water, not wanting to come up for air, hoping to stay weightless in the cool wetness forever.

When we did come up for air, we said goodbye, and I watched him walk to his car. I watched him walk away the way I always did, the way I always would, until I couldn't see him anymore, until he'd driven off into the distance, until every particle of his energy had dissipated, and until I was truly, truly alone.

I walked back into the diner and heard the dinging over my head, this time a reminder I was all alone.

I sat down, my eggs and sauce now hardened and cold, and opened the Midas envelope clutched in my hands.

The letter read like a witty poem—full of jokes and little love notes Josh had scribbled. Whimsical stories of how we'd met, how he'd wanted to break down my walls and really know me, and how he was so bummed I'd be halfway across the world.

He ended the letter with this:

My mom used to always tell me growing up, "Not only do I love you, but I like you." And Rach, I really, really like you.

Yours,

JOSH

As I read his letter, I held back tears. Even though he hadn't said it, I could feel that this man loved me. And I loved him. And as we would tell each other for years to come, not only did we love each other, we *liked* each other.

I saved the letter, and the envelope, along with the hundreds of letters Josh would write me in the years to come, and always on random scraps of paper or the backs of envelopes. Napkins with drawings he'd leave on the dash of my car before going to work and longwinded love-letters on the back of old house bills. I have these letters still, collected like an archive of him, a library of us, tucked away in a box where so much of my heart lives.

I wish I had that box with me, but it's hidden away at my in-law's shed, halfway across the world collecting dust under my wedding dress.

I haven't spoken to my in-laws in almost a year—not because I don't love them or there is any hardness there—but because when Josh and I ended our marriage, it felt impossible to know what to do with the families we lost too.

Three weeks later, I left for my two-month Asia trip with my cousin. While I was away, Josh and I wrote each other. Almost every day, I'd find an internet cafe and write him a longwinded email. And every day, I'd check my inbox, eagerly awaiting his reply.

Rachel Mother Stinking Godbe!

How the heck are ya? It's your favorite pen-pal in the whole contiguous US of A, Josh K for Kenyon Havekost. In the letter I wrote you before you left, what did I say? Have fun, live life... blah blah blah, JUST AS LONG AS YOU COME BACK. Whenever you read this, I'll be thinking about you at that moment. There's a 97% chance of it. You are truly, truly amazing. I know I should play harder to get and put you down, but I don't feel like that. I think you're terrific. You make me feel good. Thank you. Get back here and let me thank you properly.

Love,

Josh.

PS. You're a beautiful person with a beautiful personality and I miss both.

Dear Josh "You will always be shirtless in my eyes" Havekost...

I've told you this before, but I'll tell you again. I want you. (If I don't voice an opinion, I don't have one or it's not strong enough for me to care to voice it. So if I do speak up, I really want it.) When I'm with you, everything feels right. When you hold me, I don't feel like I can get close enough to you. You remind me every day not to take life too seriously and that whatever way I do it is the right way. I can't seem to get you out of my head, and I've stopped trying. You deserve to hear how exceptional you are every day. You're exceptional.

Miss yer face,

Raderbane.

We'd intro our letters with ridiculous nicknames and end with equally goofy yet affectionate signoffs. We'd wax sarcastic-poetic about our feelings and attraction to each other, skirting around our emotions but directly naming our genuine interest and delight. We shared stories of our days and honest thoughts and philosophies about the world.

Sometimes we wrote each other poems, rap songs, and short stories about our *like* for one another, the way we missed the other, the disbelief we both had about how lucky we felt, and how scared we were it might not be real.

The honesty and vulnerability with which we wrote each other in those few months was unfamiliar, yet completely home. I had never opened up to anyone like I had to Josh. I had always been the friend who held space for others, letting them open their hearts and bear their stories, but never returning the same vulnerability or history. My inner world was locked away, and I was petrified of what might happen if I let somebody inside.

I asked Josh in one of our email exchanges why he tried so hard to get past my walls. I wanted to know what he saw, or wanted to see, and why he worked so hard to break them down.

Why did I want in your walls? Hmm, I have been tossing the question around in my head like a rock tumbler, and although the stone is far from polished, I wanted to try and start typing this answer to see what I say.

I think I always have this drive to really understand people and I am not altogether sure that it's a good thing. Like, sometimes I might want to know everyone's weaknesses around me so that I don't feel vulnerable. (Woah! I've never thought of that before. This could be good, I'm gonna continue.)

But I DO think that usually it is something I do for good, I genuinely like to develop relationships. (Not always sexual, it certainly changes the dynamic when the person is a gorgeous female with a body like I've never seen.) When we first worked

131

at the gym, it was fun for sure, but I knew that if I let you make sexual jokes and did the same in return, then that was going to be the pinnacle of our relationship. (This is not a conscious thinking process btw, I'm getting all Rachel-style introspective right now, which is analogous to you telling me about your life, so you had better be appreciating it.)

And since it was so fun, I didn't want that to be the top of the mountain, I'd rather try to keep climbing. There was something else, (I don't know if it was your eyes or what...we are both terrific eye-contacters) that told me you WANTED me to deal with these walls. I don't think that's too outrageous, a lot of people with walls like yours probably don't really want to keep EVERYONE out. But like you once said they are your only defense against douchers and assholes, and it seemed like you could tell I might be a rare breed that doesn't fall in at least one of those categories.

I think to summarize: 1. I thought you were sexy and wanted to have sex with you (honesty points!) 2. I could see that there was more to you, I don't know how, but I could SEE it. Maybe that's the wrong word. Sense it? I don't know, can't explain. 3. Curiosity 4. I liked the challenge. 5. I've never met anyone (that I can think of) that thinks like I do. You are better at describing it than I am, but I think you know what I mean. 6. While mine might not be as distinct, maybe a little sneakier, I think in some ways there are walls or defenses that I use too. And I think I wanted someone in here with me.

Despite my jet-lag and the fact that I had serious food poisoning from my last few days in Asia, we arranged to meet for dinner my second night home from Asia. I wanted to see him no matter how ill I felt.

I could barely eat at dinner. The combination of my stomach cramps and nerves rendered my soup untouched. All I could think about was how beautiful Josh looked and how elated I felt to see him.

We drank beers and talked for hours without a single breath of air between us. It was as if we had everything to talk about and nowhere else to be, and we were in a trance.

We went home together that night, and it was the first time I'd ever felt truly aroused during sex. It was also the first time I'd ever waited so long before sleeping with someone I was interested in, and loved. I didn't put these pieces together for almost a decade—that the safety and connection I felt with him opened me up to feel safe in my body, connected energetically, and *allowed* to be even somewhat concerned with my own pleasure.

For the next year, we spent as much time together as possible. His job took him cross-country every other month during that year, so we continued writing each other emails and building our relationship both together and apart, creating and expanding our safety circle to keep us connected whether we were physically together or miles apart.

When we were together, we were completely absorbed and infatuated. If we didn't have the language or couldn't find the courage to say the words caught like wildflowers in our throats, we'd paint pictures of our love through moments of eye contact or breaths against each other's necks in the evening hours.

In the mornings we'd lay in bed for hours. Staring at each other and tracing each other's faces. Memorizing and learning one another with our fingertips, making imprints in our minds eye so that even in the darkness we could find each other.

"Which eye do you look at when you look at me?" He'd ask.

"This one," I'd point to his left eye, which was to my right.

"What about me?"

"That one," he'd point to my right eye, which was to his left. He'd ask me this question almost daily, as if for the first time, as if excited to

133

hear the same answer again because it delighted him, and me, so much. Like giddy school kids, we let ourselves be surprised every time, because we found it to be so magical. That when we looked at each other, it was on the same side, on the same plane, and we both believed it must be why we felt we were really *looking* at each other.

We really *did* look at each other. No conversation, no hug, no moment of eye contact or connection was met without visceral, full-body *looking. Seeing. Knowing.*

I wanted to know him, and he wanted to know me. We held space for one another's fears and anxieties. Made room in our lives for the other's goals and aspirations. Held a home in our hearts for each other's hurt and past grievances. We knew each other with almost more detail, compassion, and warmth than we knew ourselves.

Come December of our first year together, and after months of a half-long-distance relationship, we decided to celebrate my birthday with a trip together.

Spontaneously, we booked a two-week backpacking trip in Thailand. We were both adventurous, loved to travel, and could be somewhat impulsive—something we became known for in years to come. And so, we leaped without looking back. As we always did, as we always would. Before we knew it, we were on the beaches of Koh Samui, running from the monsoon rain for cover, sleeping in hostels, and eating mounds of Cashew Chicken and rice.

"Happy birthday, Rach!"

We found ourselves on the white sandy beaches of Koh Samui after a week of hitting the temples and city streets of Bangkok and countless suit shops in the streets of Phuket. Josh was often upset by his notoriously impossible-to-dress tall and athletic build (which I personally did *not* find impossible or upsetting) and very excited to get a famous Thai custom suit to suit his shape.

Josh handed me a Singha, and we found a spot on the beach where we could watch the sunset outside our hotel.

I remember being angry, but I don't know what about. I was always angry on my birthday. I had high expectations that someone would surprise me, or that the whole day would be a magical experience. I'd create these lofty ideas in my head, without telling anyone what I wanted or needed to feel special, and then would inevitably be disappointed, discouraged, and assume it meant nobody loved me.

It was likely that I was disappointed that Josh's idea of a birthday present was tuna sandwiches and beer, but rather than tell him what I wanted, I just hoped he would be able to read my mind and create some romantic gesture in this tropical paradise.

As we sat on the beach, my silence thickened. Josh recognized my distance and checked-in the way he'd always done.

"Hey Rach, what are you thinking about over there?"

He was sitting right next to me—his arm around me. I wasn't far away, but he knew that even though my body was touching his, I had gone somewhere else. The way I had many times in our relationship when I felt rejected, unloved, or uncertain. I'd go far away from my body, somewhere dark, somewhere quiet, and would lose all touch with reality, my words, and my thoughts.

"I dunno. Nothing. You?"

"Well, I was thinking about this one time in college when—"

At this point, I think I rolled my eyes, or grew more disgruntled. I hated when Josh started to tell a story or make a joke when I was upset. It made me feel more invisible.

"Uh oh, what? What did I do?"

"I dunno. I just. I dunno."

"Rach, you gotta tell me what's going on. If you don't, I can't help you." He said this lovingly.

"I dunno. I don't know what to say."

"Ok, well would it help if I asked questions?"

"Yeah, actually it would." I wanted him to ask me questions. It made me feel wanted. It made me feel seen. It reminded me that he *wanted* to know me, *wanted* to understand me, and not because I opted to tell him, but because he asked.

"Ok, well, maybe we can make this like an open floor—I'll ask you anything, and you can ask me anything."

"Ok, I like that, so like, you can ask me anything and for this one time I'll tell you anything, and same to you. Open floor."

"Ya, open floor session!"

"Let's do it." I softened, and came back to my body.

I loved this with my whole being. It was complete permission to be vulnerable, open, and transparent—which I wanted to be—without the fear of being a burden, without unloading, and without the concern that I would say too much. And in turn, I could ask him all the questions I was dying to ask but too afraid to ask. Too afraid to hurt him with. Too afraid of crossing boundaries, stepping on toes, crossing the line, angering, or being inconsiderate with. It was permission to ask the real, hard questions, and not break any rules.

It was also a chance for me to tell him more about myself without the fear of taking up too much space. It was an invitation—a space full of questions I could answer and know that I could speak my truth—no matter how scary, without it meaning anything about who

I was. I was so scared, all the time, of what my words might mean about me. Like if I expressed an opinion or thought or emotion that was anything other than thoughtful, kind, or considerate, the words themselves would *make* me, and I would be as bad on the outside as I felt on the inside.

This was our first of many "Open Floor" sessions. Eventually, when we moved in together and had our own space and our own floor, we renamed them "Floor Meetings," and intentionally carved out time every two weeks for these gatherings. We ritualized our Floor Meetings. We'd buy wine and light tea candles, bring notebooks and our favorite pens, and always started and ended with gratitude, respect, pride, or affirmations. We sandwiched any hard questions with softness, so that we could begin with love and end with love.

"Ok, who's leading today?" Josh would start.

"I will!"

"Great, I love when you lead," he'd smile, relieved. I was the planner, and Josh loved playing passenger.

"Ok, so I was thinking we'd start with three things we are grateful for in the other, then have as much time as we want for things we *need* from the other or feel we aren't receiving, then end with something we're proud of in the other. Anything you really want to include or add?"

"Hmm. No, I really like that. Maybe we can start with two things we're grateful for and something we appreciate? Just to mix it up?"

"Love it! Ok, do you have anything already? If not, I can go first."

We were so gentle with each other. There was so much tenderness, and so much love.

Floor Meetings became a safe place to open up. A reprimand-free zone to express our hurt. A cushioned zone to throw our anger. The time to ask for our needs, to stand up for ourselves, and say the sharp stuff we knew might scratch the other.

I loved our Floor Meetings. And, while they offered us a place to be honest, loving, and true, they also protected us from having to fully show up outside of its safety.

Our anger became contained to these moments of truth, unless it couldn't be contained and blew up. Our needs were only expressed in the safety of the floor, unless we needed them so badly that we grew resentful. We relied on our soft sandwiching, to the point that we were so careful with all our communication that we struggled in real-time to be genuine with our anger, upfront with our needs, and courageous with our language.

We loved one another with this goodness. We spoke to one another with goodness. We expressed our hurt, anger, and resentment in *good* packages with *good* ribbons and *good* words.

We were tender, and in time, our relationship became so tender that its fragility became the most powerful thing between us. We spent our days tiptoeing around our delicate relationship, constantly in fear of hurting the tie that bound us.

It wasn't that our bond was unstable or that the slightest crack could have broken it—it was that we cared so much for one another, that the fear of being the source of one another's pain was greater than our willingness to shake the foundation.

We both had needs that went unmet. Desires that went unexpressed. Parts of self that went un-identified. Asks that went unasked. Not because we suppressed them or denied them in the other, but out of fear that the very ask would cause harm to the person we loved most.

And so, nine years later, when we started to unwrap our desires, express our needs, identify parts of self and speak our hurts and truths and ask the big asks that we'd bottled up for so long and held in breaths between our Floor Sessions, our foundation couldn't carry the weight.

thirteen.

SHAPESHIFTER

Over the next four years, Josh and I fell deeper and deeper in love.

We moved into an apartment together, and then a house. We traveled often—and we did it *our* way, backpacking often, planning as little as possible (at least, he did, and I tried my best to go with the flow), and always giving a full body "YES" to wild adventures and spontaneous getaways.

We spent time with his friends and mine, at my family homes and his, weaving our lives into a tapestry, creating a colorful, vibrant fabric with our love, adding more detail, texture, and flare with every passing day.

Shortly after returning home from my trip to Asia and during our first year together (with Josh's gentle and loving encouragement), I had gone back to school to finish my degree. I never thought I'd find the courage or strength to finish, and I'm not sure that without the nudge and loving support of someone who I trusted, and who really understood me, that I would have.

After finishing my degree, I got a teaching job at my old high school. For two years, I juggled several hats at the school: teaching middle school theater, heading the eighth-grade leadership group, directing plays, and co-creating a new role at the school designed to function as a bridge between student, teacher, school counselor, and parent.

Between these many roles I found more and more purpose. The anxiety I'd once felt about "what will I do when I come home from Asia" had faded and I started to feel that my life had direction. I adored teaching, rekindled my love for theater, and felt rewarded by the impact I was having on the middle-schoolers I worked with and so dearly adored.

Because I was young, students trusted me, and they often came to me with their stories, anxiety, or frustrations. I *was* these kiddos, and they were me—the same sense of worthlessness, unlovability, and disappointment they felt was in their bones and still in mine, being carved into them in the same years and moments it had once been carved into me. Different hallways and different times, but the same scared hopelessness, and the same uncertainty with how to cope.

I wanted to help these kiddos badly. I wanted to offer them the love, validation, and tools I didn't get at their age. I didn't want them to be left to their own devices the way I'd been, and I desperately wanted to protect them from accidentally falling into the same cycles of hurt as I had.

Without any psychology background or education, I knew it wasn't ethical for me to be offering them the kind of support I wanted to—nor was it my job. I referred dozens of students to the school counselor in those years, dreading the moment that would inevitably come in the conversations we'd have in my office where I'd have to say,

"I really want to help you more with this, and, because I'm not the school counselor, this is as far as I'm allowed to support you. I think it would be so brave of you to talk to her, and I'm happy to walk down there together."

Simultaneously, I was falling in love with the theater again. The classes I taught and the productions I directed with these same kiddos brought such joy, life, and play back into my life. I longed to be back on the stage again, and with every passing month the courage to try grew stronger.

After leaving NYU, I told myself I wouldn't act again until I was mentally and emotionally well. I knew the pressure of auditioning and performing triggered my body dysmorphia and sense of worth, and I needed to be in a highly stable state before re-engaging with the theater as a performer.

After three years in a healthy relationship, sturdy roots in a single city, a rental home with my partner, and proof that I could land and hold a steady job, I felt ready. I believed I was in a place where I could finally step back out into the acting scene.

I gave my notice at my work, and I started auditioning.

As soon as I started auditioning, cracks in my self-confidence thickened. The acting world is strict, exclusive, and unforgiving. Castings are like animalistic interviews, where the actor's physical appearance matters just as much if not more than their talent, and any error is inexcusable and grounds for beratement. It's not uncommon to be cut-off, dismissed, or asked to leave in the middle of an audition, or simply asked not to show at all if you don't "look the part."

"Casting: 5'3", brunette female, 110lbs, soft features."
I could weigh that much by the time I audition.
"Casting: Petite, young-looking female, must be able to pass for fourteen or fifteen years old. Not casting child actors, adults only."
Ok, I can look fourteen. I'll wear pigtails to the audition.

"Casting: Twenty-five to twenty-eight-year-old female, ethnically ambiguous, mysterious, sexy."

What does that even mean?

With each character description that rendered my self-image muddled and confused, the cracks in my foundation eroded. With each audition and subsequent rejection, my footing flailed. For every role I *did* land, there was the added pressure of a potential bad review, the imperfect and fallible nature of live performance, and the reality that once the show was done, I would have to start the process all over again.

For every good review I *did* receive, there was an equivalent bad review. And while my friends, family, directors, and fellow actors applauded and congratulated me, all I could see were the small failures, the roles I didn't get, and the occasional criticism written in the pages of a local blog.

These are and were *real* pressures of being an actor, and I know that my mental health or insecurities aren't the root of how detrimental acting was for my well-being. An arena that focuses on appearance, who you know, and *getting it right* is one that instills a sense of impending fear, anxiety, and insecurity. There is nothing, nor was there anything, wrong with *me* inside that system—the system itself was unforgiving and hard, and it is natural and normal that I felt the suffocation inside its walls.

And, there was the reality that within those walls my foundation was still shaky. I walked into the acting arena carrying the insecurities, fears, and uncertainty I already owned, and upon entering the arena I began brewing a convulsive recipe that silently eroded the ground beneath me.

For a year I tried to make a living as an actress. I auditioned for dozens of plays, short films, commercials, and music videos. I landed several roles, had some success, and made just enough money to pay for my headshots, which were $350. Josh kept us afloat with his job, and he kept me afloat with his love.

With every passing week, I was losing my ability to hold onto the foundation I'd built for so many years.

The walls of the acting arena caved in so slowly, so sneakily, that I didn't feel their pressure or notice that I was making myself small to fit inside them. I was losing sight of everything and everyone around me, fixated on landing the best roles, always looking the part, and the unrealistic expectations I'd set for myself to be the greatest actress in all of Seattle.

And so, my Eating Disorder came to visit me again. Asking for a seat at the table, offering her services to me like an old, trusted friend. And I let her.

In spite of Josh's love, in spite of the support I received from friends and family, in spite of the success I was experiencing, I turned to my Eating Disorder and said, *"Help me, I'm drowning. I'm drowning and I can't get out. It feels so heavy, I'm too tired, and I can't breathe."*

I used old, familiar tools to carve my uniqueness. I leaned on cigarettes to stop me from eating. I cut out food groups and reduced my meal sizes. I exercised frequently and took to the scale. And while much of what came up remained easily undetected (dieting, coloring my hair, shopping, wearing more makeup, and so many other "normal" behaviors that were mainstream and acceptable), the cracks in my foundation were silently chipping away.

The dieting grew more and more extreme, and as it did, my body started to slowly shut down again. I was losing my sex drive, losing menstruation, and seeing the gauntness once again in my face. And I loved it. It made me feel high. Powerful. Like I'd set myself apart, made myself different, and once again tapped into the secret wisdom I'd found so many years ago.

This was how I'll stay unique. I'd think. *This is how I'll make sure they see me.* I believed this was how I would hold the attention of directors and critics. How I'd instill envy and awe in the actors and players I'd yet to meet.

In some ways, my Eating Disorder was also a way for me to stay small. Because while I longed to be unique, while I longed the attention and validation that I was somehow good and right and real, I was also terrified of what would happen if I was actually seen.

As soon as there was any hint of recognition, affection, or attention, I became startled, as if it couldn't be real. It was too unfamiliar—the very thing I wanted—so I'd either run from the praise, hiding from the certain prank that was to come, or seek it elsewhere, hungry for more, longing to feed the gaping insecurity with enough love and affection so that I was so full of it that I couldn't *not* feel it.

I wanted to be known and to belong, but the idea of being seen scared me so much that I thought the best of both worlds was to become invisible—translucent—a chameleon or shapeshifter that allowed me to be anyone, anywhere. I wanted to be small enough that I could fit into any space that I occupied. I so badly wanted to belong, that I thought shrinking was how I would accomplish it. I thought if I could fit into every sliver into every nook and every cranny and every corner, that no matter where I went, I could slither in. I could fit in and I could belong.

This longing consumed me. I couldn't focus on the beautiful fact that I'd courageously quit my stable job to pursue a craft I was passionate about. I couldn't focus on the friendships and connections I was building with likeminded souls—the family I was weaving with my creativity and their artistic expression. I couldn't focus on the way Josh admired me, and how proud he was of me, both in the adoration he expressed to our friends and family and in the private moments where he kissed me and said, "I'm so proud of you."

I was unable to see the love and care that already existed in plain sight. The arena full of teammates, the crowd full of fans, the sidelines lined with coaches who trusted me enough to put me on the playing field. I wanted more, and the real, good, and true acceptance right in front of me wasn't enough.

Josh watched all of this unravel and he did his best to help me. He tried so hard. He was kind and he was true. He told me I was beautiful, held me when I cried, and encouraged me to take breaks when I became so focused and obsessed with work or memorizing lines that I feared I'd never succeed.

But like so many other people in my life, he had no idea how to help me. He didn't have the tools, he didn't have the knowledge, and even if he'd tried to find them, tangible and accessible resources to support someone with mental illness (especially Eating Disorders), were few and far between in 2015.

I felt, as I had many times in my life when my mental health deteriorated, like a burden to him.

Like my lack of ability to care for my body and mind was a nuisance, and to keep him happy and free from stress, I needed to slowly fade away. That to belong to him, the way I wanted to belong in the theater, the way I wanted to belong to the social norm and societal presentation of beauty, the way I wanted to belong in the world, I would need to become small, quiet, and easy to deal with.

I wanted to belong to Josh. Not *to* him—not as his possession or a belonging, but to his world. To his friends. To his family. To his values, his interests, his pleasures, his needs, his hobbies, his delights. I loved him so much and I wanted to *belong*—to him. I thought this was how I'd get to stay—I thought it was how I'd get to be *with* him forever. If I belonged in *his* world, in the safety of *his* circle, in the fabric of *his* tapestry, in the wetness of *his* river.

It never occurred to me that our world was *ours*, that the circle belonged to *us*, and that as long as we were *both inside* of it, I'd always belong simply because I was there, and I belong everywhere. I just thought I was a visitor in his world, and in order to stay there, in order to belong, I'd have to fit in the spaces provided. So I made myself small.

He didn't ask me to. I did that all on my own.

145

I folded myself up neatly so that I would fit in. I hiked when he hiked. I ate what he ate. I slept when he slept and slept with him when he wanted. I befriended his friends. I grew into the person I thought I was supposed to be with him.

I know now that when I take up space—I know now that when I get big (and not physically, but, yes, also physically) I don't fit in everywhere. I am not able to squeeze into those small corners. I can't just "slither in."

But when I take up space, I'm seen by those who are looking for me. When I take up space, I am seen by those who've been looking for me but couldn't find me when I was so small. When I take up space, I'm seen by those who love to see me. And who invite me in and create space for my bigness. For my enoughness.

Ironically, all along, Josh saw me. All along, he believed I belonged. All along, he had been looking for me, and once he found me, he'd spent years creating space around us because he wanted me to have room to stretch and breathe and grow. And while I continued to shrink and try to make myself small, he kept looking for me. He never stopped looking for me. And the smaller I got the harder he fought to find me. And the harder he looked, the smaller I became.

Until one day I grew so small that he was afraid he might lose me. He was afraid that he might not be able to find me the next time. So when he asked me to get help—when he looked at me one winter night as I picked through the scraps of my raw food dinner and said, "Rachel, you have an Eating Disorder. I want you to get help," he pulled me out of the cracks. Out of the spaces I'd slithered into.

And I let him.

part four
the deep end.

My Eating Disorder was, and still is, one of the most difficult relationships to end.

She was so beautiful when she arrived. She showed me all the people she'd saved. The women she'd transformed. The lives she'd changed for the better.

Desperate and naive, I saw her success stories through glazed eyes. I didn't see the scars her victims bore. I didn't see the secrets they held. I couldn't hear the cries they muffled. I was hypnotized by her promise.

I trusted her, even when she robbed me of any opportunity to be present in my social environment and build relationships.

When she convinced me it wasn't safe to show up in my life.

When she made me believe I didn't deserve to seek joy and feel pleasure. I still trusted her to make it all okay again.

And once I gave her my trust, she'd tear me down, rip me to shreds, and beat me into a small, scared, lifeless little girl.

When I was hurt enough, she'd extend her hand, offering her sweet and sparkly services to heal me from the hurt she'd created. Loving me, cradling me, soothing me, offering me so much hope and promising so much change.

Leaving her is like saying goodbye to a friend—a horrible, toxic, abusive friend—but a friend who knows me better than anyone. It is like killing her slowly. Letting her die, as I hold her head underwater and watch the life drain from her eyes.

fourteen.

UNLEARNING

Why is he looking at me so weird? I thought as I neatly coiled a piece of raw Zucchini around my fork. I had recently learned how to make "zoodles" from one of the raw-food blogs I followed, and I was eager to see if it tasted *just like* spaghetti, *just like* they promised.

Josh sat quietly across from me at our kitchen table in our first house together in West Seattle—an odd scene considering Josh typically spent the dinner hour gleefully carving out a giant bite of red meat and grinning ear to ear while telling some fantastic fable he'd heard at the office that day.

I had reduced myself to a raw food diet that winter in an attempt to heal my recent outburst of hormonal, cystic acne. I was clueless that my hormonal acne was likely, in fact, a symptom of the years of stress I'd put my body under and a natural result of a completely exhausted and confused nervous system. I just assumed it was related to my diet like all the health blogs told me.

After a deep dive into Google, I'd discovered a raw food diet could eliminate the cause of my inflamed and painful cheeks, and I was more than happy to have a valid reason to restrict my diet.

I wanted my skin to heal because it hurt, but more than that I wanted it to heal so I could be beautiful. And a raw food diet was more excusable, understandable, and less conspicuous to my friends and family if I could claim it was for my skin.

At this point in my life, my immediate family knew I had an Eating Disorder. Josh knew too—before we started dating, I told him that I'd once struggled with disordered eating, but that I was "past it." My friends had sometimes expressed minor concern, but nothing to the point of, "I think you need help," or "I think you have an Eating Disorder."

My weight and eating habits continued to fluctuate, and I oscillated between somewhat underweight and somewhat overweight throughout my early twenties. My weight/shape/size never reached an extreme that one might consider "out of the ordinary," and in many ways, it wasn't physically obvious that I had an Eating Disorder based on the narrow understanding of what Eating Disorders *look* like.

Still, the rapid fluctuation in my size, the bouts of depression and alcohol abuse, and the obsession with calories, exercise, and my appearance still ruled my life, whether others noticed or not.

Asking for help did not come naturally to me. I was uncomfortable with seeking support, and I felt more like a burden than a normal human needing co-regulation when I mustered the courage to say, "I'm having a hard day."

In many ways, my Eating Disorder was a way for me to ask for help without asking. Changing my body was a way for me to physically display my pain. If I looked sick, *wouldn't someone notice?* Wouldn't they realize I wasn't ok, *without me having to say it?*

For years this became a pattern. If I was struggling with fears of inadequacy, lack of self-worth, or crippling depression and anxiety, I would turn to my Eating Disorder. I never asked for help. I was too afraid that someone would think my problems weren't that bad or that I was overreacting.

So instead, I made myself physically sick, because maybe then someone might take my pain seriously.

I also believed that unless I was sick enough, I didn't need treatment. I believed that if I wasn't underweight, fed by a tube, or forced to go to treatment by concerned family members, I must not be disordered enough.

The same not-enoughness that led me to my Eating Disorder followed me with her. Keeping me in a perpetual cycle of not good enough for the outside world, not sick enough for my inside world, and caught in the suffocating in-betweenness where I felt there was no way out.

So when Josh looked at me from across our kitchen table and said,

"Rachel, you have an Eating Disorder, and I want you to get help," I suddenly had a way out.

Nobody had ever so clearly seen my hurt and blatantly named it. Somebody I loved saw me, and somebody who loved me wanted me well. I don't think I ever felt more loved than I did in that moment. It was the same relief I'd felt when my mother told me I could come home for a break from college. It was an invitation to breathe, permission to rest, and the validation that my suffering was real, and that it was bad enough to get help.

"Ok." I murmured.

I didn't question him. I didn't fight the way I had with my mom for years. I didn't try to convince him he was wrong or that I was fine the way I had with therapists in the past. I didn't deflect or change the subject like I always would with friends and family who skirted around the subject.

I heard his directness, I felt his love, and I just said, "Ok."

The day after Josh asked me to get help, I made an appointment with my primary care doctor.

When I arrived at the doctor's office, my plan (ok, my Eating Disorder's plan) was to get some medication for my depression and have that be it. My Eating Disorder had already intervened—she was not interested in leaving without a fight. She convinced me medication was all I'd need—that if I solved my mood problems with medicine then all the other symptoms would fade.

After talking to my doctor for a few minutes, she recommended I see a therapist at an Eating Disorder facility in town. *That's fine.* I thought. *I'll see a therapist, take some medication, and that will be good.*

A few weeks later I was scheduled for my intake at The Emily Program. The program was located on the fifth floor of an office building just off Lake Union just a few minutes from downtown Seattle. The building seemed caught between decades—new enough that I trusted the elevators, old enough to remind me of my neighborhood public library.

On the day of my intake, I took the stairs. The same ones I'd sneak up on for weeks after being admitted, hopping out at the fourth floor to take the elevator one story up so the staff wouldn't know I'd broken the no-stairs rule.

The fifth floor felt like a makeshift hospital inside a corporate office: a confused mix of, "we're here to help, but not *that* much." The waiting room resembled a basic Western doctor's office: blue spotted fabric chairs, bright incandescent lighting, and a mysterious orange hallway to who-knows-where.

Maybe the therapist's office.
Maybe some strange woo-woo room.

152

Maybe the place I'd learn my deepest fear was true: *I wasn't sick enough for treatment, and they'd turn me away.*

"Rachel?"

I sat alert in my chair.

"That's me," I said, fumbling the handful of intake papers in my lap.

"Come with me."

How humiliating. *She was just going to call me out like that?* I felt completely naked.

I could feel my newness in the waiting room. I could sense the experienced, aged wisdom of the other women sitting near me. I imagined their eyes peering at me from behind their Good Housekeeping, eyeballing the fresh meat.

I didn't want them to smell my weakness. I didn't want anyone to sense my fear. I wanted to be better than all of them. More sophisticated. Or maybe I wanted to be sicker. So they'd pity me. I wasn't sure. But as I walked down the mystery hall, I felt their gaze on me, and I wanted to run.

"My name is Anna; I'll be doing your intake."

We were in Anna's office now—the irony of her name mocking me like a sick joke. *I wonder if she knows "Anna" is a nickname for Anorexia.*

I felt so small. I could have sworn her seat was five inches higher than mine. I sat, legs uncrossed, with my hands in my lap. Like a good girl.

I waited for her to speak. I had no idea what was going to happen. I had been in therapy before, but I'd never done a proper intake. *Was she my therapist?*

Nobody had told me.

"I'm going to ask you a series of questions. It's important you answer as honestly as possible. Ok?"

Why wasn't she looking at me?

"Ok. When was the last time you binged?"

Wow, ok straight to the jugular.

153

"Yesterday."

"When was the last time you purged?"

Jesus Anna.

"Um, last week."

"How many days per week do you restrict your caloric intake?"

Alright, here we go.

"Um, I guess I try every day, but I don't always do."

"On a scale of one to ten, ten being depressed, how depressed have you felt in the last two weeks?"

"Nine?"

"Have you ever had thoughts of hurting yourself?"

"Yeah…"

"Have you ever had thoughts of killing yourself?"

"Uh huh…"

"Have you ever attempted suicide?"

"In 2008. I was in a hospital for a few days."

She never looked away from her computer. She just kept typing. And as she did, I started to fill up inside. Filling up with something. I didn't know what. I just started to feel full, and with every question I grew more and more afraid that I might explode.

We went on like this for an hour. A back-and-forth exchange, a clinical interview that cut straight to my sorrow with no softness, no ease, and not a single glance up from her computer.

I felt invisible in her room. Filling it with my history, flooding it with my hurt and insecurity, yet nowhere to be found inside its orange walls.

Finally, Anna stopped typing. She put her hands in her lap and looked at her screen, as if waiting for it to compute my therapeutic resumé. As if some electronic slot machine was spinning on the screen, and in just a moment my destiny would display with a final, "ding, ding, ding."

She swiveled in her chair, looking at me for the first time in over an hour.

I wonder now if she looked away all that time to protect herself from the panic in my eyes. In the eyes of all the people who sat in my spot. From the longing we must exude. From our sad, sorry faces that long ago she'd once tried to soothe, but whose hurt and pain she could no longer hold in her heart without losing her sanity.

"I think you would be best suited for our Intensive Outpatient Program. It's three days a week, and includes group therapy, skills clinic, individual therapy, yoga, and one meal per day. How do you feel about that?"

How do I feel about that?

Her prescription was so curt. So abrupt. So final. I had no chance to ease into her words. No opportunity to let the recommendation sink in.

Her words pierced the welling bubble in my belly, and I, in turn, erupted.

How do I feel about that?

As if I'd lost all control of my body and voice, I choked out words I never imagined I'd utter:

"I'm relieved."

The next week, I was admitted into their Intensive Outpatient Program (IOP), which was their medium-level treatment program. The other programs included a Partial Hospitalization Program (living at a residential treatment facility) an Adolescent Program, Binge Eating Intensive Outpatient, and less intensive outpatient programs which offered weekly therapy and group sessions.

Each day followed a schedule: I was in the day program, which meant my first activity of the day was lunch. We would wait in the lobby until IOP was invited into the dining hall. We would then gather around the clinician in charge of lunch that day, while she told us what was for lunch, and reminded us how the meal worked.

We would then line up, cafeteria-style, and fill our plates with food. This was challenge enough. Each dish was labeled with a recommended (mandatory) serving size. "Fist-size of meat," "one cup of beans," etc.

I would fill my plate in terror.

This can't be right. I'd think. *This is way too much food. Nobody eats this much. They just want to make me fat.*

We would sit down with our homeroom group and check-in before our meal. We would pass around a feelings wheel and announce our emotions before eating. This was bizarre to me, as I'd never identified my feelings (let alone used a feelings wheel).

I remember not knowing what the hell I *felt* those first few days. But I wanted to be perfect for the dietitian monitoring our table, so I was ready to perform. I wanted her to see I was going to do this right. That I was wise.

"How are you feeling, Rachel?" My dietitian asked before my first meal.

Sternly, I looked at the laminated feelings wheel. There were so many feelings I'd never seen before. The longer I looked at the wheel, the more discouraged I became.

What do I feel? Fat. That's not on here.

"I don't know," I mumbled. "That this looks like a lot of food."

"Ok, I understand it looks like a lot. And this is the right amount of food for your body. Can you look at the feelings wheel and tell me how you *feel?*"

I started bubbling up. The feeling that I got in Anna's office was coming again. Surging. I wasn't doing a good job. I was doing this wrong. I started to feel a choking sensation in my throat and tears welling in my eyes. I wanted to run.

What the hell am I doing? I'm twenty-five years old, afraid to eat a fucking meal, and I can't even name my emotion? What the fuck is wrong with me? This can't be my life. How did I get here?

I felt so powerless. Like a failure. A disappointment. An imbecile.

I don't know how much time passed, but I couldn't look up from the feelings wheel. I held it, frozen in my hands. My head down, holding back tears, slowly starting to dim inside and lose all sense of myself, my surroundings, and any thought at all.

I often went away like this when I became too overwhelmed. When someone asked me a question I couldn't answer. When I was meant to express or explain myself, but I didn't have the words, didn't know how, or feared the repercussions of my honesty or vulnerability.

I later learned this was a way my brain coped with perceived threat— it had learned long before that if something was too scary, it could cope by shutting down.

I couldn't bear the idea of exposing myself and being wrong. Of being seen as stupid, immature, or less than. Of not having answers. Of someone not liking what I said or disagreeing with me. Of having an opinion, idea, or voice that belonged to me and only me, because the possibility that someone might not understand me—or worse, might not accept me—was too terrifying to imagine.

In this moment, sitting at the cafeteria table, there was no threat. All the dietitian wanted to know was what I was feeling. She wasn't quizzing me or challenging me. She wasn't accusing me or blaming me of some wrongdoing. She wanted to know a part of my internal world, something that was true for me, and something only I could know.

Still, it triggered so much fear in me. I was already on edge and panicked about eating the meal in front of me, and my brain and body were teetering a state of panic.

I learned many years later how the brain functions, and the physiology of how fear, anxiety, and panic live in the body. That when our minds sense danger, they bypass all unnecessary processes like memory storage, digestion, and reasoning, and instead flood the body with hormones to prepare it for survival. That when this happens, our minds sometimes choose to shut down altogether, because they are unable to process the terrifying experience before them.

In that moment, though, I knew none of those things. I didn't know that I'd turned food into something so terrifying my brain believed it was dangerous. I didn't know that my fear of being bad or wrong or misunderstood was so grievous that the very possibility of it caused me to dissociate. I just knew I was "blacking out" as I had once coined it, and I felt as though I might die.

"I can go if you're not ready."

I looked up. The woman to my right was holding out her hand, as if waiting for me to give her the feelings wheel. As if my complete shutdown was normal—like I was part of some freak show that no longer phased the experienced residents.

"Thanks," I gurgled.

Kennedy was tall, well-postured, and her energy was palpable. Her red curly hair tightly wound behind her neck, her blue eyes piercing with longing desperation and perseverance.

As she spoke, I drifted off. I vaguely heard her identify her feelings, somewhat effortlessly, then continue to talk about her day. She had so much to say. I remember this bothering me. As if the more she spoke, the less opportunity I would have to speak.

After lunch was homeroom. This was our hour of time to process anything we needed.

Jade checked in briefly. She had soft, milky skin, and her dark, wispy hair fell gently around her doughy, gentle eyes. She reminded me of a bunny, and I found myself wanting to protect her in some way. As if she was fragile. As if she needed me. As if she needed someone.

"I'm really proud of myself," she said slowly, as if words themselves were exercise.

She had recently been moved to IOP from PHP and had her feeding tube removed. She was finally eating on her own, and she was genuinely excited to be making progress in recovery.

I remember thinking to myself how she was a better Anorexic than me. *Could I even call myself Anorexic if I couldn't stick to my Anorexia well enough to need a feeding tube?*

Her story was heartbreaking. I won't reveal the details for confidentiality purposes, but her history was far worse than mine in terms of trauma and hardship.

I couldn't help but feel like I didn't belong there. I wasn't sick enough. I didn't have any trauma (that I knew of). I thought trauma was some singular event or clearly defined abuse—reserved for broken homes and catastrophic events. I was certain my upbringing was perfect. Happy. Nothing was wrong with my childhood or my life. *So what right did I have sitting in this room?* Surely there'd been some mistake, and I would need to get sicker in order to deserve this treatment. The treatment I'd already been assessed, diagnosed, and recommended to participate in.

After both Jade and Kennedy shared, it was my turn.

It was not unusual for me to remain very quiet in settings like this. Where something important was meant to come from my mouth. In classrooms, I waited patiently until everyone had spouted whatever thought rolled off their tongues. I waited until my thoughts were crafted carefully. I waited for opposing ideas to be expressed so I could fold them into my final statement. Everything had to be right. Careful. Perfect.

So when it came my turn to speak in group, I was prepared. I was ready to share my story. To explain how I got here. I had the words perfectly lined up.

When I opened my mouth, I blacked out like I had when Josh asked me about my life for the first time. My life story came out in spurts, like uncontrollable hiccups that came up without warning, and only stopped when I held my breath for long enough.

"I stopped eating when I was fifteen," *or something oddly blunt and insensitive.*

"My mom made me go to therapist later that year. Our relationship is terrible."

159

"My dad was an alcoholic. But I didn't really even know that, so, I don't really know if that matters."

"In college I was really depressed. My high school sweetheart died, and I tried to kill myself."

"I was fine for a while after that. I got everything under control."

"I met my boyfriend, and I don't know, I guess I just wanted to be thin again."

"I really just want to learn to stop binge-eating. Other than that, I'm fine."

My words came out like calculated bullet points. Void of any emotion. Lacking any insight or awareness.

At least, that's how I experienced it.

After a long pause, Kennedy asked if she could respond, and I happily passed her the talking stick.

"I have experienced almost every single thing you've just said," Kennedy said.

"I mean, obviously not the exact same thing. But I've tried to end my life. I can't get anything under control. I hate my body and never wanted to go to therapy. Sex is like a fucking minefield and I've been assaulted, a lot. Oh, and my relationship with my parents is whack."

I looked at her perplexed. I had never really talked to anyone about my Eating Disorder besides my boyfriend, and even then, I barely scratched the surface with him. I was too ashamed—too disgusted by my thoughts and behaviors to put words to the gruesome ways I treated myself.

To hear my inner thoughts mirrored in a stranger freed something in me. It reworked a cog that had been sternly fixed for decades: that I was the only person having my experience, that no one else thought or felt what I did, and therefore, I was entirely alone, doomed to suffer silently, and completely broken.

To know I wasn't alone laid the foundation for me to see a possibility of change. If I really wasn't as twisted, off, and damaged as I felt—if someone else, someone I had never met, shared my scariest thoughts and behaviors—there must be more like us. There must be more like us, which meant *there must be hope for us.*

I spent the next four months bussing from our West Seattle home to the bright and orange waiting room. Tuesday to Thursday, I'd share a meal and several hours of group therapy with women, who became my friends, trusted confidants, and supportive others.

Meals were nothing short of eventful. Someone would typically experience some kind of challenge: either panic over the type or quantity of food, triggered by how someone else was (or wasn't) eating, or other feelings that were previously present that erupted at the dining table.

Sometimes we'd hear the cries or frustrations from surrounding tables, and we'd sit in silence while girls we shared the lunchroom with, but never spoke to, cried, yelled, or stormed out of the room.

For the first few weeks, I had regular panic attacks or shutdowns at mealtime.

"Rachel, what are you feeling?"

Dead. Fat. Fuck. Stop. STOP. JUST MAKE IT STOP.

"Ok Rachel, can you stand up for me?"

Can you go fuck yourself?

"Great, ok now just take a look out the window and name what you see. Just name it in your mind."

Fucking house. Dumb fucking truck. Stupid shit.

"Try not to add any judgmental or qualitative words—even 'positive ones.' Name only what you see. Notice any thoughts that arise or judgments or distractions, and just witness them and let them float away."

Get out of my head. Fuck. Ok. House. Trees. Firetruck. Clouds. Street. Sunshine. This is so dumb. Ok, I notice you, thought. Buh-bye. Ok. Lamppost. Car. Person walking.

"Ok, good job. When you feel calmer and more grounded, you can come back and sit down." She said this kindly—not punitively. I was surprised at how well this worked, and as I named what I could see in front of me, I felt the blackness lift and I could feel my toes between my socks.

I learned more about how to ground and reconnect with myself in those meals than I had in twenty-five years of life.

Sometimes we were instructed to bring our own meals, and on these days, I was always scolded (or at least, I interpreted my dietitian's suggestion about my portions as scolding) for not having enough on my plate. On these days, I was required to pick something from the stock fridge—a chocolate milk, piece of bread, or leftovers from the day before.

"Ok Rachel, what do we have today?"

"Brussel sprouts, quinoa, and chicken." *Duh, it's right in front of you.*

"Great! Hm. It looks like there's not very much oil on the brussels sprouts. How much did you use?"

I used a spray, ya dummy. I'm not voluntarily putting oil on my food.

"Oh, probably one to two tablespoons."

"Hm, well, it doesn't look like that, and often the oil cooks off. You'll need to grab something from the fridge to make sure you have enough fats in your meal today, ok?"

This infuriated me. My dietitian infuriated me in general. Her voice was toothy and tappy, and she reminded me of an obnoxious neighbor. Someone who always visits at the inopportune time with useless advice or a handwritten note that says, "gentle reminder not to feed my cat."

I was convinced she was trying to make me fat, that she secretly despised me, and that her plans for me were malicious and laced with ill-will.

At our appointments, she'd track my weight on her computer, which was shaded by a privacy screen-protector so only she could see the results. If I lost weight, she'd tell me. If I gained weight, she wouldn't. This reinforced the idea in my head that weight-loss was attention-worthy, and weight-gain was not.

Even in treatment, I wanted to weigh as little as possible. I was scared that if I gained weight, they would make me leave, and no one would be worried about me anymore. Concern was how I knew I was cared for, and I started to twist care and love for something that only came when I was suffering.

Though I couldn't stand her, my dietitian forced me to question my fears about fatness. When I pressed her to tell me my weight, she pressed back.

"What are you afraid of?" She'd tap mousily with her mouth.

"I can't get fat. I don't want to be fat."

"Why? What does being fat mean?"

"I don't know, I just hate the way it feels. It's not me. I'm not fat."

"Ok, what would it mean about you if you were fat?"

"I'd be disgusting. It would mean I didn't care about myself. That I didn't take care of my body."

I'd say this through angry tears. Still not understanding the belief itself, still unaware of where this belief came from, still clueless to my own internalized fatphobia, still unaware of the word or concept, still wrapped up in the simplicity and narrowness that was, "I just want to be thin."

In group we learned skills to cope with our emotions, behaviors, and thoughts. The Emily Program used Dialectical Behavior Therapy (DBT) as their therapeutic intervention, and a big portion of the DBT model is centered in skills-acquisition.

I learned hundreds of coping skills during my four months there. Skills focused on keeping my mind present, managing painful emotions, understanding the connection between my mind and body, and learning to effectively communicate and ask for my needs. Skills for navigating the real dialectic that so much can exist at the same time—that the world is not made of black and white, of either or, of good or bad. That the sun can shine while it rains, and that two very seemingly opposite realities can coexist.

I had been in therapy so many times before, but not once had I learned the skills I did at The Emily Program. They were the life skills I lamented not learning as a young girl—the ones I wished all of us could have learned in school long before growing up.

I started to believe my therapists when they talked about duality. That I could make mistakes, *and* still be good. That I could be ready for change, *and* still feel scared.

I learned to name my emotion so that I could properly identify what I needed. *Oh, I feel anxious. That must mean I feel scared or unsafe, so...I need to seek safety. I can do some grounding techniques, like mindfulness or paced breathing!*

I learned what "validation" was and discovered how soothing it was to receive it when I was upset. I learned to say things like, "Josh, I feel really nervous about this test coming up. And I don't need you to tell me how smart I am or help me find a solution. I just need you to validate me and say, 'Aw man Rach, I'm sorry you're so nervous. That makes so much sense, tests are nerve-wracking, and you have every right to feel that way. I'll sit right here with you while you feel nervous, ok?'"

For years I had operated under the guise that people could read my mind, and that people who loved me should just know what I needed and when. I had no clue that it was ok and normal to actually ASK for what I needed, and that my needs *themselves* were nothing to be ashamed of.

I had also never learned that it was ok to say "no." I spent most of my life saying yes to everything and being reinforced positively for my spontaneity and "yes-man" attitude. My people-pleasing tendencies and lack of boundaries were so bad that I constantly felt under-appreciated, drained, and taken advantage of.

I was learning how my Eating Disorder served so many of these functions.

How she regulated my anxiety (eating food is grounding, and restricting offers a sense of control which manages fear), soothed my insecurity (I received attention, and whether positive or negative, it created a sense of being seen), called on validation (when someone saw my sickness, they said, "You look so skinny, are you eating?" which validated the emotional pain I felt), inadvertently set boundaries (having an Eating Disorder was the ultimate isolator, and skipping social outings, saying no to certain foods, or binge-eating allowed me the visceral experience of personal privacy and saying "no," but not in a way that was productive or healthy for my interpersonal or personal development).

Everything my Eating Disorder did was in an attempt to create the fabric of a healthy, interdependent, human, emotional and cognitive reality, but in the sickest, most twisted, and life-sucking way possible.

Unlearning this was like erasing an entire operating system with a single button, then getting spat out into the world as a newborn baby in a twenty-five-year-old's body and being told, "Here, learn this new operating system, you have four months to catch up."

I had to learn these necessary skills first.

I had to rebuild my operating system.

I had to learn I wasn't alone so that I could continue to seek help when months and years later I'd find myself meeting my Eating Disorder for coffee.

I had to come to grips with the reality that if I wanted something, I had to ask for it. That nobody could read my mind, and that real connection happens in the words that are shared—not the ones that aren't.

I had to learn that my Eating Disorder *was* about so much more than just my body, so that when I learned a decade later *how much my Eating Disorder actually was about my body,* I could see the whole picture: the both/and, the dialectic, and where my worth and insecurity intersected with the real cultural and systemic pressure to be thin.

When I graduated from The Emily Program late in the summer of 2015, I felt different. Changed. Proud. Solid. I'd learned so much in those few months, and I wanted the world to know what I'd learned. I wanted to share the insights I'd gained, the tools I'd accrued, and the wisdom I'd discovered.

I told my close friends and extended family about my time in the program. I named my experience for the first time openly, telling people in my life who'd seen me struggle for so long, "I have an Eating Disorder, and I finally received help for it."

A lot of my friends and family were confused and didn't really understand what that meant.

"What, like, so you eat your feet?" someone close to me legitimately responded.

"Okay, so, is it ok if I eat around you?" someone else close to me said.

"Ugh, yeah, I get it. I sometimes wonder if I have that, I have so much trouble losing weight," someone else replied.

I started to realize how unspoken Eating Disorders really were, and with each new response and conversation, I felt more and more compelled to keep talking about my experience.

The more I named my diagnoses, however, the more ostracized I felt.

I started to feel the opposite experience from my program: I went from a space where uttering, "I have an Eating Disorder" made me feel seen, connected, and safe, to a world where, "I have an Eating Disorder" made me feel invisible, isolated, and othered.

I spent the next five years vocalizing my experience. I spoke at National Eating Disorder Awareness (NEDA) fundraisers, wrote blog posts about my symptoms, and studied mental health counseling in graduate school with the hopes of destigmatizing and supporting other women in their recovery.

And as I did, I tried to weave these new discoveries into my identity, and into the identity of my relationship with Josh.

I taught him what I learned, and he adopted the tools I shared with him. I practiced my new communication skills and set boundaries with him I'd never set. I asked if we could engage with sex differently—in a way where my voice was louder, my pleasure *mine*, and my desires expressed.

He tried so hard to accommodate me. He did everything I asked, and more. He validated my feelings. He let me take the lead in sex (which I had no idea how to do because I didn't even know what I wanted). He listened when I felt misunderstood. He respected my boundaries, and he supported my advocacy plight.

He was…good.

And still, this newness strained us.

My changed and altered state in the bedroom threw him. What I'd told him I liked and wanted for almost four years was suddenly off the table—not *really* what I'd wanted, and a show I'd put on because I thought it was what he wanted.

This wasn't the full truth, and of course there were so many times I felt pleasure, satisfaction, and deep connection when we made love. And there were many times where I checked out, performed, and acted how I thought he wanted me to. Not because he made me, and never because I felt powerless. Ever.

Josh was never forceful or inattentive. When I said no and asked to stop, he always did. Still, I folded myself up so many times because it was what I thought I was supposed to do, and I didn't have the tools until my time in treatment to know there was another way.

His confidence started to waver. Our intimacy dwindled. My ability to connect to my body was so stifled that I was often frustrated, scared, and panicked when we'd try to have sex. This scared me, and it scared him.

Over time, it became the unspoken part of our relationship: a place we cushioned, a conversation we kept soft, and an area we tried not to look at with too much hardness because we were afraid of what might happen if we couldn't fix it.

I was also trying to find myself again. Trying to figure out who I was without acting, what life would look like if I no longer needed to be perfect, and who I'd be without my Eating Disorder. I gave up two big parts of self, two massive senses of my identity in a matter of months, and I was grasping to figure out who I was.

Josh was patient, and he let me look.

So when I looked to study psychology and talked to him about the possibility of moving across the state so I could go to grad school, he supported me. He did everything he could to help me make it happen. Studying with me for the GRE, working with his employer to arrange for him to work remotely, and helping me name five things I could see when I had my first panic attack on our way to Spokane, where I had an interview that eventually secured my spot at Eastern Washington University (EWU) as a Graduate student.

And like we'd done at every fork in the river, we held each other's hands, squeezing each other tightly as we braced for impact, trying as best as we could to contain our cries from the scratches we were enduring as our backs grazed the rocks below, and let the river take us. Hoping, as we always did, that it would always be just him and me.

fifteen.

FIRE

In August of 2017, Josh and I got married in the hot summer sun.

Our wedding venue was supposed to be a barn in the forested hills of Idaho, but two weeks before our wedding, the barn burned to the ground.

I suppose in hindsight, some might see this as a big fucking sign. But we didn't. I still don't.

"Hey man whatsup?"

Josh was in the kitchen, which was a split level above in the completely oversized house we'd rented in a cul-de-sac situated perfectly between the EWU campus where I took my courses and downtown Spokane where we took our date nights.

It was hot that day—a typical dry heat for summer in Spokane, and one we were still adjusting to after only living there for just under a year.

I was in the living room icing my knee after my most recent injury (my second ACL repair and a timely one with our wedding two weeks away) and frantically printing return labels for all the honeymoon attire I'd purchased while knocked out on pain medications when Josh's phone rang.

There was a moment of silence, and then Josh blurted, "Oh my god."

I was alert then, and quickly removed the ice from my knee and faced the kitchen, as if that would somehow help me hear the conversation better. Josh rarely panicked. Though he would often come home from work, immediately lay face-down on the carpet, and pass out to cope with overwhelm, it was unusual for him to let something spark a frantic reaction.

He was pacing and running the palm of his hand over his face, as if wiping invisible sweat from his forehead to his chin. He only did this when he was stressed, so I knew something was wrong.

Still on the phone, he looked down at me from the kitchen and said, "Rach, Settler's Creek burned down."

"What!?"

"Thanks man, yeah we'll check it out now."

He hung up the phone and looked at me bewildered.

We looked at each other, almost laughing in shock.

"Wait, what do you mean it burned down? Like, the whole thing?"

"I don't know, Daniel just said he was watching the news and it came up and he was like, 'isn't that where Rachel and Josh are getting married?'"

We stood hovered over Josh's phone for the next few minutes, googling "Settlers Creek fire" and "barn burns down Coeur d'Alene."

As one news story after another popped up, we saw the big red barn that was meant to be the backdrop for our wedding engulfed in flames.

Once we knew it was real, we put the phone down and looked at each other.

I don't remember the specifics of what happened next. But I do know, in some way or another, we sat down together on the couch to check-in.

Josh and I were really good at checking-in. After years together, we'd developed communication tools to help us navigate tough times, and frequent "check-ins" were one of them.

Check-ins were less formal and romantic than Floor Meetings—they were more about business: quick "how-ya-doins" and perfect for crisis scenarios or moments when we had little time to evaluate one another's emotions and our own.

"Let's check-in," we'd say. Or "Do you mind if we check-in tonight after dinner?"

Check-ins were a way for us to carve out intentional time for a conversation dedicated to presence, openness, and honesty. Sometimes our check-ins presented an opportunity to let something off our chest. Other times it was simply a way to evaluate how we were doing—individually, and as a couple.

I wish I could say this system was seamless, but we were and are not perfect beings, and there were some holes.

On this day, the check-in was of the crisis-intervention type: something big had just happened, and we needed to check on each other's wellbeing before making any rash or big decisions.

"How are you doing?"

One of us asked, then the other. I don't know who first. Maybe we said it simultaneously. Maybe we didn't say it at all.

"I'm ok, to me this doesn't change anything. I just hope they're ok—that's their livelihood."

"Me too."

"I think we should message them just to let them know we're thinking of them, but not bombard them with any questions right now."

"Yeah, that's what I was thinking."

"Still wanna get married?"

"Even if we have to do it in our backyard."

We hugged. We kissed. We smiled.

We called our folks and recited what we'd said to each other. We texted our bridesmaids and groomsmen respectively. And we went on with our day.

We went on, as we normally did, not letting ourselves feel angry, focusing on the feelings of everyone around us, and modeling what we believed was calm in the eye of the storm.

I don't think our reaction was wrong or bad—I really don't. I look at how we responded to the news of our wedding venue burning down as a window into the heart of our relationship.

All we ever wanted was to be together. All we ever tried to do was love each other the way we thought the other needed to be loved. All we ever hoped for was to be good and be good for each other. And as hard as we tried, neither of us were equipped to navigate the unconscious workings of our love, and the small weights we were adding to our connection that eventually broke it.

Two weeks later, Josh and I got married in the presence of our family and friends.

Where the barn had once been was a white tent and newly laid gravel. The staff had poured hours into cleaning the ashes of their historic landmark, and we were grateful to even have the space to use at all.

That morning, while powder painted my face and curls formed in hot rods above my head, my bridesmaids sipped their mimosas and asked me if I was nervous.

"No," I said, beaming.

"I'm just so, unbelievably excited."

In my heart, Josh was already my husband. The way I felt about him and the way he was to me was more than a boyfriend, more than a fiancé, more than a husband. He was my partner, and to honor this partnership with a ceremony and celebration felt like a sacred gift to our already existing union.

I had been to enough weddings (and been *in* enough weddings) to know that nobody—not even the wedding planner—is capable of reading the mind of the bride or groom. I had been in enough therapy, too, to understand that *nobody* is a mind reader, and if I wanted something, I had to be clear about it.

So, for our wedding, Josh and I were clear about what we wanted—with each other, with our bridal party, and with our family.

I was particularly clear (so clear that I made binders for the entire bridal party).

I created schedules and color-coated outlines of the entire weekend. I delegated tasks, like who was picking up who at the airport, who was helping with set-up and tear-down of the rehearsal dinner, and who was responsible for contacting catering for Sunday brunch. I had copies of speeches, vows, and recessional line-ups tucked away in the folders of the binder.

As completely controlling as this sounds, it was how I was able to let go of everything as soon as the weekend of our wedding began. I trusted that our friends and family knew what we wanted, how to support us, and where to be and when. Nobody asked me or Josh a single question all weekend, and we got to completely relax, be present, and enjoy each other.

I floated through the entire weekend in bliss. It was difficult at times to stay focused on anyone but Josh—I knew I needed to be polite and talk to everyone who came and thank them, but mostly I wanted to spend the weekend locked in the arms of my best friend, laughing, kissing, dancing, and creating memories the way we knew best.

We had written our own vows, something that was so natural for us after the hundreds of love letters we'd written and the countless vows we'd already made and spoken to one another over the years.

I still have my vows, which I've included here because they're important in this story. I don't have Josh's vows with me. They're folded somewhere in the box that holds all the letters Josh has ever written, in the box with the Midas envelope, in the shed that I'm not sure I'll step foot in for years to come, if ever again.

Josh,

You probably already know everything I'm about to say, because for some reason you seem to know me better than I know myself. You are so in tune with me that you know when I need a good cry before I do. You've been in tune with me since the day we met, and I know this because you told me I was going to fall in love with you before I even knew I liked you.

Around that same time, you said something to me that I will never forget: *"Rachel, there is no right way, there is only the way you do it."* In just a few words, you had given me the freedom to make choices based on what my heart wanted, not based on unanswerable hypotheses or social norms. It had never occurred to me that if I made a choice based on what I wanted, the only person I would have to answer to is myself. I think this mantra has infused our relationship too. Together, we have always chosen *our* way, not the way that is prescribed by society or the culture we live in. And I believe that has allowed us to create our very own love that is uniquely ours; a love that is undeniably the *right* way for *us*. Thank you for showing me *my way*, and for giving us *our way*. This is a fun life we're having, Josh, let's keep doing it the way we choose to.

As for our future, I have some promises I would like to make to you as we begin our married life together. And while most of these will not be new to you, I want you to hear on this day that

I am committed to them. I promise to help you zoom out when you're too zoomed in. I promise to make sure I preface every planning question with, "may I ask you a planning question?" I promise to love every motorcycle you buy, *and* sell. I promise to talk to you. I promise to travel the world, and I promise one day we will ride on a motorcycle through South America. I promise to tell you I'm proud of you. I promise that my love for you is unconditional, and there is nothing you can do to make me love you any more or any less. I promise to learn from you and let you teach me. I promise to give you attention when you need it, and to give you space when you want it. I promise that no matter the direction life goes, I will lean into it with you. I promise to be on the same team as you in life, and to have fun playing. Most of all, I promise to not only love you, but to like you.

I kept every promise I made him, except the last one. Except the one that was the most important to him, and the one he couldn't forgive me for in the years to come. The clue he gave to me in the Midas letter as how to love him, and the one thing I stopped doing—or knew how to do—years later when he started to question if I still liked him at all.

There's a photo of us from our wedding day, probably an hour after the dancing had started (and hours after the champagne had started) where Josh is holding his hands up to his face in a little square. Grinning from ear to ear, he's peering through the finger-made shape and gazing right at me. You can't see my face in the photo, as my back is to the camera and I'm facing him. But I know exactly what I looked like.

I'm smiling with my entire face, my chin pressed back as if mid-laugh, my eyes squinted in glee.

We had decided, in that moment, to take a mental photo.

We had been doing this all weekend—snapping mental photos together so we could pause and remind our brains to store the moment as memory, even without a real picture.

Now that there are hundreds of photos from our wedding, it's hard to remember what images are those we created together, and those I'm recalling from the albums.

When I do see these images, they come with sounds and smells. I can feel the piercing heat of the day when I see my parents walk me down the aisle. I can smell Josh's skin when I see him holding his wedding vows. I can taste our wedding cake, and feel his body pressed against mine as we embrace during our first dance.

I can feel his lips, the softness of them on mine, when I see our faces pressed together, just moments after our best friend and officiant said,

"You may now kiss the bride."

After we walked down the aisle together—officially married—Josh pulled me close in the dry wheat fields. He held me there, in our safe circle. His hands pressed to my shoulders. His eyes on mine, my whole world in those eyes.

"It's just you and me," he reassured me.

I wish, so badly, that it had been. I wish that it had always just been him and me.

But as Josh said to me in the weeks after he asked for a divorce, there was always a third person in our relationship. She was there the day we met. She was there at every fork in the river, and she was there the day we got married.

She's still here, haunting me with her vapid cruelty, her insipid sneakiness, and the ruthless way she just won't die.

Like a hunting mistress, she floated right beneath us, wading there in the cold frosty wetness, sliding silently between us so quietly that neither of us felt her until she was all we felt.

And as the water grew more turbulent, as the pace quickened and the eddies thickened, we did everything we could to stop her from coming between us.

sixteen.

FROZEN

Psychology fascinated me.

Graduate school was, for me, a fast-track to understanding my own pathology, and my curiosity was insatiable.

I was ferociously devouring the information my professors fed me. I learned about trauma and the brain, medication and the problems with pharmaceuticals, healthy (and unhealthy) childhood development; diagnostics and the way mental health diagnoses were never *actually* meant to be used for therapeutic intervention; play-therapy for children; suicide prevention and crisis-counseling; micro-skills for listening and attending to clients; theories of counseling and different hypotheses for *why* people are the way they are; ethics and morals of the counseling profession; research and how to *read* research to know if it is actually valid or reliable to use as evidence; group counseling theory; and, a short and disappointing attempt at culturally-competent-counseling, which was taught by a white man and placed far too much attention on *the white man* as a misunderstood and prejudiced group.

Pathology, mental health diagnostics, research, and the interventions designed to heal what ails our minds and bodies both excited me and frustrated me. *How,* I thought, *can there be this much information about our mental wellness, yet so little access to resources for those who need this knowledge the most?*

While I was learning the tools and knowledge I knew would prepare me to eventually sit with clients (we were thrown into an internship in the spring of our first year), I was also harnessing a deep awareness of my own childhood, my own biases I'd need to work through, and a window into the world of trauma that changed my entire framework for understanding myself and future clients.

In my second semester of school, a professor assigned my class *The Body Keeps the Score* by Bessel Van der Kolk. I am not a very good reader (my mind gets distracted, I lose my place, and I generally struggle to focus), but I could not put this book down. It was as if the "secret trauma" I had been convinced never existed all those years ago in therapy had been written in his pages. An account of hundreds of patients with varying types of trauma, and, ones with nuanced, not so-singular, grey-area experiences that accumulated to the very symptoms, thoughts, and existence as me.

I was learning the ways in which the subtle happenings in my upbringing *were* traumatic—not that my *parents traumatized* me, but that a culture of independence and stoicism, schools and social systems that perpetuated perfection, and the subtle ways in which my home itself felt more like a stage than a home was *traumatic*.

Because, as I learned in school and in the pages of Kolk's book, trauma is not just one singular glaring event.

Trauma is any event or enduring experience that is too incomprehensible for the brain—an instance or series of events that are outside the realm of normal, safe, and predictable *for that human being*. An event or series of events so unbearable that the body and mind briefly part. Disconnecting while the body tries to protect itself from the dangerously unimaginable, while the mind is busy sending signals through the nervous system, working together yet separately to survive. And in the wake of such a fight the mind has lost all sense of that moment as reality, lost touch with the physical self, and struggles to recalibrate if no help to do so is present.

> Traumatized people chronically feel unsafe inside their bodies: The past is alive in the form of gnawing interior discomfort. Their bodies are constantly bombarded by visceral warning signs, and, in an attempt to control these processes, they often become expert at ignoring their gut feelings and in numbing awareness of what is played out inside. They learn to hide from their selves. (Kolk 2015, 97)

I wasn't aware of this then, but I now know that my Eating Disorder was the most traumatic thing to happen to me—and the guilt and shame I feel for *doing it to myself* is one I still live with and haven't forgiven myself for.

Because while I can blame society, or my parents, or premature exposure to sex, or peers, or lack of education for being the funnel that led me to choosing her, I'm the one who held my hand from my mouth and stopped eating.

I'm the one who put the thousands of calories in my body in under thirty-minutes.

I'm the one who ran on the treadmill until my feet went numb and contorted my stomach to make myself vomit.

I did that.

My hands. My body. And the result was and is, a connection between my mind and body so severed that I no longer trust my body, and she no longer trusts me.

I couldn't make this connection then. I was barely scratching the surface of trauma and what happens in the brain when we experience stress or a traumatic event, and how the mind and body are inseparable when it comes to the cause and treatment of mental health.

As I dove deeper into my studies, I started to see how much overlap there was with so many mental health diagnoses.

Often, Eating Disorders, Borderline Personality Disorder (BPD), Post-Traumatic-Stress-Disorder (PTSD), Complex-PTSD, Depression, Anxiety, Panic Disorder, and Substance Abuse Disorder go hand-in-hand. There is a ton of overlap with symptoms, coping mechanisms, beliefs about the self, and history of childhood trauma or sexual trauma for folks with these diagnoses.

Marsha Linehan (creator of DBT and Wonder Woman of all things BPD), believed some of us are simply born more sensitive. It is this sensitivity that makes some people feel the stressors of life more sharply, as if they are living "…with third degree burns over 90% of their bodies. Lacking emotional skin, they feel agony at the slightest touch or movement" (as cited in Greenstein 2017).

I first discovered Marsha's theories in my Eating Disorder treatment program where DBT was the therapeutic model. I learned a tremendous number of skills and tools for how to navigate living "without emotional skin." I was never diagnosed with BPD, but over the years I've grown more aware that I have some interpersonal traits that fall within the umbrella of BPD traits and symptomology.

While I was comforted by the fact that maybe all of my mental health troubles were due to an innate sensitivity (and that in fact, being sensitive was okay as long as I was aware of it and tended to it), I was also discovering how being sensitive was only one part of the picture. That sensitive or not, some of what happened in my life (and *certainly* what happened in the lives of my clients) was traumatic—sensitive skin or not.

I saw this firsthand when I started interning at a community mental health facility in Spokane. I was serving clients with BPD, and while most folks in this program had BPD as a primary diagnosis, many had comorbid Depression, Anxiety, and PTSD.

It was not uncommon for my clients to have a history of severe trauma even *without* a PTSD diagnosis. It was, in fact, the norm.

Most of my clients were not only managing symptoms of their mental health, but they were also trying to find housing, jobs, and survive. Many of them were homeless or relying on the Department of Health Services (DHS) for food, money, and the ability to enter the community mental health program.

For some, the program was mandatory post-arrest or a pre-requisite for housing. For many, it was an umpteenth attempt at recovery, and just another walk around the block. For others, it was the last, and final attempt to start their life, or end it.

Most of my clients had attempted suicide at least once. Almost all of them were actively suicidal. I saw them one-on-one weekly and in group therapy daily. The program was centered in DBT—the gold standard for BPD and personality disorders.

I loved my clients dearly. And I felt powerless to help them. This was a time in my life where I still believed it was my responsibility to save, fix, and heal those who needed it.

If a friend needed me to hold space, I dropped everything. It was my job to help them. If Josh had a problem, I dropped everything. It was my role to find a solution for him.

So, naturally, in a helping role and profession, I dropped everything to help my clients. And by everything, I mean everything.

I stopped caring for my body. My Eating Disorder took a front seat in the car and took every opportunity to grab the wheel. I started drinking wine nightly, just to make homework a little more fun. I tuned

Josh out at the dinner table, because I couldn't turn off the stories my clients had shared, and I desperately needed to find an out for them.

No "out" ever came. No magic potion flowed from my constant thinking. No new tool or method was born in my desperation. All that came was rumination, panic, and a sense of total helplessness.

The mental health system does not work in favor of the people who use it. Period.

I cannot tell you how many clients I worked with whose primary concern was not their suicidal thinking or abusive relationship, but the fact that they were fired from work and might end up homeless. Their entire sense of safety and security was in constant flux.

Our basic human needs—and rights—are to have safety and security. Food. Shelter. Water. It's basic. It's so fucking basic. But so many human beings do not have these basic needs.

And when we are wrought with trauma, when our entire lives we've been told we are worthless, when our brains are working against us in the face of every single stressor life throws our way, it is damn near impossible to maintain those basic needs in a society that demands we be completely, one-hundred percent mentally "stable" to do so.

I will never forget my very first client. I was ridden with angst. She was being transferred to me by the intern whose place I was taking, and I was certain I wouldn't be good enough for her.

She was young—maybe nineteen or twenty. I remember her energy. I remember her face. I remember her matted, bristly brown hair. Her circled wire frames. Her softness. Her skin. The oversized tie-dye sweatshirt she wore effortlessly every single day.

I was a little in love with her—in the way I fall a little in love when I find a new song on my Spotify "for you" playlist. In the way I fall in love with a model who doesn't look like a model, and somehow makes me feel safe yet totally lustful all at once. In the way where I didn't actually want her, but wanted to be in the presence of her, because I could sense she was special.

Sophia was gentle, just like I thought she would be. She was kind, as I imagined. She was happy with me and our work, unlike my fears and expectations.

For months, she occupied my mind. I fell asleep at night thinking of her. Worrying about her. Wondering how I could help her. How I could give her what she deserved.

My supervisor told me it was normal to have this kind of attachment to a first client. That the first person we ever sit with becomes imprinted in us, like a first love.

I want to be clear, I never told Sophia any of these feelings. I was completely professional, and truthfully the way I felt was not romantic, sexual, or intimate. It was, I suppose, like being in awe. Like sensing someone's energy and becoming intensely absorbed and mystified.

My very last contact with Sophia was a crisis call over the phone. It was six months into our work together, and she had fled from her parent's home. She was living in a small shack with no running water or electricity, and she had no food and barely any money.

The program I worked in had a strict no-show policy, where if a client missed a certain number of groups or one-on-one sessions in a row, they were removed.

Sophia had already missed the maximum because of her living situation and lack of transportation, and I had already made a request for an exception in the week prior. My hands were tied, and I knew if I couldn't find a way to get her closer to our facility so she could come to group the next day, she would be removed.

I frantically called every service I had phone numbers for. My supervisor came into my office to help, and together we dialed hotlines, community phone numbers, and every resource we had in our wheelhouse. But because she was in another state, there was nothing we could do.

I never saw her again.

I think this was the beginning of my disillusionment with the mental health system.

I was already incredibly frustrated with some of the ethics and regulations designated by the American Psychology Association (APA), and the added layer of the community mental health system was the icing on the shitty cake that claims to support those in crisis or mental disarray.

I fully believe in the reasons for the ethical guidelines and think they are relevant and imperative. Many of the ethical guidelines keep clients safe and protected, and I am fully on board with regulations that prioritize safety. And, I felt constantly restricted in my ability to care for my clients in a way that showed them I *really* cared for their well-being out of fear of violating an ethical code.

The people working in the community mental health system are also tremendously undervalued and under-supported. The clinicians I worked beside clocked eighty-hour workweeks with highly suicidal clients, and were constantly burned out, discouraged, and lacking in the passion and optimism that I still had as a new intern. Not because their hearts were cold, but because like many of their clients, expecting disappointment from the system designed to support them became the norm.

I wondered how and why those who are most deeply impacted by trauma are the ones who are most forgotten and under-cared for in our system. I wondered how a system that is built to help people could have been made with so little care, and how a system that was so clearly exhausted might ever recover.

I saw countless clients come in and out of those doors with stories so horrific that I became paralyzed with how to respond.

How, I thought, *could my school think I am equipped to help these people? I have less than a year of education under my belt, and I'm supposed to be able to talk with a suicidal client about her paranoia and plans to end her life?*

And I wondered how I—a twenty-seven-year-old, white, blonde, privileged graduate student with no work-experience under my belt had any business trying to help the people who stepped into my office. *Why should they trust me? I can't ever know what it's like to go through what they've been through—why on earth would they want help from someone like me?*

This insecurity around my clinical experience and the guilt I felt around my privilege eventually prevented me from doing any work. Like a self-fulfilling prophecy, I guilted myself into inability.

This is why (as I learned years later both in mediated counseling with Josh, and when I started doing anti-racist work), guilt is not an effective vehicle for good. It only renders the person feeling guilty self-focused, self-absorbed, and lost in their own I'm-so-terrible that they can't actually focus on making change around the thing they feel so guilty about.

The combination of my insufferable insecurity, increase in disordered eating, and anxiety around the real suicidality of my clients started to show.

I was having regular panic attacks at work. My supervisor gave me an ice-facemask to keep on deck for when I arrived at the clinic. I started rescheduling and cancelling clients daily, and more often than not I went home about twenty minutes after arriving.

Josh was concerned. He would often softly suggest I take time off school—never as an instruction or demand, but an invitation.

I desperately wanted to finish. I was one semester from graduation, and I knew if I withdrew from internship I would have to restart in the summer, and my graduation date would be pushed back by almost six months.

I can't fail again.

I can't quit again.

I can't—just months from graduation—leave school because of my mental health, again.

But when I started hitting my face in the shower, when I had to leave Josh and his mom at the dinner table to silently scream into the bathroom mirror, when I had urges to bang my head against the walls, I knew if I didn't withdraw from my program, I would withdraw from my life.

Shame poured herself over me. Like a thick tar, she molded herself to me, plastering herself upon my skin like a familiar demon. She was so comfortable on my back. Clenching my shoulders with a gentle firmness, as if to say, *"I've been waiting, you fucking failure. I've been waiting to come back and bury you. Goodbye you worthless piece of shit."*

I spoke to my supervisor and college professors about withdrawing.

They seemed a little *too* understanding—as if they perhaps saw in me the torment I refused to see in myself.

How, I thought to myself, *how, after so much therapy, after knowing what I do from my education these last two years, after the love and support I have from my husband and friends, has it gotten to this point, again?*

Shortly after withdrawing from my program, I cut off all my hair and started working at a yoga studio. I needed a fresh start. Something to do. A safe place to be. Money. A purpose. But nothing *too* stressful— nothing *too* demanding.

I started seeing a therapist again, this time one whose focus was on attachment and the way our relationship with our primary caregivers impacts all other relationships in our adult life.

For the next eight months, I dove deeper into myself than I had in years. I started writing mantras every morning by candlelight. I paid attention to my reactions to Josh's statements and tried to decipher if they were because of an old attachment wound, or because of what was really happening in the present moment.

A friend sent me Gabrielle Bernstein's *The Universe Has Your Back* mantra deck, and I started to tap into my sense of spirituality and connection to something bigger than myself.

I wrote more than I had in seven years, and I started to share my experiences with mental health online; in a blog and on my Instagram.

Writing was always therapeutic for me. From the entry I wrote in my first diary at age nine to the pages of this book—writing has been my medicine. It is the safest and truest way for me to be fully vulnerable, fully honest, and fully me.

The blog I started in those eight months in Spokane is now gone. A lot of what I've written is. And like so much in life, I let that go.

I let a lot of that part of my life go.

The part covered in shame. The part where Josh had to pull me from the couch and take me to an urgent care because my panic attacks were so frequent and massive that neither of us knew what else to do. The part where I stopped being his wife and started being his patient. The part where I started caring more about our mental health than our relationship. The part where he stopped understanding my mental health, or maybe stopped trying. The part where our marriage was like fire: bright and luminous on the outside, but completely untouchable.

It was in these eight months that we plotted our motorcycle trip to South America. Where we had nothing to lose and everything to gain. Where we put thumbtacks on maps and spent our evenings eating rice and beans to save money. Where we focused our anxiety and uncertainty on a plan—on a route—on the promise I had made in my wedding vows one summer ago.

And so, in the wake of another breakdown, in the resting tide of my tidal unraveling, we tried to build something beautiful.

And we did. Oh, how we did.

There was nothing un-beautiful about the ten months we spent together, riding one motorcycle down the Pan-American highway. Not a damn un-beautiful thing.

Painful? Yes.

Stressful? As hell.

Beautiful? How could seeing the world in the way we did, even with the unruly challenges it forced us to face, even with the torment it caused us, even with the physical and mental exhaustion it brought—how could it *not* be?

part five
tidal wave.

For so many years, I thought love—romantic love—was supposed to be
like a tidal wave.

Like a hurricane that would sweep me and them from the rising water
propelling us from the tidal tip
into a never-ending storm of passion and desire.

That the faster we spun,
the more we would lose sight of who we were.

Like drops of water becoming one,
clasping each other's fingertips as the rapid wind
encompassed us in a giant, magnificent and roaring siphon.

Holding onto each other's gaze,
we'd be one another's anchors as we rose,
towering above the world together,
dissolving into one, and never letting go.

I didn't know that anchors weren't meant to rise.
I didn't remember that tidal waves crash.

I didn't understand

That love
like an anchor
is supposed to keep us still.

That love
like an anchor
is not the raging sea or rising tide

That love
like an anchor
is the grounding root that keeps us tethered
when the storm comes to sweep us away

That love
like an anchor
should feel no fear in the darkness
Nor care to see the storm
Nor beg to be moved
Nor be bothered by the thickening of aging moss

That love
like an anchor
is gently attuned to the current
paying close attention to when the tides are high
and honoring the water and her movement

That love
like an anchor
is tethered to two hearts and bodies,
two souls and stories,
two threads whose coils weave together
in constant awareness
of when the line grows too taught
and requires

a softening

so the anchor
can rebury itself in the dirt
and remind the coilers
that they are free to dance in the sea.

192

seventeen.

SOUTH

I wish I could blame this trip for the end of our marriage.

I've tried to. I've tried to blame our longing for independence on the constant togetherness. I've tried to point fingers at the lack of security and stability that comes with constant travel. I've tried to say, "If we didn't go on this trip, *maybe we'd still be married.*"

But I can't blame this trip—the same way I can't blame him, the same way I can't blame me.

I do believe that this trip cracked parts of us open that may have otherwise lay dormant for years. Parts of self and our relationship that may have seeped out slower and in more tolerable outpours. Revealed at separate times so we could each have the opportunity to look at and heal the hurt that came out of so much cracking.

Before we left, my anxiety was at an all-time high, and I was still having regular panic attacks.

For the first time in ten years, I was back on medication, and while I was not a huge fan of medicating myself (and Josh was vehemently appalled by the world of pharmaceuticals, and not shy about voicing this with me), I couldn't find another way to soothe the panic that boiled under the surface and the choking sensation I often felt and regularly dreaded.

I hoped that maybe this trip would save me. That an escape from our reality would give me relief. That *I* would change with the changing landscape, and the further we got from home, the further I could get from the world I seemed to crumble in.

I think, in some ways, Josh hoped for this too.

As much as he tried to help me with my mental health over the years, his efforts were often surface-level and solution-oriented. His beautiful, analytical, logical mind—the same one I fell in love with—kept him stuck in a cause-and-effect loop, constantly looking for the reason I was suffering and the solution to stopping it.

Sometimes this was helpful—he'd find out that certain foods might be causing my bloating or find vitamins online that were supposed to assist with sleep.

Other times, I just wanted him to hold me.

Many times, I just wanted him to say, "I got you, Rach, we're gonna fight this thing together."

And most times, the constant fixing made me feel more broken. As if I was a rusty machine that needed some oiling, and if I just did a little fine-tuning, I'd be fixed forever.

In hindsight, I think Josh *wanted* me to be fixed forever.

He wanted there to be a solution to my problems: a Band-Aid for my blood, a remedy for my sickness. Because if there was, he wouldn't have to face the truth that what ailed me might be something I was

194

going to fight for the rest of my life, and that perhaps, he wasn't prepared or interested in fighting it with me.

"I'm worried that blogging about your mental health is going to make things worse, not better, Rach," he said in the months leading up to our southern-departure.

As if to say,

By naming and honoring what you've experienced, you're glamorizing it. You're making it too known—too public—too available to people.

You're contributing to the problem rather than fixing it, and I don't want you to talk about it anymore because by doing so you make it more real, and I'm not interested in a reality that includes suffering.

It didn't occur to me that his disapproval of my writing might be fueled by his refusal to acknowledge a real part of who I am, and in doing so, his attempts to help me were clouded efforts to protect his own worldview and keep himself comfortable.

Josh had a high-on-life attitude—an optimism for living, a joy for existing, and a firm belief that *life was easy.*

Josh's life *was* easy.

He was a white, handsome, cis, straight man with social tact, an education, and natural athleticism. He hadn't experienced much hardship in his life, and while he struggled with general anxiety, insecurities, and fears, his capacity to grasp *why* I suffered and why it was difficult for me to recover from setbacks was limited.

"I just don't understand, Rach, you seemed fine last week. Something must have happened to set this off," he'd say.

And in my attempts to remain real, to be known, and to find some semblance of validity in my own not-knowing around my mental health, I'd exhaust myself trying to find the answers to his questions so that maybe he *could* understand, and so that maybe one day I wouldn't have to explain my existence to my husband anymore.

While he did the best he could to *care* for me, there was always a tiny disconnect for him in *recognizing* me—a small yet harrowing gap

195

between him and my mental illness that he simply could not (or maybe didn't want to) bridge.

And that maybe his desire—whether conscious or not—to avoid a reckoning of what it means to live with mental health conditions, was more important to him than actually supporting me how I needed to be supported.

I think, in that year before we left for Argentina, I carved a part of myself away. I resigned to the fact that my husband might not ever understand my mental health.

That perhaps, it was a part of me nobody would ever fully understand.

That like I'd always feared, unless I molded myself to be who he wanted me to be—happy, healthy, and optimistic—he would no longer love me, no longer accept me, and I would no longer be real.

Looking back, I think a lot of my mystery anxiety and panic in those months before we left for Argentina was rooted in a feeling of being deeply misunderstood—not only by society and culture at large, but by the very person who had committed to understanding me for the rest of my life, but who so adamantly refused to do so.

But at the time, my anxiety was still a mystery. To both him and me. And in our hopefulness and love for one another, we did what we'd always done, and dove headfirst into the frosty wetness together, hoping the rushing river would take us where we needed to go.

Everything that year happened so fast.

In October of 2018 we sold everything we owned (save the boxes that live at my in-law's), packed our belongings onto one motorcycle, and rode down the Pan-American highway without ever looking back.

For twelve months, we rode south.

Every three or four days, we'd pack our bags, load the KTM1190, gear up, and head to Argentina.

We had a vague plan:

"Head south, and focus on the journey, not the destination."

No two places were the same. No two places spoke the same language—even if Spanish was the baseline tongue. We traversed greenery that resembled English countryside, cliffs with roads unfit for curves, and cities with twinkly lights and vibrant music.

I wish I could put every inch of the beauty of this trip in the pages of this book. That I could honor each country, each city, each person we met in the spaces of this chapter. But to do this trip and the places we visited justice, I would have to write an entire novel, and that story is not all mine to write. At least not here, at least not now.

We'd made a few promises to each other about our rides, and we stuck to those for the sake of our safety and sanity.

"We'll never ride in the rain."

"Or the dark!"

"How about, we never ride longer than four hours a day, and we stop every hour for stretches and breaks. We aren't in a rush."

We kept to these few rules, and the rest we let unfold completely naturally. We planned just enough to know the direction we were headed and the places we hoped to see, but not so much that we couldn't be flexible. We wanted to feel free. We wanted to wake up each day without a plan, without a schedule, and without having to be any particular place at any particular time.

Sometimes this worked out in our favor—we'd fall in love with a town and decide to stay another night, sometimes several nights that turned into weeks.

Other times, we'd arrive somewhere we'd fantasized about, and upon arriving look at each other and say, "Well, this place sucks. Wanna leave first thing in the morning?"

We communicated well, and often. We had to. Every single move required a decision:

Where we would eat breakfast.

Where we would stop for gas.

What time we would wake up and what time we'd start to ride.

Who would write the next blog post.

Who would watch the bike while the other got groceries.

The decisions themselves were not stressful, but the constant *making* of decisions depleted our energy, so when it came time to actually connect, we were exhausted.

I'd only been on the back of Josh's motorcycle three times before the trip, and I had no idea how physically and mentally tiring it was to endure such long rides.

By the time we'd arrive at our destination, unloaded the boxes and bags from the bike and lugged them up the inevitable three flights of stairs to our hostel, taken off our sticky, sweaty gear, and found a restaurant (one that satisfied our vegan diet), we were too tired for intimacy, too tired for long talks, too tired for anything other than a, "Goodnight, I love you," and inevitable crash.

Between ride days, we made huge efforts to rekindle the lost connections. We'd schedule date nights and carve out floor meetings. We'd make each other morning coffees, hold space for each other's panic or anxiety, and tell each other how much we loved one another.

While I was struggling with the panic attacks and anxiety that I couldn't find seeds or reason for, Josh was growing restless and overwhelmed about money.

He'd always had anxiety about money—something we were aware of and trying to work through together. An old belief adopted from his parents about deserving nice things, about being worthy of buying quality food or materials, and general enoughness associated with money.

We fought often about money, and I witnessed Josh spiral more and more into a state of insecurity over the months.

One day in March, about halfway through the trip, we were staying in Limon, a black-sand beach on the eastern coast of Costa Rica. We stopped into a small grocery mart to get some lunch—where most items were under three dollars. I followed Josh through the aisle, the way I'd learned to do over the course of our trip.

He would lead—picking up items and checking labels, monitoring prices, then returning them. I'd follow, quietly, giving him the mental and physical space he needed to calculate whether he really needed it, if we could afford it, and ultimately either allow himself to put it in the cart or return it to its shelf.

I'd learned that when I led the grocery runs, Josh's anxiety would spike—I'd put dozens of things in our cart—yummy crackers, chocolate, a beer or two, and some back-up treats for later. It was easier, I found, to let him lead and decide what we could eat to keep his anxiety at bay.

I watched Josh pick up item after item in delight in the mart in Limon, then grow weary as he checked the price label. He'd pick up a can of beans, review the price, and put it back. After a few minutes in the store, hands empty, he looked at me in panic.

"You don't want anything?"

"Ah, I dunno Rach, I dunno what's going on. I gotta leave."

"Ok bud, no worries—" I turned to the shopkeeper who looked mildly confused and disgruntled by the gringos who entered his store and left emptyhanded, "—*gracias señor, vamos a regresar más tardé.*"

I met Josh outside, where I found him sitting in the hot sun on the curb outside.

He was crouched on the ground with his head in his hands, and he looked sullen. He'd lost weight since the start of our trip—both from lack of options, and from his anxiety about money and not wanting to eat more than rice, beans, and bananas.

"Josh, I'm gonna go inside and get us something to eat and I'll buy it, so you don't have to think about the cost, ok?"

"Ok," he said.

I returned to the shop and quickly bought what I knew Josh would eat and not get anxious about—a can of beans, some tortillas, a jar of salsa, and a Gatorade. I paid the shopkeeper and returned outside, where Josh was still curled inside himself, now soaked in sweat from the heat.

"Ok bud, I got it, let's go back to our Airbnb and eat, ok?"

He nodded—the way I imagine little Josh might nod, as if to say, "*What's happening to me? I don't understand this. Please take care of me.*"

Our Airbnb was just up the road, a small studio and one of the only Airbnb's in the town. Most Airbnb's that fit our budget were reminiscent of a grandparent's spare bedroom. Décor that was homey but not intentional, bedding that was sometimes nothing but a child's fuzzy blanket, and distinct yet unidentifiable odors that lingered in the upholstery.

I remember this Airbnb being particularly green—as if we were in some kind of hospital room. The space was large, and we were lucky enough to have a kitchen, so we were trying our best to cook most of our meals and make the most of being in our own space instead of a shared hostel.

We ate in silence around the small coffee table in the center of the green studio, the hum of the air-conditioner buzzing in the background, and the occasional roar of a small truck rushing by on the main road outside.

I wanted to give him some time to decompress, and I hoped that maybe after eating his hangxiety might subside.

Finally, I turned to him and said,

"I'm worried about you bud. You just walked through a grocery store where everything was less than three dollars, and you couldn't buy anything. I understand you want to save money and you're worried about not having money when we end this trip, but you have to feed yourself. If you're that scared to spend money, it's not about budgeting anymore, it's about something else."

He put his fork down and swept his face with his palm—the way he did when he was overwhelmed or not sure what to say.

"I know Rach. It's just really hard. Like I know you want to stay at all these nice places, and I know you're having a lot of digestion problems so you need to eat better food, and I just get so worried that we're gonna run out. I don't think about money like you do. You can just make money whenever you want, and I just get really anxious about it. I don't want to feel like I don't have a choice when we get home, and I don't want to have to get another job I'm miserable at."

Josh had been in sales since I met him, and while he was very good at what he did, he wasn't fulfilled. He had big dreams of entrepreneurship and had come up with dozens of products and businesses in the time that I knew him.

"Yes, so you put the camera on your dashboard, and it records everything— like a police car. So if you get in a crash, you have the record!"

"It's a bottle cutter that cuts wine bottles and beer bottles in half, so you can make candles!"

"Think Yerbamaté meets energy drink—it's like a healthy pick-me-up for healthy college students."

He wanted—like he'd told me all those years ago at the front desk of the gym—to lead an interesting life. He wanted something more than a desk job. Something outside the box. Something that defied the norm, was on his own terms, and in his own hands.

His ideas were creative and brilliant, but I think his fear of failure stopped him from ever pursuing them long enough to bring to fruition. Or maybe, deep down, he didn't think he deserved the success he so desperately wanted.

I wanted him to feel secure about money. I wanted him to trust himself enough to believe he could make his ideas a reality. I didn't want him to feel so undeserving of good things in life that he couldn't even feed himself. I wanted, just as he'd wanted for me, for him to see in himself the worthiness that I did.

We'd have versions of this conversation over and over. This, and dozens of others about the unpacked, unseen, old wounds that had remained dormant in each of us for most of our lives and that neither of us had ever seen or dealt with.

Paired with Josh's new insecurities was a natural need for me to affirm him. To show him he was still lovable, liked, and worthy, even in this space of cracking open. And I did a poor job.

I'm not proud of this, but it's the truth.

Almost daily, Josh would say,

"Rach, I feel like you don't like me. Like you just tolerate me. *Do* you even like me?"

I had no idea how to answer him when he'd ask this.

Honestly? I don't know. You do annoy me sometimes. But isn't that expected when you spend every waking hour of every waking day with someone for six months straight? Does that mean I really don't like you or that I just need some alone time, like a normal human?

He needed me so much more than I was comfortable with. He needed me to remind him he was good. That he was beautiful. Likeable. Valuable, interesting, funny, and attractive. He needed what a normal partner needs from their partner, and suddenly, I had no interest in giving it to him.

I was massively confused by this shift in myself, and I didn't understand it. I was hopeful that it was just the nature of the trip, and not actually that I no longer liked my husband, the man I'd liked, loved, respected, adored, and wanted every day for so many years.

We started arguing more than we'd ever argued in our entire eight years together. Truthfully, I don't remember what the fights were about.

So much was unspoken—we'd sense the other's mood or hear the tone in their voice, witness a facial expression we understood to be annoyance or even disgust, and delicately we'd try and sort out the frustration that lay beneath.

Our small fights about trip logistics turned into lengthy, painful conversations about whether I liked him or not. About why we weren't having sex. About why I was depressed. About why we were fighting.

Why became our mode-d'être, and the further south we got, the further we got into sense-making everything.

It is hard for me to pinpoint where and when our relationship started to cry. When she started to screech and grow colic. When she started to say, *"You guys, you have to pay attention to me or I'm going to die."*

At times I wanted to give up. Not only was I facing my own still very real insecurities, fears, and anxieties, but I was watching my partner, the person I love most in this world, go through it too. I watched him feel pain as he faced parts of himself he'd never met. I did what I could to support him as he discovered truths within him he didn't know. And he did the same. Feeling and digesting his own self-realizations, all the while holding me as I swallowed my own.

We were finding ourselves and losing each other, holding each other and letting ourselves go, asking questions we didn't have answers to and making meaning from meaningless moments that simmered under the surface. The ground beneath us was growing too hot, and we were burning.

Our attempts to salvage our lost intimacy with floor meetings and dates and "taking it slow" had grown stale.

I was growing bored with Josh's jokes and feeling guilty for even thinking so.

Josh was starving for my attention, and his needing me started to feel invasive.

And as I retreated, he looked harder for me, trying to find the person who once laughed at his jokes and adored his advances.

I was tired of his anxiety and suffering under the weight of my own. My panic attacks had turned into rage attacks, and the further south we got, the further I felt from my body and sense of self.

I was losing my attraction to him physically, and I felt ashamed that I didn't find my husband desirable.

Was it his physical change that caused this shift in me? Or his anxiety? Am I sensing his energetic shift and is that what's making me lose my lust?

Or does this all circle back to my mental health and completely muddled history with sex and sexuality?

I had no idea how to unpack those questions, and honestly, I was terrified to. Because what if the answer was that I didn't want to have sex with my husband? How would I reconcile a truth like that? How would we?

I think it was the avoidance of these questions that kept me so anxious. That kept me in such a heightened state of panic, and ultimately a physical state of demise. I was too terrified to answer the questions I needed to ask in order to either eventually re-meet my husband in intimacy, or potentially never meet him there again.

By August, my health was dwindling, and most of our relating had moved from therapizing Josh and his money anxiety to medically diagnosing my physical condition. I had started to lose my hair, was experiencing frequent panic attacks and bursts of anger, and my digestion was so out of whack that I felt powerless in my body.

Josh's fix-it hat was at the ready, and he worked tirelessly to find me doctors in Colombia and Ecuador. He called holistic providers back home for advice. Nothing seemed to work, and my body was falling apart.

As my body and mind broke down, so did we.

We were fighting often, crying often, and our analyses were coming up short. We had no answers for what was happening to us, and we were scared.

By September, I knew I needed to leave the trip.

My body couldn't handle the rides anymore.

Our days had grown longer with the vastness of Peru.

The weather was turning cold, and the further south we'd go the longer our days would become.

Cities were fewer and far between, and the horizon looked more rugged than I anticipated being able to tolerate.

I had made it this far—would that be enough?

Could I live with myself for leaving before we finished?
Could Josh ever forgive me if I made him stop here?

We were so close to the end, and my heart couldn't bear the idea of him not finishing his dream. I also couldn't bear the idea of not finishing something, *again*.

And in the spaces between our inevitable fights, in the moments where we bowed our heads in silence, wondering how we'd gotten here, Josh would broach the idea of us ending the trip. Halfway hoping I'd say no because this was his dream, halfway hoping I'd say yes so we could stop the pain we both were feeling.

eighteen.
PERU

"Josh, why do you have these old photos of you on here?" I chortled. "They look like pictures for a dating profile!"

We were having lunch in a small town in northern Peru, just a few weeks before our eventual separation in Lima. I asked to use Josh's phone at lunch to review our photos for an Instagram post—a typical mealtime activity that kept me focused on everything but Josh, and Josh focused on where my priorities seemed to be.

I looked up at him humorously, not expecting to meet his face drooped in guilt—a face that told me they *were* photos for a dating profile, and I'd accidentally found something I wasn't supposed to.

"Wait, are they?" I asked, my heart holding the truth that his hurt was much bigger than I'd realized, much more dire than I'd thought, and much more than just him feeling unliked.

"Yeah, they are."

"Ok," I paused. I checked in quickly with my emotional state. I wasn't angry. I could sense this was not about looking for sex or even about wanting to leave me, I knew it was about filling a space in his heart that I hadn't been filling, and meeting a need I'd been neglecting for many months. I just hadn't been present enough or listening enough to recognize its magnitude.

"Why? I'm not mad, I just want to hear from you what this is about, because I am pretty surprised."

"You just don't pay attention to me anymore. And like I've told you, I feel like you don't like me. And we aren't having sex and I just started to wonder, *am I just really that unattractive and undesirable? Or is it Rachel?* So I got the app just to try and make me feel better. To boost my confidence."

"Ok, that makes sense. Did it?"

"No. I deleted it pretty fast. But obviously in Josh fashion I forgot to delete the photos."

"Alright," I stammered. I did what I would eventually do a year later in his brother's basement. I stayed steady, kept my cool, and tried to coach us through what felt like a pivotal moment in our marriage.

"Can we talk about this? Because this suddenly feels way more serious than I realized it was."

"Ya, ya I think we should."

We finished our lunch and moved our conversation to a coffee shop. Josh unpacked his hurt—how he felt unliked, how his confidence was shot, and how my lack of interest in him sexually left many of his needs—sexual and intimate—unmet.

I tried to empathize and hold space, but I didn't know how to fix the problem. I was so confused sexually, and after several years of trying to unlearn what I'd learned about sex and my role in sex, I felt like a lost thirteen-year-old, clueless with how to approach the arena, and fearful of what I'd find inside.

My relationship with sex itself was still so messy, and I'd lost sight of whether my paralysis in the bedroom was because of Josh, because of my sexuality, because of my history, or if there was just something vehemently wrong with me.

And try as we did to work through that together, I wasn't ready, healed, or prepared in my own work around sex to do so, and the fires it was starting were growing too big for us to manage.

Again, none of this was conscious to me at the time. I just felt confused, flustered, and unsure of how to move forward. My husband felt unliked and unloved, I felt disorganized and pressured, and we both felt like we were running low on patience, steam, and time.

What we could both agree on was that we were so enmeshed in our thinking and feeling that we couldn't parse out what we wanted as individuals versus what we thought was best for the other.

We decided together that we should take a few days apart to sort through our own thoughts and reconvene once we'd figured out—on our own and without the influence of the other's emotional state—what we both needed and wanted.

I took a bus from the small town in northern Peru to Lima and stayed alone in a hostel, where I took four days to sort through what I needed and wanted.

For those few days, I walked more than I had in months. I paced the streets of Lima. I'd move between walking and running, sitting and standing, staring blankly at paragliders in the foggy sky and sobbing into the palms of my hands.

"What am I doing?" I'd think.

There were slivers and pockets of time where I felt utterly free. Happy, even. I was alone, and none of my decisions had to be run by anyone. I could eat when and what I wanted, go where I wanted and how, and simply move about my day with total independence.

In just a few days many of my digestive symptoms had settled. I wasn't panicked either. This alone alarmed me.

"Could being away from my husband be the reason I feel so good? How can that be?"

I tried not to analyze what was happening, but it's in my nature to overthink and I couldn't help but make rash conclusions about what was happening.

Though I don't remember making any kind of final decision, I knew what my body and soul needed. I needed to leave Peru, and I needed to go somewhere that would allow me to harness and foster the independence and sense of self I'd lost and so desperately longed for.

While I knew I had the option to go home and stay with one of my parents or in a friend's guest bedroom, I couldn't fathom how living under my parent's roof or being in the presence of my happily married friends would support the need I felt to find out who I was outside of my marriage.

I knew I needed to care for my health, and in my heart, I knew the reason my health was suffering was closely tied to my mental wellbeing. I felt suffocated. Not by Josh, or our marriage. But by my own inability to simply be my own person.

I craved freedom and independence. Autonomy. Choice. Knowing myself so fully that I could move through life as my own container, leaning on others when necessary but keeping my sense of self solid in the mix.

Being together day in and out, being pressed against another body for hours at a time, living in hostels and waking up each day living out someone else's dream—no matter how much I was benefiting from tagging along—was draining me.

I knew I needed to spend some time alone—really and truly *alone*. And this terrified me.

A few months earlier, we had flown to Bali to film a friend's wedding. I fell in love with the culture, people, and way of life, and for some reason it was calling me back.

After four days alone, we reunited at an Airbnb in a new part of town. I honestly can't remember if he picked me up at my hostel or if I met him there—I recall lugging our boxes and bags up two flights of stairs and bartering in Spanish with the woman who greeted us about whether or not we could leave the motorcycle in the gated parking lot.

The apartment was spacious—it had a living area, dining room, kitchen, bedroom, and full bath. The décor was eclectic and floral, somewhat scattered and mismatched in a way that made it unclear if the aesthetic was intentional or the result of throwing together leftover furniture from a family estate.

Somehow, we found ourselves sitting in the living room. I don't remember how long it took us to get settled or who made the first mention of "are you ready to talk about this?"

It was midday, and there was plenty of light seeping into the third story apartment. Josh sat across from me on the plastic-covered floral couch, his eyes teary and hopeful. He looked so optimistic. So eager. So wanting—of me, of us, of the possibility that we would make it out of this together.

I could see in his eyes how badly he wanted to save us. To save me. His love and goodness poured over me, and I turned it into sticky guilt. Like tar, I turned black and heavy inside. I knew I was going to hurt him.

With his hands clasped in front of him, he said, "I think we should go home. I don't think you can be on this trip anymore. I think we should end the trip, go home, and have everything go back to normal."

I felt a lump swell in my throat. I kept my hands in my lap and remained motionless. I shifted slightly, as if hoping to stir the courage from my seat up and out of my mouth. The plastic underneath my own bum squeaked.

"I think I need to leave the trip. But I don't think going home together is going to make everything go back to normal."

"Ok, so what are you saying? We go home and do therapy? Let's do that."

"No," I said, beginning to lose myself, beginning to leave my body, beginning to darken and blacken inside as I tried to find the words for what I needed to say.

"I think—and you can think about this because I want you to decide for yourself and not do it because you think it's what I want for you or what I think is best for you—I think you need to finish this trip. No matter what happens with us, I'm worried you might resent me for the rest of your life if you leave now. We've made it this far, and you're so close. And this is your dream. So I think you should stay and ride to Argentina. But I can't stay."

He nodded. I could feel him beginning to understand what this meant and put the pieces together of the reality that we may spend the next several months apart—something we had never done in the course of our entire relationship.

"So what will you do?"

"I think…I think I'm going to go to Bali."

I explained my reasoning to him, and he understood. He didn't question me or challenge me or say my idea was selfish or crazy. He simply said, "Ok Rach, I get it. I understand. If that's what you need, I support you."

We cried. We sat there, across from one another in the Peruvian Airbnb, in teary silence. Not touching, not speaking, not knowing how or what to do with the words we'd filled the space between us with.

He wiped his face, and I watched his heart collapse and his throat close. I felt mine do the same. I loved him so much. And he loved me. And neither of us could understand how this made sense. We sat there and made a decision to separate, unable to fathom how it could be both the right and wrong decision at the same time.

The next few days happened quickly. I bought a suitcase in a downtown shopping mall and packed what belongings I had. We paired down what I would take and what he would keep, bargaining gracefully over plugs and pill boxes.

We shared awkward silences and strange embraces.

We kissed. We didn't.

We called our families and received equally confused and befuddled reactions.

My mother couldn't grasp the decision. "But you look so happy on your Instagram…" she challenged.

We did look happy on our Instagram. And we were. Very often we were. But laced between the photos and stories was the thick veil of truth that never really permeated the surface. Even in real life. If you'd met us on our trip, you'd say the same thing: *but you seemed so happy, and in love.*

And we were. That isn't untrue.

This was what made our decision so confusing. We were both perplexed.

How could I love someone so much, and yet long to be so alone?

I couldn't answer that question then, and it took me a year to find the answer. My last night in Lima, Josh and I sat in a hotel lobby drinking cocktails while we waited for my airport shuttle. We barely spoke. I think we tried to engage in some small talk, avoiding the inevitably painful goodbye that was coming.

We sat at our cocktail table, our legs dangling around the sides of the riverbank, toes dipped in the shallow end, knowing the rushing water was coming but too novice to know when it would be time for me to jump into the cold—this time alone, this time without the firm grip of his hand on mine, this time without knowing if he'd find me somewhere down the river once again.

My phone pinged, and suddenly it was time. Without warning, the wave was coming, and it was time to let go.

What was I doing? I thought.

We held each other close in the cold darkness of Lima's evening air. I didn't want to let him go.

Last week I was riding to Argentina with my husband, and now I'm flying halfway across the world alone, with no plan, no money, and no timeline of when or how I'll see him again?

The water was rising.

What the fuck am I doing?

His hand was slipping.

Am I making a terrible decision?

I felt like I might drown, and I was so scared I wouldn't make the swim alone.

Tell me to stay, tell me I'm wrong, stop me from going—

"Vamanos," the driver said curtly, as if bored by our long goodbye.

I looked at Josh. This was it.

He held his hands to my shoulders and looked at me. He didn't bow his head or meet me the way he'd always done. As if his body was there with me in our safety circle, his mind unsure if his heart could join us.

"I love you, Rach."

"I love you too, Josh."

He gave me a half smile—his best, *this is hard for me, but I love you enough to let you do this,* and my insides crumbled.

Shouldn't his goodness be enough for me to stay?

Shouldn't his goodness be enough for me to want to?

I climbed the stairs, looking back at him when I could.

I found my seat and pulled myself close to the window, muffling my tears in my Peruvian turtleneck. I peered out at him, and as the bus pulled away from the street, he put up his hand in a wave. Pressing my hands against the window, I watched him disappear into the darkness, wondering if I'd regret this decision for the rest of my life.

214

nineteen.
PATIENT PAKSHI

"The good news is, all of this can be fixed by healing your relationship with your mother."

You've got to be fucking kidding me.

I sat in Pakshi's small healing room and felt the humid Bali air swell through the wooden crevices in the floor. My own internal heat rising, as I tried to wiggle my way out of feeling the sweat from my back meet the cloth of my market-bought jumpsuit.

Stickiness is inevitable in Bali. I had only been there a week, and I hadn't yet learned that being outside meant being drenched in sweat. There was no way around it.

I'd chosen to go to Bali in the hottest, dampest part of the year. Rainy season was about to begin, and little to my knowledge I'd spend the next three months welcoming a tropical winter filled with fat, plum-drop rain and electric thunderstorms.

But I didn't go to Bali for the sun or warm beaches. My decision-making process was less concerned with high or low season, and more with safety, healing, and empowerment.

Still, the decision was impulsive, and I spent the first few weeks in treacherous doubt, covered in sweat, and second-guessing myself.

This was how I arrived in Pakshi's office. Overdressed, overheating, and overwhelmed.

I call it an office, but it was more of a cabana. Each healer at The Yoga Barn had their own little cabana—a sacred space to practice their magic.

Energy healers, meditation masters, lightworkers, gut specialists, sex technologists, chakra healers, and so many other incredibly talented experts from around the world held astute positions at the renowned yoga center in Ubud.

The sprawling grounds seemed to defy the density of Ubud center—tucked away down an alley wide enough for two or three yogis, The Yoga Barn materialized as a utopia to those who entered.

Pathways wove through coy ponds and rice paddies, revealing towering open-air studios and secret nooks for prayer and meditation.

Six months prior, I had come to The Yoga Barn for lunch during my first visit to Bali. Josh and I were filming a wedding in Uluwatu, and the bride and groom had graciously offered to host us for two weeks so we could experience Bali for ourselves.

I fell in love quickly.

I fostered a childlike wonder for Balinese culture: the slow pace of life, the value of spirituality, and the immense priority of community over personal gain.

Bali gave me a sense of peace and satisfaction—something I struggled to find on a daily basis.

I went to Pakshi that day because I needed relief. Relief not only from the lack of peace I felt, but relief from the guilt, confusion, and shame surrounding my decision to go to Bali in the first place.

When I arrived at The Yoga Barn, I completed a short intake form— it was no different than any form I had filled out for a therapy appointment in the past:

History of mental illness? *Yes. Eating disorder. Depression. Anxiety. Suicide attempt. Panic disorder.*
History of physical illness? *Yes. Digestive issues. Hair loss. Hormone imbalance. Loss of menstruation. Knee injuries and countless broken bones.*
Presenting concern? *My marriage is falling apart?*

The check-in lady escorted me to Pakshi's cabana, where I was instructed to sit on a small stool outside his door and knock when my hour began.

I watched my phone and waited for the clock to tick to the exact hour. I saw two shoes outside his office and started to panic. *Was there someone still in there? I'm supposed to knock on the hour, should I still knock?*

Rules paralyze and soothe me. It just depends on the context.

Sitting outside Pakshi's office, debating whether to knock like I was told, or wait like my intuition told me, I felt the trembling child within me bubble to the surface. Painstakingly, I knocked. And as I did, I knew I should have trusted my gut.

The door creaked open, just enough for a small, bearded face with ageless eyes to peer sideways through.

"I am with a client," he gently muttered in a thick Indian accent.

Horrified, I apologized through whispering teeth, and proceeded to curl into the smallest ball I could outside his office.

What a first impression.

I waited with bated embarrassment for another five minutes, wondering if I should just bolt instead.

He probably already knows everything he needs to about me now. I'm a rude, inconsiderate white girl who thinks she can just go knocking on people's doors. Fuck me.

Unable to get over my own neuroses, but able to hold myself accountable for making what felt like a grievous mistake, I prepared my apology to the renowned guru.

A few minutes later, the door opened and a young girl left. I waited for his gesture to enter, and as I did, I began to apologize in the most gracious, honorable way I could muster.

Pakshi seemed to barely notice my groveling, and my attempts to recover maturely suddenly felt childish.

His cabana was fairly empty, except for two sofa chairs facing each other to the right of the entrance, and a massage table by the window.

Pakshi gestured for me to sit down and took my sheet of paper. He glanced at it briefly, then placed it gently on the coffee table between us.

As the sweat beads dripped down my breastbone, I wondered how he looked so cool and dry in his long sleeve top and matching white pants.

It was then that he looked at me for the first time.

As if peering into my soul, he gently tilted his head, and scanned my body. I could sense a faint smile through his wispy black beard.

I felt insignificantly small. My hands pursed tightly between my legs as I held back tears. I could barely meet his gaze, because when I did, I felt as though he'd see how deeply shattered I was.

I desperately wanted this man to see me as wise. I wanted him to acknowledge my courage and strength for choosing to be in Bali, and somehow confirm that I had made the right decision leaving my husband in Peru.

I next expected Pakshi to ask me about the "problems" on my intake sheet. I was sure he'd ask me about my Eating Disorder. I was certain he'd question how my confidence or self-worth played a role in the unweaving of my perfect marriage.

Instead, he calmly and delicately asked me one or two questions about my family:

"Did you have a happy childhood?"

"What was your father like?"

And,

"How is your relationship with your mother?"

I am not stranger to the therapy room, and his familial and familiar line of questioning didn't startle me. For a moment, I thought I might regain control and composure. *I can answer these questions with grace and profound self-awareness!*

Still, the pain of recounting old wounds, the vulnerability attached to revealing oneself in the presence of someone with power, and the grief of potentially losing a partner are all cause for losing one's footing.

I answered his questions, drowning in a mouthful of tears and trying to keep the salty snot out of my mouth.

This is not going as gracefully as I imagined.

I tend to glamorize the therapeutic/healing experience. I imagine myself entering into a therapist or healer's space, sitting down, and wildly impressing them with my intuition and awareness. I fantasize about how well I'll perform, how beautifully vulnerable I'll be, and how they'll praise me for my insight and astute psychological knowledge.

Even in therapy I create unmanageable self-expectations. Typically, this results in one of two outcomes:

One, I overindulge, overshare, and become so emotionally compromised that I almost black out and lose all sense of self.

Two, I become so rigid, so stiff, and so presentable that I contort myself into paralysis and make no room for potential progress or healing.

My perfectionism has robbed me of a lot in my life, and my own healing has been no exception.

So, I sat there, across from Pakshi, falling in and out of dire desperation and rigid resistance. He patiently allowed me a few minutes to explain how I'd arrived in Bali.

I still hadn't figured out how to say that in a matter of one week, I had decided to fly to Bali after ten months of riding through Latin America on a motorcycle with my husband.

Even today, a year and a half later, that sentence feels too long and exhaustive, yet inexplicably hollow. The reality itself was too exhaustive and inexplicable, and I learned there was no digestible or graceful way to chew the experience into bitesize morsels.

My husband and I are having problems.

My hair is falling out.

My digestion is failing, and I can't stop crying.

My sex drive is absent, and my husband is questioning my sexuality.

My ability to live out his dream of riding a motorcycle to South America has met its limits.

My anxiety is at an all-time high.

My Eating Disorder is rearing her ugly head.

Which was I supposed to start with? How could I re-purpose this broken-down list of what was happening to me—to us—into a comfy statement that encompassed and did justice to the pain I was experiencing?

I couldn't.

Still, I can't.

I've learned I don't have to, and that unraveling the reasoning behind my Latin-American-exodus was not something I could ever fully explain.

In that moment, though, in front of the wise and powerful Pakshi, I wanted to prove my ability to encapsulate the decision. I wanted to bottle it up so nicely that when he received it, he could feel and taste the bitterness and joy, the fear and anticipation, the pain and longing. I wanted to be perfect for him, so that I could hear him praise me for what I desperately hoped was the right decision. I wanted him to absolve me of my guilt, so that I could be free.

I flailed, and briefly blacked out (as I normally do when attempting to divulge dozens of delicate details.) I have no clue what I said to him, other than something about my marriage and a motorcycle.

Pakshi was patient but swift. He nodded with a slight indifference, as if to communicate, *I see what is happening to you. You are not perfect. You can stop trying now and let me do my work.*

He folded his small hands in his lap to mirror me, and the tip of his wispy black beard almost touched his knees as he leaned forward.

He looked into my eyes, and with barely any emotion, said with total resolve:

"The good news is, all of this can be fixed by healing your relationship with your mother."

I scoffed.

I half expected him to go on—*that couldn't possibly be all he has to say to me.*

I looked at him, my mouth open and fused in a "you've got to be joking me" grin, waiting for the rest of his diagnosis.

Nothing.

He just sat there. Him looking at me, me looking at him. And when I realized that was the end of his analysis, I flopped back into my chair.

My mother? Really?

My hopefulness crumbled and I cowered at his response. *I was here for healing, not more problems. I was here to have him tell me I was on the right path, not to turn around and go further back. I was here for my husband and me, not my mother.*

Slightly angry, but with no clue or courage to feel or express it, I sat silently in response to his statement.

He must have sensed my discouragement, because he offered to begin our table work. I lay face up on his table, and for the first time I noticed the strange lights that hung over the energy-working-arena.

As I lay there, now completely drenched in sweat and utterly embarrassed that this stranger had not only seen me so weak and unaware but was allowing me to turn his massage bed into a pool, I tried to mentally prepare myself for whatever was to come next.

The Bali energy had already carved open a space of curiosity and willingness in my heart for "woo-woo" healing, and I didn't want to lose my openness just because of some back sweat and a comment about my mother-daughter relationship.

How did he know there was strain between me and my mom?

I kept thinking about this as he began his work.

"Shh. Quiet your mind. You are only here now."

God he's good.

For the next forty-five minutes, Pakshi did something I will never be able to explain or understand.

With his palms facing me, he gently hovered them over each chakra for a few minutes at a time. Sometimes he'd make contact and place his hands firmly on the area. Other times he left them hovering above the surface of my jumpsuit, inviting me to make sounds with my exhales as he did. Either way, I could feel the energy flow from him to me, from me to him, and out.

And as it did, I wept.

I wept and breathed with such force that I thought I might pass out, crying with such force that little sparkles appeared in the corners of my eyes. At times my head filled with so much oxygen I nearly *did* pass out.

In areas of particular tension (my throat was a hot spot), he would pulse his palms and encourage me to breathe.

"When you are ready, you can open your eyes and return to the sofa."

That was forty-five minutes? Holy hell.

Slowly, I rolled myself off the table to return to my original chair. The energy there now stale as I felt so much running through my veins. As I sat down, I felt lightheaded and utterly exhausted. I prepared myself for what normally concludes any therapeutic experience: processing, follow up, and action plans.

But Pakshi had only one thing to say to me:

"This work will take you a very long time. You must come back."

I couldn't have known it then, but he was right.

The work did take me a very long time.

And I did come back.

I spent the next three months in Bali, alone. Not alone in the sense that I was isolated from human contact—but alone in the sense that for the first time in my life, I was truly *on my own*.

After high school I moved straight to my NYU dorm room, and then bounced between my parent's home, Evergreen College dorm room, living with friends, and finally moving in with Josh until we eventually married.

I had not once in my life lived on my own. Initially, I was excited at the prospect of total freedom: I would be able to wake up and do whatever I wanted without the constant fatigue of navigating another person's body, needs, energy, or belongings. I carry some shame about this, but I was delightfully looking forward to not sharing a space with another human for once.

I wanted to know what it felt like to wake up and ask,

"What do *I* want to do today? What do *I* want to eat for breakfast? When will *I* decide to go outside or move my body?"

It's not that Josh or my parents ever controlled these parts of my life—it's that these mundane, simple decisions were always made with the consideration of another person.

These small little pockets of freedom, as insignificant as they seemed, sounded so delicious. And after a year of waking up day in and out and making every breathing decision together, Josh and I were decision-fatigued.

I also recognize how silly, trivial, and ridiculous this sounds. How lucky we were to even travel like we did. How privileged we were (and are) to even have decisions to make in life.

We leaned on gratitude for as long as we could to manage the weight of our silent conflict—we recognized how fortunate we were and didn't outwardly complain or make a big deal of any of the challenges we faced. We took them in stride—the same way we stood tall and firm when our wedding venue burned down—and we trusted that we could navigate all the decisions, the fatigue, and the uncertainty of what our lives would be when we reached the end of our trip.

So, when I got to Bali, ready and longing for the autonomy and freedom to be me and truly alone, I was crushed when I realized I had no idea how to actually *be* alone. I was completely void of ability to make my own decisions. Petrified I'd make the wrong one. Lost for what to actually *do* all day, because I had forgotten (or maybe never discovered) what I actually enjoyed.

I resisted the urge to call Josh daily. To ask him for help with mundane choices like "where to get the best scooter rental in Canggu." To ask him to soothe my anxiety or loneliness with his kind words and softness. To ask him if he thought we were doing the right thing, because I wasn't sure and I needed reassurance.

I fought these urges because I wanted so desperately to be able to fend for myself. I wanted to feel like the adult that I was. I wanted to see myself as an independent, self-sufficient, capable human with interests, desires, and power. But I had no idea where to start.

I spent many nights crying alone in my room. With the sixteen-hour time difference, it was rare that my cry-times would line up with my friends or family members' waking hours back home. And truthfully, I wasn't speaking to that many of them. I barely understood what Josh and I were doing, and the idea of trying to explain my uncertainty and doubt while attempting to provide some type of context for our decision to multiple people back home was overwhelming.

Daily, I questioned whether I had made the right decision.

I desperately wanted to call Josh for reassurance. *Are we doing the right thing? Are you as freaked as me? Are you ok? Do you miss me?* I was lonely, scared, and confused.

I felt like I was skating on ice, unable to slow down, unable to stop, reaching in every direction for something to stop me from slipping away.

Despite the intense urge to call for rescue, to reach for reassurance or guidance, I didn't. I skated—not so gracefully—and tried to slow myself down. I noticed I was spinning out less and finding more balance. Still, I would hit a crack in the ice, and find myself once again flailing for support.

When the urge to call him faded, I noticed a new, equally strong urge. It was the urge to call my mom.

When I couldn't depend on my primary love-person for emotional caregiving, my brain immediately recalled its previous emotional caregiver: my mother.

I've been dependent on someone other than myself for a lot longer than I realized.

In that moment, it felt like I had uncovered a deeply ingrained pattern of dependence on someone other than myself to tend to and care for my needs. I felt like I had an opportunity to break that cycle, and I chose to dive headfirst into the abyss.

For the next three months, I noticed times when I had the urge to call Josh, my parents, and even best friends for support. I focused first on trying to solve the problem on my own. If it was too complicated or overwhelming to do alone, I asked for support. If I felt I was in danger (emotionally or logistically), I asked for support.

Otherwise, I took care of myself.

I stopped looking to be rescued and started learning to paddle.

It wasn't easy. And I flailed alot. But I learned.

When I had panic attacks, I grabbed an ice pack and used the self-soothe skills I had learned in therapy. When I felt lonely, I let myself feel lonely, and used mindfulness and non-attachment to notice what it felt like to *feel lonely* (really fucking bad, by the way), rather than fight or judge it. When I felt myself falling into a depression, I outsourced to a therapist and coach because I knew having an unbiased, trained professional was necessary if I lost my way.

I was giving myself the love and care I so often gave others, but rarely gave myself. I was breaking down, falling apart, laying on the ground in pieces and saying, "It's okay Rachel, you can do this. You will not die. Be broken for a moment. Lay here in pieces. You will not die. You will put yourself back together, with your own glue, your own special recipe, your own magic fairy dust. You will not die."

And as I did—as I put myself back together, piece by piece—I knew I couldn't do it alone, nor did I want to.

So, I started to re-visit the idea of togetherness. Of interdependence.

How, I wondered, *can I continue to care for myself, without crossing the dangerous border of doing everything on my own and burning out?*

Can I hold onto a sense of independence, and open my heart back up to Josh, without falling so quickly into the comfort of his all-encompassing care?

And—the scariest question of them all—*would he still want me?*

part six

oceans away

We both wanted to be good.

He, a good boy
Me, a good girl.

And as much as we tried
out of the goodness
to prevent the hurting

it was sometimes
in the trying so hard
to build walls to stop the hurt
that we grew blind to the fact
that we were building a home for that hurt to grow.

And when the hurt grows too big
when the walls can no longer keep it inside
it has nowhere to go
but out.

And the walls
while well-made
with good intentions,
built with love
and on solid ground—
break.

•

twenty.

SEX IN STOCKHOLM

"Do you think Sweden is ready for sex?"

I laughed when I saw the message in my inbox—Ama was a sex and marriage therapist based in Seattle and was responding to a post I'd made about a TEDx speaker I'd coached while in Bali that fall. We had a few LinkedIn connections in common, all from my high school. I didn't know who she was, but assumed she was either a former teacher there or connected to the staff in some way.

"Totally, haha!" I replied. "By the way, are you taking new clients? My husband and I are looking for a therapist, and I noticed that's what you do."

We spoke on the phone a few days later, and I could feel her energy through the phone. As she talked, I felt hope. She didn't make any promises about what she would do for me or for us, and I loved that she fused her psychology education and experience with a somatic and energetic approach. She was analytical, educated, and experienced in the world of psychology, and her worldview was painted by a deep reverence for spirituality, non-duality, and the belief that our bodies are vessels for our energetic souls.

I asked Josh to have a phone call with her too, so that he could see if he felt like she was a good fit before deciding to move forward. We wanted to choose someone we both felt connected to, so that we could keep things as fair as possible. As always.

We decided she was a good fit, and I booked a plane ticket home for Christmas Day, 2019.

I met Josh at a coffee shop a few days later—one we'd been to many times in the years we'd lived in Seattle. I was so nervous. I had never been away from Josh for that long, and the circumstances were beyond any I could have fathomed.

How would I feel when I saw him?

Would I be excited?

What if I felt nothing?

What if I felt everything, and he felt nothing?

I sat outside the coffee shop under a covering waiting for him to arrive. I was always early. He was always late.

He came around the corner in the same clothes I'd left him in three months ago: dark jeans, orthopedic sneakers, and a black puffy jacket. But on that day, his clothes seemed more worn. He did too. As if he'd seen so much, and he was changed because of it.

I realized then, that he had. He had finished the trip we started together fifteen months before, and he had witnessed the land and roads I was meant to see with him. He had felt the wind and sun I would have felt with him. But now, instead of holding the memory of that ending together, it was one he carried alone, and one I would never be privy to.

We hugged, somewhat lovingly, somewhat awkwardly, and ordered coffee.

We sat across from each other and talked. He shared small stories from his ride through Patagonia. I shared whimsical tales from my sweaty stay in Bali. We laughed. We smiled. It felt like a first date, but with an ex-lover. The nerves were as palpable as the comfort—the knowing each other as real as the not-knowing.

We were strangers in love—or lovers estranged. I wasn't sure.

We had both come bearing gifts. In my last week in Bali, I'd gone souvenir shopping, and was on the hunt for a mug he could use for his Yerbamaté. After several unsuccessful attempts in the market, I stumbled upon a small stuffed animal. It was a monkey, and I recalled all the times I'd bought Josh a stuffed monkey as a gift over the course of our relationship.

He loved monkeys (he wanted a real one for a pet every year for Christmas growing up), and seeing this monkey, all alone in this market full of replicated souvenirs in Canggu, seemed like a small sign. I picked up the monkey and asked the shopkeeper what his name was.

"Oh, I don't know," he giggled, shaking his head and laughing sheepishly.

"No? What *would* you name him?" I asked, smiling. The shopkeeper was young, maybe seventeen or eighteen. I could tell he was shy, and his earnestness was endearing.

"Haha oh um, I don't know."

"Anything you want," I said kindly.

"Oh, I don't know, maybe…. Josh?"

My smile dropped and I looked at him dumbfounded.

"Josh?"

"Yes, Josh, it's not ok?" He looked almost afraid, like he had said the wrong thing.

I couldn't believe it.

In Bali, most people are named depending on their birth order—the firstborn child is named Wayan, Gede or Putu, the second is Made or Kadek, and so-on. While some Balinese people give themselves nicknames, Josh is not one of them, and I'd never encountered or heard of anyone using that name in Bali. The fact that this young, Balinese boy who spoke very little English chose Josh out of the blue to name this monkey almost brought me to tears.

"I'll take him," I said, grinning ear to ear.

When I told Josh this story in the coffee shop in Seattle, he beamed.

"No way! That's awesome. I love it. Thanks Rach."

When it came time for him to give me my gift, I wasn't sure what to expect. He'd been riding for the last three months, and real estate on the motorcycle was limited.

He handed me a rectangle-shaped package—I think it was wrapped in tissue or packaging paper—something translucent enough that I could tell it was a picture frame.

When I peeled back the paper and revealed the image, my heart started to pound. I looked at the image, grazing the glass with my fingertips as if feeling it would help me remember.

"I know that meant a lot to you," Josh said. "I know it took a lot of courage for you to get back on the scooter after you crashed it when we were there together in June. I thought you might want to remember this moment."

It was a painting of a photograph I'd taken on my scooter in Bali. The fact that he had chosen to honor an experience I had, when I was alone, when I had left him, and one that he knew mattered to me even in the absence of "us," carved a hole in my heart.

I don't know that I realized it fully in that moment, but Josh cared for me more than I could ever let him. He tended to me in a way I didn't know what to do with.

I held the image to my breast and looked at him with a tilted head.

"Thank you, Josh. This is so thoughtful. I love it."

We talked for several hours more, enough for coffee refills and ultimately, the grumbling of our bellies.

"I'm really enjoying talking to you, and you can of course say no, but would you like to come back to my mom's condo with me?"

I said this so formally, as if I had pre-constructed it in a therapy worksheet on communication. I wanted to be respectful of his boundaries, be clear in my ask, and make sure to express my emotions. This was still a sticky process for me, but one I was determined to practice.

"Yes, I would like that very much Rachel," he said, mirroring my sticky formality.

When we arrived at my mom's condo, I offered to make him a smoothie bowl for lunch, and we talked while I prepared our food.

We tried to talk—I think—about next steps. About where we might live. About what we would do. About what we wanted. About what we didn't.

I wish I could remember what happened next. How we spun ourselves into a knot. How we tangled ourselves into the heat of disconnect and confusion.

I wish I could remember how all the fights that transpired over the next five months started. But I can't.

It's as if every conversation started peacefully on the bow of a boat: both of us gazing ahead towards the open ocean. Carefully, we'd try to maneuver the ship's sails, attempting to negotiate the direction of our seafaring vessel, and arguing over the weather as if we knew how to predict the ocean wind.

And as we'd try to convince the other of the currents we both felt, fumbling for lines and slipping on the wet and salty surface of the ship, one of us would fall into the ocean. And as the waves would cascade over the boat, whoever remained on board would do everything they could to pull the other back in.

How we fell out became irrelevant. The crashing water would pound the side of the boat and the harsh tide would pull the fallen half further off to sea. And when the storm would come to an end, all that either of us could remember were the cries we made to one another, the fear and panic of losing each other, and the helplessness to control the storm.

Somewhere between blending bananas and slicing strawberries, a storm erupted, and we were drowning. And when it was over all I could remember was sitting at my mom's kitchen island, our smoothie bowls melting in the space between our cries, and us looking at each other in disbelief.

After a few moments of silence, Josh looked at me and asked with total genuineness,

"How can two people love each other so much, but be so much happier apart than together?"

I started to weep. He leapt up from his seat opposite me and pulled me close to him. He held me, and I cried into his chest, feeling safe in his arms even in the knowing that what he'd just said was so utterly true.

For the few months prior to reuniting in Seattle, we had both found a lot of relief in our aloneness. Peace in our autonomy. Joy in our freedom.

Was our apartness a revelation of what was already true? Were we already basically a long-distance couple, in a close proximity relationship?

These were the questions we grappled with along with dozens of others that arose in therapy and the spaces in between. And as these questions unraveled, so did we.

I saw Josh hurting in a way I'd never seen before. I saw him weep. I saw him furious, defensive, and at his limit. I saw him defeated, discouraged, and depleted.

At times, he looked like a child. I don't mean that in a cruel demeaning way—I mean that he looked like I imagined little Josh might if he was scared, sad, or hurting, and this innocence and vulnerability was the truest form of suffering I'd ever witnessed in him. I'd never seen him so emotionally distraught, and I was certain it was all my fault.

I retreated in the face of his suffering. I turned into myself with the only way I knew how to cope with seeing someone I loved in pain— self-blame, self-hatred, and guilt. I became passive, withdrawn, and lifeless. I responded to the pain of our conflict with a hopeless victimhood, believing that if I blamed myself enough and wore my guilt on my sleeve, he would see my sorriness and forgive me. I believed my own display of hurt would stop his.

And so, we became two hurt children, fighting over who had the biggest wound. Bleeding before one another, neither one of us with enough wisdom or courage to offer the first Band-Aid.

We didn't mean to fall into these roles. We didn't mean to fall into any of the roles we so blindly tumbled into over the years.

We simply did what we thought we were supposed to.

We co-managed the symptoms of my mental illnesses the only ways we knew how.

We traversed our individual differences the best we could.

We tried. We learned. And we practiced.

We built a foundation we were proud of over the years— "our communication box" we called it.

In many ways, the roles we played kept us safe from discomfort and far from conflict. We thought this was good, and we were reinforced for our ability to stay so in love.

"Your relationship is honestly so beautiful," my friends would tell me.

"I wish my husband was like Josh."

"You're so lucky to have a partner like him."

"You guys seem so in love."

We *were* in love.

I *was* lucky.

Josh *was* a husband and partner I was proud to be in relationship with, and who I was deeply grateful for every moment of our partnership.

What others saw on the outside was truly how we felt *inside* our relationship: in love, deeply happy, and lucky as hell. We loved each other fervently. We were fond of one another. We were kind. We were caring. So much so that we needed nothing and no one else but each other after a time—he took care of me, and I of him. I soothed his worry and overwhelm, and he cradled my insecurity and perpetual anxiety.

Somewhere along the way, our toolbox we so coveted and the knobs and screws that fixed and healed us became a weapon.

We had grown so accustomed over the years to saving one another. To caretaking. To leaning so heavily on one another, and in return caring for and supporting one another with such vigor that our dynamic had become a seesaw of doctor and patient, parent and child, caregiver and vulnerable other.

And in the months that came after Josh asked for a divorce, I started to question if our love was really the kind to be jealous of after all.

What if all our friends had love right—connected enough to feel a partnership, but disconnected enough to have autonomy and individuation?

In so many ways, we had lost that for ourselves. I had become so comfortable with the fact that Josh took care of my needs that I forgot how to take care of my own needs. Not only that, but I lost sight of what my needs *actually were.*

I didn't know what I liked or didn't like. I had a vague idea, but for the most part, I looked to Josh to decide those things for me. Or to tell me. Or to help me find out.

We were so engulfed in one another that we had lost our sense of *self,* and the natural flow of give, take, ask, respond, and the space between us that kept us autonomous and free had dissipated.

I think after a few months apart and tasting what it felt like not only to have no one to care for, but learning we could care for ourselves, created a firmness within us. A hardening of sorts, and new walls covered in signs that said, "I'm not your caretaker anymore. And I don't need you."

We didn't mean to do this—it was a natural retreat. A normal withdrawal after years of playing these roles. And I don't fault him or me for moving so far in the opposite direction.

He needed to.

I needed to.

We needed to.

We needed to learn autonomy. We needed to be reminded of our independence and ability to show up for ourselves and say, "what do *I* need?" We needed our freedom. Our selves as separate others.

And so, when we reunited in Seattle that January, there was fear and curiosity. Hope and trepidation. A willingness to reconnect and reunite, and a willfulness to relinquish the power we'd both so proudly discovered.

This was our work in therapy: coming to know our *selves* while trying to reunite our separate containers into a Venn Diagram of sorts, without falling back into the complete overlap and singular container of him, me, and our marriage that we'd been in for so long.

We spent countless hours in Ama's office doing everything we could to find a way back to each other. We put our heads together and attempted to re-fuse the tethers that once bound us. Try as we did to reconnect our wires, we came to discover time and time again that our systems had changed, and no matter how we configured them, our plugs no longer fit. And the more we tried to reconnect, the more we shocked the system and electrocuted our circuits.

When March 2020 came, we'd decided to try and take more time apart. This time, with more intentionality, more conscious communication, and more hope.

"I'll get the RV I've been wanting and tour around the US."

"I'll go back to Bali and keep writing and try to start my own business."

"And in six months, we'll reunite—"

"—Either here, there, or somewhere."

We shook on this, and on March 4, 2020, just one day after the first COVID case in the US, just miles north from my dad's home in Seattle, I flew to Bali, alone, again.

twenty-one.
CALLS WITH CARA

When I landed in Bali for the second time in March, I was flooded with memories. The landscape had changed, the trees had grown, and the landmarks I'd once recognized had somehow shifted. As if they too had been through something in our separation.

I still couldn't shake Pakshi's comment about my mother all those months ago.

In order to heal, you must first heal your relationship with your mother.

His words lingered in me, and while I felt I'd made steps towards his prescription since seeing him in October, I still couldn't see how it would help me heal my marriage.

As I worked on the parts of myself I perceived most important in healing my marriage (codependency, self-worth, boundaries, sex, and values), I kept returning to Pakshi's words:

In order to heal, you must first heal your relationship with your mother.

Pakshi wasn't wrong.

My relationship with my mother was particularly strained when I saw him, but I didn't connect it to my marriage, and I certainly didn't see how focusing on that first would allow me to salvage the kinks and cracks in our relationship.

Sure—the conversation I had with my mother before leaving Peru that October was nothing short of dreadful, but did that warrant a full pivot to remedying that conflict, and not the more pressing marital upheaval?

It was not abnormal for my mother and me to struggle with communication, and it wasn't surprising to me that when I told her Josh and I would be taking some time apart she responded with a gruff, "I had no idea this was going on," and a curt, "But you look so happy on your Instagram."

I was used to my mom personalizing my experiences.

If I was sad, she was sad. If I came to her with hard news, I hadn't told her soon enough. If I erected boundaries and wanted privacy, I wasn't fulfilling the expectation of the "close mother-daughter" relationship she hoped to have.

I was also accustomed to letting her down—the bed wasn't made quickly enough, the dishes not returned to their proper home, my depression not remedied in due time.

Nothing my mother ever said was outwardly cruel or hurtful—most of the criticism I experienced was packaged in nuanced, passive language, which made it that much more difficult to stand up for myself once I discovered how untrusted I felt—I had nothing to refer to, no single act or blaring event I could point to and say, "This is why I am constantly afraid of disappointing you."

Recognizing the patterns in our relationship took over a decade of therapy, and when I'd arrived in Bali the first time in October, we were still in the trenches of discovering why it was so hard for us to connect.

When the time came to call her from the plastic-covered couch from our Peruvian Airbnb and tell her the news that not only was I going to Bali, but my marriage was on the rocks, I was petrified.

I knew she would have some kind of reaction—whether it was to question my decision, to wonder why I hadn't confided in her previously, or say something about how hurt or sad she was in response to our marriage falling apart.

Curled in terror as I prepared for what I could only imagine would be a painfully upsetting telephone call, I coped ahead for all the concerns or line of questioning I might ensue:

I don't understand why you're doing this.
Have you really thought this through?
Is this what Josh wants?
Why didn't you tell me sooner?
I had no idea; you never tell me anything.
I'm shocked.
Have you considered any other options?
You really think this is a good idea?
You really think this is what you want?

I opted for a brief, boundary-laden representation of our plans, and was determined to keep the conversation short, cool, and neutral.

I wanted no fuss, minimal flare ups, and as few emotions as possible.

I'm a thirty-year-old woman, I reminded myself. *I'm an adult. I can make my own decisions.*

My heart pounded as I dialed her number. She was the first person I called—not because I wanted her to know first, but because I knew she'd ask who else I'd told, and I was worried about how she'd react if she knew her true place on the phone tree.

"Hi sweetheart, how's it going?"

"It's ok. I need to tell you something."

"Ok…"

"Josh and I have been having some problems, and you know I've been having health issues. We took a few days apart last week to try and clear our heads individually, and we both agreed I need to leave the trip. And rather than come home and live with you or dad and just feel really like, I dunno, like I don't have my independence, or something didn't feel right, so…I'm going to go to Bali."

I think at this point, my mom said, "Wow," and then remained silent for a few moments.

She said "ok" a few times, the way someone says "ok" when they have a lot to say but don't say anything at all.

I could feel the confusion through the phone. The shock. The disapproval. I sensed an utter sense of disappointment.

"I'm just in shock." She said bluntly.

"I know. It's a lot," I said, beginning to care for her feelings.

"I had no idea, you guys look so happy on your Instagram, and you haven't really shared any of this with me."

"I know, but you know Instagram doesn't show everything, and we've been private about some of this stuff."

"Why Bali?"

"I feel safe there, and I want to rekindle my relationship with myself. And it feels like a good place to do that."

"Ok."

I sat through a few sighs and scoffs. I waited, hoping to hear something else, hoping to hear an "I support you," or "I can't imagine how hard this decision must have been," or "you must be going through a lot," or "how can I be there for you?"

Instead, I got a few more questions, a couple more I-don't-understands, and a general sense of "well, good luck."

I spent weeks thinking about what I could have done to alter the course of that conversation. How I could have offered a longer backstory to soothe her shock. How I could have let her know exactly what I needed from her, rather than hoping she would know how to support me.

I would remind myself of what I'd learned in therapy:

"It is not the job of the child to care for the parent."

"It is not the child's job—no matter how old—to soothe the parent. It is not the child's job—no matter how mature—to tend to the parent's emotional needs."

She is my mother—my caregiver—the person who cradles and holds me when life is painful, the woman who offers wisdom when I am lost or don't know the way, the human who bears her natural gift of unconditional love no matter the mistakes I've made.

I know this now, and she and I know this now together.

But as Pakshi said, it took a long, long time for us to arrive here.

When I finally returned home in January and Josh and I started couples counseling, my mom was still completely baffled and unsure of how to speak to me. Our interactions were laced with passive undertones and anxiety, and she'd often make small comments like, "I guess I'm not allowed to know that" or, "I know I'm not supposed to ask these things."

One afternoon in late February, she came to say goodbye to me before I went to Bali for the second time. We had a few logistic things to go over (I was living in her condo that she normally rented out on Airbnb). I was prepared for her to arrive with a list of to-dos, a checklist to ensure the house was perfect and clean, and some doubt that I had done or would do what I needed to unless she wrote it down, read it to me, and reminded me.

We sat in the living room with the list of to-dos on the glass coffee table between us. My mother, legs crossed under a blanket, hands clasped on her knee, lips pursed and eyes watery from her own nerves. The heightened emotional state was palpable, but I couldn't bear to confront it.

"Well, I guess I'll go then," she said, as if creating a space in the room for me to finally share my deepest secrets with her, tell her the juice she wanted to know, divulge in the stories she thought she deserved to hear if we were ever to be close.

"What?" I said sternly.

I could feel my temperature rising. My cheeks were flooding, and my heart rate started to flutter. I felt like a fifteen-year-old teenager, stifled by my mother's passive air and determined to keep my world private no matter how hard she pressed.

"Well god Rachel, I don't know. I'm not allowed to ask you anything, you don't tell me anything, and I worry about you, you know. And I know I'm not supposed to say this, but I have to be able to tell you when I'm worried about you. I have to be able to tell my child when I'm worried about the choices they're making, I'm sorry but I do. I guess I'll just have to resign to the fact that I'll never have the close mother-daughter relationship all my friends have."

You have got to be kidding me.

Years of anger flooded my chest. I lost all control of my emotional state, and I started to weep and yell and do the best I could to use the language I'd learned to hold my truth together.

"Mom, you are allowed to be worried about me. You are. And you need to find a different place to direct that worry. You need to process your feelings about me and my marriage and what I'm choosing to do somewhere else, because this is not about *you*. This is about me, and Josh, and it is fucking hard enough for me to deal with my own confusion, guilt, shame, and fear, let alone carry yours.

"And I want us to be close. I do. But telling you everything all the time is not *how* I get close to you. And yeah, I know I've set a lot of boundaries in the last year, but that's because I'm going to therapy and doing the work to figure out how to have healthy relationships. What the fuck do you think I'm doing in therapy? I'm doing my work so that we can have a healthy relationship too. So, if you want us to have a relationship, you have to do your work too, because I've been doing mine for ten years and I can't do it by myself."

My whole body was on fire.

In thirty-one years, I had never stood up to my mother.

I'd run out of rooms and slammed doors and written notes in the margins of my diary for her to "keep out," but I'd never entered the space of real conflict where my anger and hurt was given space to breathe.

She sat there, paralyzed, and in terror.

"Rachel, I don't know what to say to that, I really don't." I half expected her to rebuttal—to come back with a "well you're wrong," or "that's just not true," or "I don't see how boundaries creates closeness."

But she didn't. She sat there, motionless, processing what I'd said and attempting to digest how viscerally I was experiencing this moment.

"Well," I said, mustering the only courage and breath I had left in my body before leaving it, "I don't know either. But I can't sit here with you anymore, and I need to go for a walk and calm down. So, I need to say goodbye to you. And I need you to know that this doesn't mean I don't love you or don't want to talk to you or for you to know me. It means *I do*, and this is the part where it gets really hard and painful, if you're willing to do this work with me."

I'm sure what I said wasn't as eloquent. It certainly wasn't graceful. I was flooded to the point of losing all connection to reality, and I couldn't be sure if anything I'd said was warranted or fair or cruel or even real.

I felt, as I had many times when trying to confront her in the past, unreal: as if my whole existence would suddenly be taken away from me.

"Ok," she said. I think she agreed because she didn't know what else she could do. She was shocked, and as I felt her trying to hold herself together, I felt myself resisting all the urges in my body to help her.

"Ok," I mirrored.

We stood up and walked to the front door together.

"Bye mom, I love you. I will call you when I'm in Bali." I smiled, just enough so she would know I meant it, but not enough to erase the truth of what I'd said. I wasn't going to erase myself to protect her feelings anymore.

I hugged her, and she left.

I immediately took a long brisk walk, monitoring my breath by the fog I produced in the cold Seattle air as I huffed up the streets of Queen Anne Hill.

I did it. I thought. *I am not responsible for her anymore. I am only responsible for me. And any feelings she has right now are not mine to hold. It's not mine. It's not mine.*

I repeated this as I climbed the hills, letting my heartrate simmer and my mind return to my body.

I didn't know it then, but this moment changed our relationship in ways I would never have imagined.

I had, at that moment in time, resigned to the fact that my mother and I might never be close. That maybe, we might instead, never have a relationship again.

In the months that followed I started writing more openly and with less concern than I ever had. I felt free to express myself and make choices without the fear of how it might affect her. I found more courage to tell her how what she said or did affected me or angered me, and I kept promises to myself about my boundaries and "nos." I made choices without running them by her, and instead I told her what I was doing without explaining myself or seeking her approval.

"I'm coming back from Bali and Josh and I are going to live in his brother's basement while we figure out where to live," I told her on a Zoom call late in March.

"Ok, that sounds great," she said genuinely.

As I found myself freer from concern of her emotional world (and not in a way where I suddenly had permission to intentionally hurt her: I want to be clear that absolving oneself of being responsible for someone else's feelings is not the same as never needing to take responsibility when your actions directly harm someone), I found myself more in tune with my gut, more aligned with my passion in life, and freer to fill the space in the world that I longed to occupy.

Days after arriving in Bali in March, the news of the COVID-19 virus was sweeping the globe, and like some kind of apocalyptic film, I watched hundreds of people flee Bali to their home countries—some who had been in Bali for years, others who had just arrived for a two-week vacation.

For weeks Josh and I went back and forth about whether I should stay or come home.

"I just don't know what will happen with the borders. I don't want to get stuck here for six months and not be able to see you."

"Me neither. I know we said we'd take more time apart, but I wouldn't want to *not* have the option to see you if you got stuck there."

We'd been working through The Gottman Institute's *7 Principles for Making a Marriage Work,* seeing Ama virtually on a weekly basis (together and separately), and working hard on our individual goals and self-work.

We were hopeful, confident, and more in tune than we'd been in almost six months.

"I'm going to think this over on my own and come to a decision without any input—I want to decide this from a place of what I need and want, not what I think my parents or society will approve of."

"You got it, Rach. I support you."

After a few days of meditating, journaling, and reflection, I decided it would be best to go home. While I was disappointed to have only been in Bali for a month (but truthfully, only in my guesthouse as I stopped leaving the house after the news of the virus), what I cared most about was reconciling with my husband. Bali would always be there.

At the beginning of April, I flew home.

At that time, there were no travel instructions or testing requirements—they didn't even have COVID tests in Bali yet. There was, however, a scramble to find plane tickets, as flight after flight got cancelled last minute. I was hearing horror stories of women showing up at the airport with all their belongings, hoping to fly home to their families for the first time in years, only to find their flight had been cancelled or their country's borders shut down during the time they'd left their nomadic homes and arrived at the airport.

There were only four flights back to Seattle in the month of April, and I bought a ticket as soon as I made my decision. I was lucky—my flights weren't cancelled, and I was able to get home.

I remember the woman I sat next to on the plane ride home. She called herself "Kitty Kat," and she was having a full-blown panic attack for the entire ten hours of my first flight to Tokyo.

"You don't understand, Rachel. This is my third time trying to get home. All my flights were cancelled. My uncle died of COVID, and these people won't even back away from me on the bus. *They* are just so disrespectful," she'd say while pointing her eyes towards the Japanese passengers in the seats beside us, "not caring at all about any of this, I mean, *we are in the middle of a pandemic*," she'd gripe, leaning towards me, holding my arm with her bare hand, and occasionally elbowing me as if to say, "we're the good guys."

In Tokyo we passed through "Quarantine," a lineup for temperature checks to clear us onto our next flight. Kitty Kat was nervous, and she was certain her temperature would rapidly increase just at the moment it would be her turn.

I lost Kitty Kat at baggage claim, where she waved her arms at me as if saying goodbye to a shipmate on the Titanic. I felt her panic in that wave, and hoped she'd find whatever she was looking for back home, not understanding that the interaction I'd just experienced was a tiny and real window into the xenophobia, racist violence, and trauma done to Asian people in the year to come.

Hours later, I landed in Seattle. Josh was waiting for me in his RV, and though less time had passed since our last separation, it felt as though I hadn't seen him in years.

We embraced, and I awkwardly climbed into his RV.

At rest stops we'd try to kiss and touch each other. Our hands wanted to remember where to go, our lips looked to find the nerve endings our tongues once delighted in.

I could feel Josh's eagerness to be with me, and I could feel myself recoiling. We drove the five hours to his brother's home in Leavenworth, and in that short window of time, I felt the thickening of my own anxiety fill the RV.

Ama continued to work with us via Zoom for the next month. After two weeks of self-quarantine, cyclical conversations about where we might live and what our futures held, and endless battles over the hurt Josh still felt and the suffocation I started to feel again, we had quickly fallen back into the cavernous hole of you vs. me, my hurt vs. yours, and the ominously unspeakable question:

Can we survive this?

It was in these weeks that Josh lost hope.

It was in these weeks that I lost patience.

It was in these weeks that we tiptoed around the real possibility that we might not be able to recover—at least not there, at least not then, and not in an honest or mutually agreed upon way.

We had so many brutally honest conversations in those last few days. About whether we were just friends. About whether we just needed to be alone, and for longer. About whether the problem was just that we had no home to live in, no jobs, no community to involve ourselves with, and no security or stable foundation to hold us while we forged the rising tide of our turbulent waters.

After Josh asked me for a divorce, I called my mom.

I was scared, again, like I'd been on that day in Lima. Scared of her own hurt filling the phone, scared of her own confusion robbing me of mine, scared that while my world was collapsing, she'd ask me to hold hers.

"Mom, hey. So, a lot has happened this week, and I don't even really know how to make sense of it or even explain it, but I'll try."

I told her about our charts and graphs for where to live. I told her about how hard we'd been trying in therapy. I told her how Josh asked me for a divorce, and how I'd moved to a condo down the road to be alone. I wept intermittently, trying to stay present but struggling to hold myself together.

I held my breath, prepared to field a line of questioning or disgruntled sighs.

Instead, my mother inhaled and said,

"Oh darling. Oh, my sweetheart. I am so sorry. Oh, my sweet girl. Imagine I'm right there with you, holding you. I am so sorry."

A hole that had been carved inside of me for decades suddenly flooded with warmth. I wept with gratitude, as if sealing the tender place that had just been mended with her words.

Days later when I shared the news with my brother, he asked the obvious question that we'd both been waiting to address: "So, how did mom take it?"

"Bro, I have no idea what sorcery has occurred, but she was so loving and supportive, and I felt closer to her than I ever have in my life."

"Wow, Rach, I'm so happy to hear that."

"Yeah, me too. She felt, for the first time in a long time, like my *mom*."

twenty-two.
TIGER'S NEST

"I'm realizing that even amidst the absolute shitshow that is grief, I am growing," I said to Ama in one of our weekly Zoom sessions.

By January 2021, I'd managed to find my way back to Bali—again. After almost a year of going into debt in LA and scrambling to stay afloat while managing my depression and grief, Bali opened its borders to foreigners, and I leapt at the chance to return.

I moved into the same guesthouse and room I'd stayed in the year before. Found the same views on my morning run. The same faces in the cabanas next to me. The same, but different.

When I landed in Bali, I expected to panic like I had the last time I returned. I expected to ask myself what the hell I was doing there, and why I thought it was a good idea to fly halfway across the world alone, *again*.

When I had returned the last time, so much had changed. The grass was a different shade of green. New construction paved the roads. Bali wasn't how I remembered it, and I had panicked.

This time, as I looked outside the window of my taxi from the airport, there was no panic. But not because nothing had changed.

As I witnessed the greener grass, the empty streets, and the changing buildings, I smiled.

As rice fields whizzed by and the scent of sambal seeped inside my mask, I thought, *of course. Of course things have changed. Trees fall. And new ones grow. Everything changes, but that does not change me.*

It was as if I recognized for the first time that what made me *real*—what made my life and existence stable and secure—is not what happens or doesn't happen *around* me.

I am real because of what happens inside me.

I am stable and secure because of what grows within me.

Wherever I am *is* the real world, because *I am the real world.*

I held these mantras close to my heart, hoping they would keep me safe in the next chapter of my life.

For the first few weeks after arriving, I was socially awkward and overstimulated.

Bali's COVID policy was:

"Wear a mask on your scooter or do fifteen pushups if the Banjar catch you without it."

Their measures for social distancing and wearing masks were next to none, and life there was, for the most part, normal.

Most restaurants are outdoors or open air in Bali, and most activities are done outside. Many people in Bali believed COVID was a hoax, while others were convinced Bali had reached herd immunity, so masks were a futile attempt to stop any spread.

Information in Bali is also not incredibly reliable, and while the government put out data about the numbers, I learned from the doctor who did my nasal swab after my first week in Bali that he was only required to report positive tests if the patients were locals.

As I grew more comfortable with socializing, I found myself wanting to have sex. There's not really a fancy way to put this. I wanted to be intimate with someone. I wanted to see if I could rekindle my relationship with sex, the way I'd hoped I could for years, the way I'd wondered about for months, the way I, like many human beings, had a natural and healthy desire for.

I downloaded some dating apps and tried my hand at internet flirting. I was clear that I wasn't emotionally available for a relationship, and, that I didn't want a one-night stand. I wanted a friendship, some kind of connection, and good sex.

I found out this was much harder than it sounded, and I gave up many times.

One Friday night, I went to a bar with some girlfriends. It was one of the first times I had been to a bar in over a year, and I was excited.

I put on an outfit I felt completely myself in, wore my hair in a half-pony (my new signature style), slapped on just a dash of mascara and strapped my fanny pack to my chest, and met up with my girls.

It had been so long since I'd felt joy. Since I'd been in the presence of other bodies and beings. Since I'd heard loud music and ordered a drink at a bar.

After too many drinks and a lot of laughing, I met the gaze of a guy across the dance floor. He was cute, and I liked his scruffy shoulder-length hair. We started talking, and I learned he was my age, also just out of a long relationship, and didn't live in the immediate area. Perfect.

We danced and talked, he bought me drinks, we held hands, and kissed. There was no spark or connection, just the right place, right needs, right time.

I went home with him that night, and this next part is not so easy to write, nor will it be so easy to read.

When we got to his cabana, I had been drinking for about five hours, and I was drunk. The kind of drunk where I lose pockets of time, where my memories are fragmented images, and where I lose my agency and ability to make decisions.

Immediately upon arrival, we clumsily undressed each other and started to have sex. He was rough, and I remember him pulling my hair, bending me over, and at one point, choking me so hard that I couldn't breathe.

I started to cry, and he stopped.

"Are you ok?" He asked.

"I don't know," I mumbled.

"Is it because this is the first time since your ex?"

I started to cry harder.

I wanted to say,

"No, you're hurting me, and I can't breathe."

"No, I'm having sex with a stranger and broke a promise to myself."

"No, you started choking me without asking first."

"No, you didn't put a condom on and didn't offer to."

"No, I am flooded by every other time in my life when I've been choked, when someone has put their hands on my neck without asking, when I let someone penetrate me and it hurt and I didn't say stop, when I left my body during sex because it was easier than saying no, when men pulled my hair and scratched me and didn't consider the fact that it was a person they were interacting with, and how I can't believe this is happening to me again.

I wanted to say all of this, but I was drunk, I was scared, and I had already in many ways resolved that I had lost my power. My body settled into her familiar place—into the safety of immobilization, and my mind had fallen into hers—into the belief she didn't exist here—in the sex arena—and that I was just a pawn now.

254

When I stopped crying, he started again. I lay on my stomach, motionless while he inserted himself in me. My cheek pressed against the pillow, my throat closed, my heart empty. I thought, "I just have to lay here until he's done. I just have to lay here until he's done."

When he finished, I got up and I left. He offered for me to stay, but I wanted to go home as quickly as I could.

When I got home, I couldn't stop crying.

I tried to stop the thoughts that flooded my head.

This isn't that big of a deal—Yes, yes, it is.

You should have said stop—I was crying, he should have seen that as a stop sign.

He was really drunk, he probably didn't know—Being drunk isn't an excuse for murder, and it's not an excuse for sexual assault.

You chose to go home with him—You are always allowed to change your mind in sex.

Maybe if you hadn't drank so much this wouldn't have happened—You getting drunk isn't the reason men think it's ok to choke a woman without consent.

I noticed the shame, the guilt, the self-blame, the protecting him, the lessening-of, the minimizing, the total internalization of everything I fought so hard against in my day-to-day life and advocacy erupting inside of my brain.

When I got home, I knew from years of education about trauma and the brain that it wasn't safe for me to be alone—my mind was too erratic, I was teetering on a state of panic that bordered suicidality, and I needed to feel safe.

My neighbor at my guesthouse had always told me that I could come to him, night or day, if I was struggling. He knew about my mental health issues, Josh, and my history. He'd been living in the room next to me since my first day in Bali sixteen months before, and he had become like a big brother.

Still balling uncontrollably and very drunk, I stumbled next door to his patio and gently knocked on his door. No answer. I tried again. Nothing. I felt the panic welling inside of me and clutched my face with my hands.

This can't be happening, this can't be happening, not now, not here, not this. Not this.

I curled up on his patio and started to rock back and forth. The air still hot and sticky, my body hard and cold, my heart losing her hope.

A few minutes later, I heard a creaking sound behind me.

"Rachel? What's wrong, what happened?"

I saw him, sleepy eyed and scared, peering out his sliding door.

"I—I can't, someone hurt me, I can't—"

"Ok, ok, it's ok." He came outside and sat on the ground with me. He put his arms around me and rocked me back and forth.

"Who hurt you Rach?"

"A guy, I was at a guy's house, and he was choking me, and I cried, and then he kept going and I just, I don't know I just lay there."

I heard myself say it out loud, and in my mind the thoughts came back.

You are so pathetic.

This is not a big deal.

You're being so dramatic.

People have rough sex all the time.

Why are you so upset about this?

You're overreacting.

He probably thinks you're such a drama queen and that you bring all of this on yourself.

I wanted to escape my body. To escape his gentle embrace. I was wrong—I didn't need his help, I should have coped with this alone, this wasn't a big deal, and I was being a fool.

"Did you know who he was? Where is he?"

"No, I met him tonight," I sobbed. "He's at his place, I came back here."

"Want me to report it? Or go after him?"

"No," I said, but I was somehow comforted by his wanting to protect me. By his wanting to track this person down. It was, somehow, validating. His reaction told me that what this man had done was wrong, that I was not overreacting, and that the hurt I felt was warranted.

"This shouldn't have happened to you. What happened wasn't ok. He shouldn't have done that."

I sobbed.

"I don't want to be alone, can I stay here?"

"Yes of course. I'll get you some water."

I stayed the night—the way I may have stayed with a good girlfriend, the way I may have stayed in my parent's bed on nights I had nightmares, the way I would with someone who's only intention was to keep me safe and protect my heart.

The next morning, I was still really shook up. The thoughts in my head had returned, and I did everything I could to combat them.

I knew, after so much work in therapy, after so much schooling and research, after social justice advocacy and working with victims of sexual assault, that what had happened to me was not okay.

I also knew that the panic I felt in the wake of the event, the tears I cried and the breaths I couldn't control, were also the ones I had been holding onto from every occurrence of non-consensual, unsafe, and terrifying sex I'd endured over the last eleven years.

I spoke to several friends the next day to tell them what happened. I'd learned in therapy that the more I talked about what happened to me the less power it would have, and the less shame I would feel.

I connected with people I felt safe with and told them what support I needed.

"Hey, so something really scary happened to me last night, when you have the space, it would be really helpful if I could talk about it with you. I just need to be able to tell someone—I don't need you to say or do anything, I just know this is the kind of thing that gets worse if I don't speak up."

Almost everyone (all women) I spoke to had a similar response.

"Ugh. That's disgusting. I'm so sorry that happened. What is wrong with men?"

It was one that said, "I've heard this story before. This has happened to me. And I'm used to hearing about this."

Not in a way that dismissed or excused it—but in a way that reminded me how normalized this behavior has become, and how conditioned we are to think "this is just the way it is."

One of my friends in Bali immediately offered to hold space, and we arranged for a phone call. After telling her what happened, she said, "Aw babe, well maybe this is a good reason to kind of take a look at your alcohol consumption. You know?"

I hung up the phone immediately.

"OH HELL NO." I said out loud, to myself. "HELL NO." I repeated, pacing rapidly back and forth in my bedroom, trying to stop the bubbling of rage building in my belly.

No. I thought. *That is not what this is.*

Immediately I had a flood of texts from her apologizing—she knew instantly she had said the wrong thing—and a harmful thing. I wasn't ready to talk to her, and I didn't reply. I didn't need to forgive her or absolve her guilt in that moment. I needed to honor my anger, feel it, and calm down so I could stay grounded and firm in my self-respect when I did tell her how her words impacted me.

Whether or not my drinking was an issue was a moot point. Even if I had drank too much, even if she was concerned about my alcohol intake, even if my level of drinking was in absolute direct connection to my risky behavior and carelessness with my own life, *it was not the same issue.*

When I was ready to talk to my friend, she asked if we could FaceTime so she could see my face and properly apologize. I said yes, and told her that first I wanted to say my piece before she said hers.

"Hey girl, so I know you feel bad and want to apologize, and I appreciate that. First, I need to tell you why I'm upset, and have you hear me. And I don't need an explanation from you, I just need an acknowledgment.

"Ok babe, totally. I'm here."

"Here's the thing. I know that I've been drinking more than normal, and that I'm using it to cope with my grief. I'm aware of that. *And*, it's a separate issue from this. My drinking and what this man did were two separate issues, and my alcohol consumption did not cause, create, or invite his actions.

"If an adult, *human being* has another adult, *human being* in their bed, and in the middle of intercourse that human being starts crying, an adult, human being should see that behavior and respond with, 'Oh my gosh are you ok? Let me get you a glass of water, I'll give you some pajamas and let's curl up and we can just talk or sleep, ok?'

"There is no reason—no matter how drunk someone is—to see a crying human in your bed mid-intercourse and think it's ok to *keep having sex*. The problem wasn't that I was drunk, or that he was drunk. Him *being* drunk isn't an excuse for him not knowing better. The problem is that if he had known better or been taught better or raised better, he would *already know* that those actions weren't ok, and even in his drunken state, would have known to stop.

"The same way that if I'd known all those years ago that my pleasure mattered or communication was important or I could say 'no,' I would have been prepared and practiced in doing that, even in a drunken state.

"And the fact that your response was, 'This is a cue for you to drink less' is part of the problem, because as women we internalize the same fucked up lie that somehow, it's our fault. That we asked for it. That if we had dressed differently or behaved differently or drank less, we wouldn't have attracted or allowed this.

"No. We are not the problem, we are not the ones who have to make a change. This is not acceptable—not for me, not for anyone—and we can't perpetuate that. I can't perpetuate it."

She inhaled and nodded, her gaze fully locked on me in a way that told me she was genuinely hearing, witnessing, and agreeing with me.

"You're so right. And I am so sorry. I knew immediately it was the wrong thing to say, and I fucked up."

I forgave her, and we went on to have a conversation about all the internalized messages we'd received. About the times we had been uncomfortable or felt unsafe in sex but thought we couldn't say no or tried to but weren't heard.

The next day, I received a WhatsApp message.

"Hey Rachel, it's Kurt, how are you? Hungover? Lol."

My heart started racing and I felt queasy. *Do I respond? Do I block him? Do I ignore him?*

I debated for a week whether I should reply. Part of me wanted to tell him how he'd impacted me. Part of me never wanted to speak to him again. Part of me felt anxiety and fear just thinking about what might happen if I did text him, and I imagined all the replies he might have or defenses he might put up.

I consulted my friends, and ultimately, decided to message him. Not for me, but for the girls he might meet in the future. So that he could know what he did that hurt me. So that maybe it wouldn't happen to someone else. Because maybe he had done this before, and he just had no idea how much damage he was doing, because so many other women like me felt terrified (and rightfully so) to speak up or face the person who hurt us.

I know that what happened to me is not nearly as horrific as what some women have endured. And I'm not suggesting that it is our responsibility as women, or victims of sexual assault, to teach our assaulters.

No.

It should never fall in the lap of the person hurt to educate the person who hurt them, nor should they be expected to confront or ever speak to their assaulter again.

Because I felt supported by my friends, eager to break a pattern in my own story, and safe enough to do so, I decided to message him. I drafted a text and ran it by my friends.

"I'm going to send this, and then immediately block him. I don't want to hear what he has to say or engage in conversation. What do you think?"

"Ok babe, whatever you need to do. We support you."

Ok, I can do this. For me. For some other girl. For future Rachel so she can remember her courage instead of what happened.

"Hey Kurt, I'm ok. Honestly, I was a bit shook up after last weekend. I know you were really drunk, and I was really drunk too. But I do remember crying at one point, and you were choking me while we were having sex and there was one point when I couldn't breathe. I debated saying anything at all, and I don't really want a response. I just felt it was important for me to tell you I was pretty freaked out the next day and decided to tell you, so you know how it impacted me."

Block contact.

I threw my phone on my bed and paced my room. I felt slightly panicked, a little relieved, and proud. As soon as the relief and pride came, the maybes poured back in.

Maybe I should have reported him.

Maybe I could have pursued something further.

Maybe, as the voice in my head still whispers, *I made too big of a deal out of it and I'm acting like a total baby.*

The courage I felt in the wake of that night kept me afloat, but the aftermath of the event itself soaked me like a thick, heavy rain. Not drowning, but not at peace. Halfway above the water, my face drenched in wetness, wondering when I might find relief from the storm.

In one of our sessions in the weeks to come, Ama said to me, "You have been mistreated in sex far too many times. More times than any human should—because one time is one too many.

And yet you keep showing up. I say this not to shame or judge you. I say this to reflect to you how *in spite* of the times you've been mistreated, you still have hope. You still believe in intimacy. You still want the closeness and specialness of sex. You keep entering the arena, because you haven't given up."

I choked back tears and thanked her for this reflection.

It was the hopeful line I needed to be fed, the strand of courage I needed to hold onto so I could know that maybe, someday, I might find myself in a safe and loving arena once again.

That what she said was really true, and that despite the hopelessness I felt in the months that followed, I hadn't given up, and I still didn't want to.

twenty-three.
LEAVE WHAT'S HEAVY

"Hey, so, I know I've sort of been skirting around this but, I found out how to get our divorce papers signed electronically."

I let out an audible sigh. Josh and I were rarely speaking, and when we did, it was only over the phone. I still couldn't see his face without breaking down into tears, and his voice alone was enough to stir a deep sense of sorrow.

I had dreaded this particular moment. I hadn't brought up the paperwork in conversation because I didn't want to have any part in the *wanting* of the papers to be signed. Still, it was the ever-looming topic that hovered over us, and eventually, we needed to address it.

In some ways I wanted to sign the papers—not because I wanted a divorce, but because I hoped it might create some ending to the limbo state I was in. A finality, of sorts. A line in the sand, a clear moment and action that could swiftly cut the middle-space so I could finally face forward knowing we were truly no longer husband and wife.

While logistically I knew it wouldn't be very hard to do, I could feel the weight of its finality approaching.

I wasn't wrong—it was one of the most emotionally taxing experiences of the year.

It wasn't so much the actual signing—although that event alone was full of sorrow and disbelief—as it was the weeks leading up to the moment, the anticipation, the dread, the revival of shock and grief, and the instant numbing and emotional paralysis that followed.

In the weeks before signing the papers, I knew I had some letting go to do.

I suppose I knew I'd have some letting go to do for a long time, but in that moment, I felt as if I had to squeeze in more—like I needed to wring out the juices of a year's worth of grief and prepare for a new cycle, a new fruit that might grow and ripen in the wake of a single signature ending an entire relationship.

I took myself to Uluwatu, a surf spot known for its beachside cliffs and crystal turquoise waters on the southwest tip of Bali.

With me, I brought a crystal I'd purchased while living in LA. It was a Bismuth crystal, which was rainbow-colored and looked like a tiny pyramid whose bricks had all been pushed slightly out, like a Jenga game or three-dimensional model of Mahjong. I'd read it was a helpful crystal to have while going through deep change and transformation, and I thought it was beautiful.

Somewhere along the way—I truly can't remember if it was before or after I arrived in Bali for the final time—the crystal broke.

I didn't think much of it other than, *bummer, my crystal broke!*

I kept both pieces, certain that getting rid of one of the halves would be bad karma.

One day I made a poll on my Instagram: "Does anyone know anything about crystals, and the significance of one breaking?"

Many people responded saying the breaking of a crystal symbolizes its completion: it has done what it was meant to do for the owner, and it's time to take it back to the earth. To bury it in the ground, and let it return home.

So, I brought the crystal to Uluwatu. To bury it.

On the last Thursday in January 2021, I walked from my hotel in Uluwatu to a beach nearby.

After walking down a gravel road just off the main road, I found a small temple and a steep staircase heading down the cliff to the beach below.

From the top of the stairs, I could see the white sand and blue waters below, lined with colorful fishing boats and little beach houses.

I took off my shoes and started down the stairs, trying not to move too quickly, but feeling a sense of urgency—almost excitement—around how what I was about to do felt so terrifying yet utterly important.

Lyrics whispered to me through the headphones in my ears.

"Breathe, go slow," they sang, and I tried to listen.

As I hopped down the steep stairs, I unraveled my dress and let my skin breathe in the heat of the sun. Barefoot and sweating, I made my way past the stilted houses and quiet rooms of what I imagined might be homes to older expats, lost souls like me from generations long ago.

When I hit the sand, I heard the giggles of children to my left. A Balinese family was sitting outside what looked like an abandoned restaurant, and I wondered if this beach had once been a bustling tourist attraction before the pandemic.

I dropped my bag, dress, and shoes on a rock above the tideline and walked towards the water holding the crystal in my hand.

I kept my headphones in, hoping that maybe the music would guide me or offer me some kind of sign as it once had so many years ago.

"Heavy" started to play in my ears as I approached the water's edge.

When I'd first heard these words almost fifteen months before—during my first round in Bali—I thought *leave what's heavy* meant *he* was the weight—*Josh* was what is heavy, and that it was him I had to leave behind.

When I heard those words that day at the beach in Uluwatu, it was as if I'd finally heard them for the first time; for the way they'd really been written. Or maybe, I heard them with a softer ear, and I allowed them to mean something more expansive and true than I'd once narrowly assumed.

Leave what's heavy behind.

I had to let go of my guilt and shame and fear—I had to let go of the weight that shrouded me, so that I could open my heart to love.

I had to leave behind the heaviness of my guilt for what I'd done to unravel our marriage. I had to leave the shame I carried for such a love ending at the water's edge. I had to leave behind the fear that I may truly be unlovable.

I had to leave *those* weights, *those* clouds, and *those* cloaks behind so I could let love in. I had to let go of the extra weight I'd carried all year so I could finally release my grip on *us*—and be left with the only thing that really existed, which was my still-present but never-the-same love for him.

That was it. I loved him, and we were not us. Those are both true, and when I let go of all the weight that clouded the simplest of truths, which is love, I could finally let him go. And I could still love him.

Holding the crystal out in front of me, I looked out at the horizon. I looked at the sky and water I'd seen so many times over the last fifteen months, each time in a new version of myself, at a new reckoning, and always with the question in my heart:

What happened to my marriage?

This time, the knowing and finality lay in the palm of my hand, and it was time to let go, and bury what was dead.

Without really thinking, I started speaking.

266

"I let go of guilt. I let go of shame."

As the wind swept up and the moment became real, tears started to well and my throat clenched.

"I release my guilt. I release my shame. I release my fear."

I knelt to the sand, and against all my bodily desires to run, I dug a hole. Placing the crystal in its crevice, I felt a surge of sorrow flood my body. I was burying my husband.

Not *Josh*, not *him,* but my *husband.*

A role that no longer was, a relationship that no longer could be, a way of knowing him and us and our togetherness that had finally died, and one I needed to bury.

As I covered the spot where I buried him—where I buried us—I wept.

Just as soon as I patted the sand flat over him, the ocean came and swept the spot clean, leaving no trace of where he'd been buried. As if now it was final—he was there, buried and gone, someday to wash to sea. Someday to be rediscovered by someone who would glean from his colorful and shiny edges.

I cried and placed my palms over the earth, longing to dig him back out but knowing this was goodbye. That this was when I finally let go.

And just as is true with all burials and death—this goodbye did not stop me from loving him.

We never stop loving those we say goodbye to. And yet, I could now love him without him being mine. I could love him without the possibility of reprieve. I could love him, and hold that truth, while knowing firmly in my body and heart that this was the end.

I stood up, choking on my tears, my body shaking and heavy with grief.

As I rose, the song playing in my headphones faded. And I wept more. I stood tall, growing. The sky turned dark to my left. It was time to go.

I started up the steep stairs, and as I did, I felt strong. I felt powerful. Not because I'd shed some kind of burden or freed myself from some man or some *one*—but because I'd freed myself from myself.

I'd shed a part of me that I'd created, a shadow I'd covered myself with so I could know just how dark of a world I'd created for my partner. A cloak I believed would prove my still existing love for him, demonstrate my remorse, and serve as a universal sign of for just how much I wanted another outcome.

But just as it was never important for me to prove our love to anyone but Josh, and just as I mistakenly showcased our love through my writing, photos, and social media, nobody needed to know that I loved him but *him*, and in my shrewd miscalculation, he was the only person who didn't feel it.

I was determined not to look back. To look forward as I walked sturdily and steadily up the stairs. I did, though. I looked back. Just over my shoulder to see the sea, to remember where I'd buried him, and to see where I had come from. I glanced behind me, took a mental photo, and turned to face the hill in front of me.

And as I did, a new song started to play:

Few thousand miles and an ocean away
But I see the sunrise, oh, just like the other day
Picture your eyes as I fall asleep
Tell myself it's alright, oh oh, as the tears roll by
Ooh, I wish I could feel your face
Ooh, I'm helpless when I'm oceans away.

part seven
wade in the water.

"But it's cold!"
I squealed.

"I know it is, darling."

"But it's dark!"
I giggled.

"I know it is, darling."

"But it's hard to swim!"

"I know it is, darling."

"Well, so why do you still get in?"
I inquired.

"Because, my darling, it is in the cold that I am reminded that I have a body. It is in the dark I remember there is light. And it is when the kicking and paddling becomes hard that I know I have something I am fighting for."

twenty-four.
LOOP OF LIFE

Sometime in February of 2021, after a month-long depression that left me cradled in the depths of the not-knowing—I started to think about dying again. In a way that I hadn't really thought about dying in almost twelve years, since my suicide attempt in college.

I was googling things like, "how many Xanax will kill me?" and "how tall of a building do I need to jump off to die?"

I would lay down to bed at night with the thought, *I probably won't last that long anyway,* and wake up to, *what's the point?*

Ama asked me one morning during this state, "When you have these thoughts, about dying, what is it you are hoping to stop?"

I paused.

I hadn't thought about it like that before. I wanted to answer her question, though—and this time not because I wanted to show her how wise or self-aware I was—not because I wanted to impress her or be good for her, but because I'd finally learned that her questions weren't for her benefit: they were for mine. Because I finally understood that not-knowing isn't dangerous, and questions from people who care aren't tricks to catch me in the not-knowing.

"I guess, I just want to stop the 'doing,' the responsibilities, the having to pay my bills and work, the 'supposed to's' and just the everyday things that for some reason feel so hard."

I let my shame show. I knew I didn't need to be shame-free for her. And while I felt ashamed about a reason for dying that felt so pathetic and unworthy of wishing I were dead, I didn't let the shame stop me from being true, because maybe the truth would lead to something I hadn't considered.

"I also just want to stop this cycle. This cycle that feels never ending, where I feel well and alive and like life is enjoyable, and then feeling out of control, lifeless, and hating myself."

Why, I thought to myself after our session that day, *why do I hate myself so much?*

I imagined myself at every age from birth, picturing little me in my mind's eye, asking, "Do I hate *this* version of me? Do I hate this four-year-old girl? Do I hate eleven-year-old me?"

The answer was "no" at every age, until I imagined myself at nineteen or twenty years old. At the height of my Eating Disorder, when she first found total control over me, and when I lost full agency of my body to mind.

"Ama," I said through tearful hiccups, "I think, I think that it's not me I hate so much. I think it's my Eating Disorder. I think it's her I want to kill. It's her life I want to end. But she's been with me for so long that I cannot separate her from me, and I'm afraid that I don't know how to kill her without killing myself."

272

"Ok," she said in her knowing and wise way. "Ok, this distinction is one we get to know now, and one we get to sit with, listen to, and honor. This is an important discovery, and we are walking this path together."

We talked a bit about pressure. About generational pressure, and the pressure to perform, succeed, and meet some bar that has become so impossible for the majority to reach and designed only for a small, certain type of person to achieve.

We talked about how many kids lost their lives at my high school to the pressure—while I was a student and in the years that came before and after me.

We talked about the intensity of the education system, and the hope and possibility that the way it is now might someday crumble, so that we can rebuild a home-away-from-home for our children that offers them tangible skills and support for life, rather than a funnel towards a slim and narrow chance of success, or a crushing and impending sense of failure and disappointment.

Ama's brother committed suicide a decade ago, and I always feel a slight pang of guilt when I tell her I'm thinking about dying. I know it's her job to hold that space for me, regardless of her personal experience, and still I know it can't be easy to relive losing him in the possibility of losing me.

When she asks me questions about my suicidal thoughts, I wonder if some part of it is so she can make sense of her brother's death. And I don't mind, because in her trying to understand him through me, her curiosity opens the door for us to deepen our own understanding of what it means to think about ending one's own life. And in our micro chasm of personal research, we learn to add language and color to a subject that has remained wordless and colorless for so long.

Suicide is hard to talk about.

I have thought about dying and ending my life more times than I would wish for anyone, and I still don't know how to talk about it.

I'm scared of hurting someone with my words. I'm scared of scaring people I love with the truth of my thoughts. I'm scared I'll worry people when they don't need to be worried and confuse them with the intense delicacy of the dialectic that exists in the reality of, "I want to die, but I'm not going to kill myself."

This dialectic lives in me.

When I am low, when I am lost, when I feel rejected or neglected or like I've failed. It lives in me like a constant truth.

"I want to die, but I'm not going to kill myself."

How do I explain this to the people who love me, who want to be there for me, without confusing them or discounting the also, very real moments when I actually *might* want to kill myself?

Suicide, like everything else and nothing else, is not black and white.

It is not, "I want to die," or "I want to live."

It is sometimes wishing everything could stop, it is sometimes thinking about death or dying, it is repeating the cruel words, "You'd be better off dead," it's the planning of and actual preparation for a true completion, it's the letter-writing or thinking about letter-writing, it's the attempting and failed attempts, it's the almost attempting and sudden intervention, it's the reaching out in moments when I don't trust myself, it's the reaching out in the moments when I fear it might *get* to a moment of not trusting myself, it's the days of hope and the days of joy, it's the wanting to live and choosing life, it's the *I'm still here*, and the *how long will I last?*

It is a complete spectrum, evolution, cycle, and *alive* experience.

It is suicidality.

It is a condition I live with at times, a state of being I battle, and I am carving out language and words for my experience of it daily.

In a session with Ama a few weeks later, I told her something about my suicidality that I had never told anyone.

"I often feel like my urge to end my life is not one of no longer wanting to be here, but one of longing to go home."

I held back tears as I said this.

"It's as if the constant battle is one between my soul's longing to return to the stars, and the knowing that I am here to experience life as a human, for whatever reason. It's as if every day I choose to be here is an effort my soul makes to remain in this human life, against all suffering, in order to fulfill some soul mission. The fight isn't not dying. The fight is staying alive."

It is in the belly of these conversations that I start to think I've made some sense of it all. I feel perhaps an upward turn, where I finally understand the *why*, so maybe I can stop the cycle.

While I've learned not to hold on too tightly to these insights, I sometimes still do.

I grab onto them, because for a moment, I think I've discovered some meaning, some answer that might finally end all my potential suffering, and why *wouldn't* I want to hold onto that possibility when it's hurting so bad?

Do I struggle so hard to make meaning because it offers me that sense of control I so long to have?

Or do I make meaning because I know in my soul that suffering is the human condition, and meaning is how we survive?

And do I not want to survive?

It was later in one of my conversations with Ama—when we started to check in daily because my suicidal thinking had grown bad enough that she asked that we touch base every twenty-four hours—that she said,

"I read somewhere, that for people who are suicidal, it is not the external reasons for living that keep them alive: it is not the people or experiences or jobs or passions, but the reasons that have to do with no one but themselves that are factors for survival."

I welled up when she said this.

I don't have a reason that's just for me. It's not that I don't have purpose or feel like I don't have value on this earth—I do think I have a lot to offer

and a lot to give. But I don't feel like there's anything for me to receive. Or maybe I don't believe I ever will receive what I long for. Or that I even deserve it.

My nights and days started to blend together between these conversations. I was losing track of time in the daily crying, losing track of purpose in the constant panic, and losing hope in the constant fighting.

I had grown too tired to find any reason. Too exhausted to be purposeful with my purpose. I had surrendered so gravely to the idea that I had no control or agency in my life, and beyond the space where surrender is productive and into the place where I had simply given up.

This, I think, is the paradox of purpose and the delicate walk that is surrender.

We fight suffering with purpose, and we use purpose to feel that we are in control.

We surrender control to ease suffering, and the loop continues.

To exit this cycle is to give up on life. To exit this loop is to choose death, or an unconsciousness that renders our soul equivalent.

This is how I often find myself: just between the circle of living and mystery of death, in a half-waking state. Dead to my conscious life; soulless, and teetering the edge.

To pull myself back into the loop of life, I have to find my reason.

And like Ama said, I have to find one that has to do with *me*.

This balance is what gives me grace when I over-control my life. This balance is what gives me strength when I lose control and feel helpless.

This balance is where I try, to the best of my human ability, to find myself again, and again, and again.

It is also why my Eating Disorder has been so difficult to let go of.

I equated my ability to control my body to purpose, and I mistook the attention I received when I was ill as reason. My Eating Disorder— yet another paradox—kept me in the loop of life while slowly killing me.

Year after year, I'd fall out of the loop of life and into the liminal space between living and not-living, and I'd choose my Eating Disorder as the hand to pull me back in.

What I was clueless to—at no fault of my own—was the misconception that the control I sought would keep me safe, and that the body I longed for would make me special.

The more I took her hand, the more familiar her grip became. And time and time again, I chose her familiar fingertips, hoping that *this time*, I would be strong enough and wise enough not to fall from her lofty promises and expectations.

I did, though.

I always fell. I still do.

There have been seasons of my life where I've chosen differently—and those choices were some of the most uncomfortable and terrifying ones I've ever made.

Somehow, though, when I'd start to teeter the edge and lose my balance in the loop, I'd fear falling outside of life and cling to her familiar grip.

And in doing so, I'd find myself again in a relationship with a part-of-self so cruel and abusive that I'd lose the longing to live all over again.

This is how I found myself in the hazy days of late winter, early spring of 2021. Teetering the edge, losing my balance, and engulfed in the abusive turmoil that is my relationship with my Eating Disorder.

"Ama, I think I need to go back to treatment."

She tilted her head, the way she would when she tried to hold back tears.

"I think, that if I want to keep Rachel—the real me, the one I love and like and care for—alive, I have to *really* kill my Eating Disorder. And as much as I want to be able to, I can't do that alone."

"Ok," she smiled—in a way that said, *I am so proud of you. I am so glad you came to this decision. I am so glad you are choosing life.*

As soon as I said this, I felt relief. I felt hope. I felt, for the first time in a year, that I might have some semblance of structure, some feeling of being understood, and some relief from the trying so hard to fight against something I couldn't fight all on my own, and that I didn't have to. That maybe, I could find a way back into the loop of life without her.

twenty-five.
SWIMMING LESSONS

"You know Rachel, you do not need to hurt to be a healer. You've been living with that story for a long time. And you do not need to hurt anymore."

I welled up a little, the way I do when Ama says something so simple yet perfectly made for me. The way I do when I know I'll remember those words forever, the way Josh's rolodex love lines would sit carefully on his shelf in my mind—a special place reserved for his wisdom, now next to a new shelf made for Ama and hers.

I never thought of Ama as someone who contributed to my marriage ending. I saw her as someone who contributed to our ability to reckon with the inevitable truths that Josh and I had buried in our bellies, and the ending was something we chose and came to all on our own.

Ama never told us what to do or not to do—she simply allowed us to be fully in our truth, present with our bodies and each other, and open to the possibility that there wasn't any rule book to follow when it came to mediation other than the one we made.

Ama did so much for us. For me. For Josh.

Some days, I really thought she must have favored us.

If she didn't, she did a really good job of making us feel like her only clients, and as though our relationship—both to each other and to ourselves—was the most important thing to her in the world.

So much so, that I sometimes wondered if she grieved our marriage too.

Did she feel responsible? Ashamed? Or did she know all along we wouldn't make it?

I asked her in one of our sessions in the spring of 2021 for her experience of us during our mediated sessions.

"Ama, you don't have to answer this if it crosses a boundary, but when I look back at those months in therapy, I know I can really only see what was going on through my filter, which was still so dirty and foggy and full of old gunk. And while I know that any amount of knowing won't change anything, I am curious to know what you saw."

"You know, Rachel, I've said this to you before, but you and Josh were so loving. So gentle. So kind. You're both incredibly self-aware and compassionate. And, I think you were both living in some stubbornness around what you weren't willing to budge on.

"Him on the fact that he felt unliked and unwilling to let go of that hurt until you accommodated him in the exact way he wanted. You in your resistance to be changed or influenced, and hostility towards him that wasn't his to bear.

"I think you spent so much of your childhood accommodating your parents that you were tired of it, and the pent-up resentment was coming out on him when he started to need it most. And I think he could never meet you where you needed to be met, and you have spent far too long falling to your knees to meet *him*.

"I think you both just needed a little more time to go inward individually and find these things. And I had hoped that you would get that time, but you didn't."

I cried when she said this. She was fair, and she was true. Her words resonated, and they landed softly. They didn't bring up shame or anger the way they may have a year ago. They didn't spin me into fury towards Josh for not giving us time or guilt for how I'd misconstrued old hurt for present-problem. I simply understood, and thanked her.

While our work together didn't result in the continuation of or healing of my marriage, it did result in the evolution of my own becoming. Of a massive reckoning with the ways I retreated and neglected my husband, and of a deep and lasting shift in how I've also neglected myself, and allowed so many people to neglect me too.

The lessons I learned during our work together—even as a result of the utterly gut-wrenching couple's sessions with Josh—have opened my eyes to possibilities I didn't think existed.

So much of what I learned happened in our sessions together, and so much happened in the moments between our sessions when the work really began.

When I'd break down in tears on the bus ride home from therapy in those first months in Seattle, wondering if this really was the last few threads of my marriage unraveling.

When my heart would fall to pieces as I lay awake at night, and I'd hold myself gently like I was just a little girl.

When I started to open my heart to my father, and he started to open his to me.

When I finally felt safe and empowered to tell my mother how I felt triggered by a conversation we'd had, and she held the space and listened.

It happened when I practiced saying "no," expressed anger, and showed up vulnerably and truthfully in the presence of male friends.

It happened when I witnessed growth not only in myself, but in the important people in my life who showed me how deeply they also valued our relationship and wanted to be a part of the web of work I was hoping to cultivate, not just for me, but collectively.

It was in these spaces and moments that I learned.

And it was with the unconditional support, tenderness, and wise space that Ama created in her therapeutic arms that I was safe to learn, experiment, fail, and try again.

I learned that everything in life is a give and take.

It is an energy exchange—always. When we give too much, we resent, retreat, and push others away. When we take too much, we hurt, undervalue, and pull others close.

If we are in a pull-pull, we are not in any state of harmony, flow, or tenderness. If we are in a push-push, we are barricaded against one another, forcing ourselves and our needs against a wall that will not budge.

When one person in a relationship is always in push and the other in pull, we live inside the world of only the one who is receiving, and the relationship lives inside the body and home of only one half of the whole.

Give and take is not a trade, nor is it about keeping score.

It is gentle attunement. It is paying close attention to when the tides are high, and honoring the boundaries of the water so we can carefully put our boats to sea. It is a delicate dance, a weaving of hearts and bodies, and two threads whose coils run smoothly together, in constant awareness of when the line grows too taught and requires a softening.

I learned I am not responsible for anyone's feelings but my own.

Yes, I am responsible for my actions, and if my actions hurt another human being, I am responsible for acknowledging, owning, and repairing my mistake. But the emotional turmoil, the suffering, and the hopeful recovery of another being's pain—that is not my responsibility to bear.

It is not my job to fix or solve the hurt that other's carry.

To help another is to offer the safety and space for them to make those changes. I can offer my knowledge and tools, bear witness to them so that they may be seen, and hold them in my arms so they know that they are loved. But what they ultimately *do* with that love, how they choose to move forward and carry on, that is not in my power.

Nor is it in anyone else's to save or fix my own hurt.

Yes—to soothe and be soothed by those who love us is a real and biologically valuable part of healing. We are meant to co-regulate, and to seek comfort in our communities. And, soothing does not mean mending. Only I have the power, agency, and choice to mend what hurts me.

I learned there are no "bad" feelings.

Our feelings are normal, physiological responses to our experiences. Everything that happens in our life stimulates a physiological response: our brain interprets what it observes through our senses and uses both historical reference and survival instinct to determine how to "feel" about what is happening. Our brains do this for both sensory information that comes "in" from the outside world (the unfriendly face of a stranger, being hit by a car, smelling a foul odor) as well as what comes "up" from inside of us (our stomach grumbling, an infection, preparation for a bowel movement).

Not all senses initiate a large emotional response: a hunger cue might quickly communicate our appetite and cause us to find food to satiate that well-oiled response. But sometimes, both our internal and external experiences can stimulate an intense emotional response, whether because our brains use historical, traumatic references to misinterpret the present moment as dangerous, or, because the event itself stirs up the hormonal response that is appropriate for the occasion.

When our boundaries are crossed, when we are taken advantage of, when we are betrayed, rejected, or abandoned, we *feel*.

We feel angry, we feel confused, we feel sad, we feel insecure, we feel disappointed, and so much more. These emotions are stirred by the real hormonal burst that occurs when our brain detects that what our bodies and minds had created as a reality is now altered, changed, or immediately destroyed. This sets us out of equilibrium, and we *feel*.

Our feelings do not mean there is something wrong with us: it is quite the opposite. It means we are *working*. It means our brains and bodies are working in tandem to observe and respond to our world tangibly and viscerally, so that we can learn what we need to return to equilibrium.

I learned that trauma causes these working wheels to have error.

When we experience trauma, the brain struggles to cope with an event that is so beyond the scope of imaginable hurt. This leaves our systems in a state of constant confusion, where we misinterpret non-threatening events as threatening, safe experiences as unsafe, and associate generally "normal" senses with danger. This is when our feelings misguide us, and this is why trauma work is so important.

Discovering how our trauma has impacted the function of our physiological system allows us to repair and rewire the cogs that are either on high alert or completely dulled, so that we can accurately appraise danger *and* fully embrace pleasure. Because pleasure, joy, and delight are just as much a part of the physiology of our emotional spectrum, and they too are meant to be felt.

I learned that love—*real love*—love that is tender, safe, and fluid, love that is built on deep connection, trust, and intimacy, love that honors differences, freedom, and independence, love that seeks to honor and support, not own and merge with—is boring.

It *feels* boring—at least to me or those who's measure of love is built on chaos, scarcity, or not-knowing—because it is safe, stable, and tender.

I learned that many of the challenges I faced in life—many of my personal insecurities as well as the corners I found myself in when in relationships—were born and bred from a long, long history of capitalism, misogyny, patriarchy, racism, sexism, homophobia, fatphobia, ableism, and gender inequality.

And if I want to feel fully alive, well, and in flow with life, part of that work is dismantling every single belief I carry that is a result of the systems who have prioritized money, whiteness, men, heterosexuality, ableism, and power over all other humanity for generations—a reconciliation with a system that harms me and a system that I benefit from.

I learned that the culmination of my years and years in therapy is not about unlocking some secret trauma or wound, but rather about constantly cultivating self-awareness, harnessing life skills for better living, and leaning towards support instead of away. And that the reason I've turned away from support for so long is because we aren't taught how to help each other with mental health, and I started to believe it would be easier to turn inwards than feel misunderstood again and again and again.

I learned that ultimately, self-awareness is only the foundation for everything that's to come, and that no amount of knowing can un-change, undo, or erase what has happened to me.

That self-awareness, like a rich soil, must be well fertilized and tended to. But unless we plant seeds for flowers to grow, we simply live our lives digging holes in the dirt, looking for a rose that will never bloom.

"I have spent the last year—from May until about a week ago—sense-making," I said to Ama in a session in late February, "trying to answer the question *why?* And *how?* And *what happened?* I realized that the answers to those questions only led to more questions, and that more questions only led to more suffering. And it wasn't until I stopped asking *why* that I finally found what I was looking for."

Divorce—at least for me—was a cataclysm of not-knowing. Of returning to deep insecurity. Of shaking foundations and stability. Of rebuilding from scratch. Of a deep dive away from what's been true and certain and known into an abyss where nothing is certain, and nothing is known.

And ultimately, this is what human life is.

Great uncertainty. Great unknowing.

We don't have the luxury of knowing everything, and we don't have complete control. And in the trying so hard to lasso life—we move

285

through the world like wild animals, trying to capture a wet hurricane in our hands.

But when we do, we simply become storm chasers—perpetually caught in the eye of the storm, spinning faster and further from earth, and swept away from the stability and calm below that we thought we might find in the capture.

So one day that spring, I stopped asking why. I stopped chasing the storm.

I watched the hurricane as it grew smaller in the distance.

And when I did, I felt some peace. I felt some calm.

And for the first time in a long time, I didn't blame myself for what happened to us. I didn't blame him. I didn't blame anyone or anything, because blame is never what it was about.

He was not the hurricane.

Neither was I.

Neither were *we*.

And now that the storm has passed and I am sitting still, I can see him there on the other side of the dusty plane. I can feel myself here on the ground. And while my heart still hurts, I'm not asking why, and I'm not suffering in the tethered space between here and there, between wanting and longing, between not-knowing and knowing.

Time and time again, I am reminded that these lessons are just small seeds.

That in time, they will have grown into something completely different, the way all things do. And I will look back and laugh at how in this moment, they feel so new, so important, and magnanimous.

This is also one of the greatest things I have learned.

That ultimately, I know nothing.

And as soon as I think I've learned it all—as soon as I think that I've reached the final place or the finish line, I'm simply at another fork in the river, preparing for a new flowing stream.

twenty-six.
BRIDGE

On March 3, 2021, Josh and I spoke on the phone for the first time in a month—the last time we'd talked was to discuss the logistics of our divorce paperwork, taxes, and anything else clerical related to the end of our marriage.

Since the moment Josh asked for a divorce, he had told me he wanted us to be friends. How he hoped and still hopes that somehow, someway, we could still know one another and be in relationship.

I wanted that too. I really did. But I had no idea how to do that. I had no idea how to make the leap from in-love to regular love. From lover to friend. From person who knows my every move, breath, and nuance, to person who catches up with me every couple of weeks.

How could I build that bridge with so much hurt, pain, and loss underneath it? When the river that bellowed below was so turbulent and full of memory? When our hearts, tears, and history lay behind me?

How, I wondered, *do I leave behind the story of us that was so real, so potent, so loving, and cross over, knowing we can never go back?*

I lived on this bridge for all of 2020.

Taking one step closer—trying to move my body across the river, clutching the railings of the bridge, and looking over my shoulder time and time again. Wondering if I turned around and went back, if he might come with me.

Each time I'd look up, I'd see him there on the other side.

Probably eating a banana, laughing, or patiently waiting for me to be ready.

He was already there, on the other side.

He moved there, I think, as fast as he could because he knew one of us needed to. That if neither of us crossed the bridge, we'd be stuck in limbo forever.

I couldn't see it this way for a long time. As an act of love. I saw it as a dismissal of our love. I saw his ease or quickness to move into friendship as an insult to the realness of our relationship. A sort of metaphorical fuck-you to the grief I was feeling, and the uncertainty and trepidation with which I set foot on that bridge.

I wanted him to honor our marriage the way I was honoring it: I wanted him to feel sad, to feel torn apart, to be unsure, to question if it was right. I wanted him to hurt like I hurt, because then I would know that what I felt we lost was real.

I didn't want to imagine a world where the ten years we had together weren't as magical and important as I believed them to be. And if he wasn't hurting too—if the other half of that ten-year equation wasn't in as much pain as I was for losing it—then there was a very real possibility I had been wrong all along.

288

I'd like to think that Josh crossed quickly because he honored our relationship. That he crossed quickly so that he could be there to receive me when I was ready. That he crossed quickly so there could remain a bridge between us, so that there could be a path for me to meet him again somewhere new. And in some ways, I wonder if he sacrificed his own grief so that I could have mine.

In the days, weeks, and months after That Day in May, I had so many acquaintances and new friends in LA and Bali respond to the fact that I was in the middle of a divorce with,

"We'll help you get over that ass hole!" or

"You must be so relieved!" or

"You'll be better off!" or

"Congratulations!" or

"You'll find someone better."

These people didn't know me very well, and they certainly didn't know Josh.

I was appalled that this was the natural response for so many. I understand that divorces can be terrible and nasty and end for reasons much worse than what Josh and I endured. And still, it is not enjoyable, fun, or exciting to end a relationship.

To these comments I would always sternly turn towards the speaker and say, "Don't talk about him like that. Josh was and is an incredibly good man, and I care deeply about him. And when you make comments like that, you're also insinuating that for ten years, I made a poor choice. And I didn't. I made a great choice, day after day after day."

Even for people whose relationships are abusive, traumatic, or confusing—those people did not make a poor choice. They made the best choice they could based on what they knew, and to tell someone at the end of their relationship, *"you'll find someone better out there,"* is to add a layer of already existing shame onto that person that who they partnered with the first time around wasn't right, and they will need to choose better next time.

Love doesn't work that way. We don't select people from a panel—and while dating shows and dating apps might condition us to think otherwise—love and relationships are so much more complex than a single choice.

For me and for my relationship with Josh, I regret nothing. I am proud of the relationship we had, the love we created, and the way we have and still are navigating what it means to be in relationship now.

When I spoke to him on the phone that day in March of 2021, I told him that I was going to be done with this book, and soon.

"So, you're in my book. And, you couldn't really not be, because you've been in a third of my life, so naturally you're a part of my life story. The same way my parents are, the same way my friends are. And I plan to talk to them too. I don't expect you to read it, but if you wanted to review it before I publish it, I'm open to that. Also, if you don't want me to use your name, maybe this is your chance to finally be called Abraham."

We both laughed.

"You remember that?!" He asked gleefully.

"Of course!"

"You know it's funny, I was actually thinking about that today—how growing up I always wanted to be called Abraham and even made my teachers call me Abe in elementary school. You know Grandpa Abe—he's going to die soon—that isn't even his real name?"

"What?!"

"Yeah, I never told you that? His real name is Thomas. He just started telling everyone to call him Abe. So, I figured when he goes, I'll take on the role of Abe from now on."

We both laughed—big, real, belly laughs.

"Look, Rach. I knew I would be in your book. And the thing is, I know you would never paint me in a light that is hurtful or malicious. I also know that if you write something about me that makes me look like an idiot, it's probably because it's true and I did something dumb. I'm

290

not perfect. And, I like myself. I think I'm a pretty good guy. So even if someone else reads it and thinks, 'Aw this guy's a total dummy,' I can handle that. This is your life, your words, and your experience. I'm not going to take that away from you."

I started to cry.

"Oh no, what did I say?"

"No, no, these are tears of gratitude, respect, and appreciation. That is just such a kind and loving response. Thank you, Josh."

"Oh, ok good."

I choked back tears and thanked him again.

We went on to talk for the next forty minutes—about our philosophies, about the thoughts we'd had recently about consciousness, about his big ideas discovered while hiking solo and my idea dumps on my notepad app. We laughed. I cried. We didn't caretake, we interrupted each other to say if we'd been misunderstood, and we flowed.

I felt, in that moment, that I'd met him on the other side. That the work I'd done for myself over the year in order to cross the bridge was met by the work he'd done to keep himself there. And there, on the other side, we met again, as once lovers, as hopeful friends, and as two separate, but equally interested and supportive others.

Before we hung up the phone, he said one more thing to me.

"Just remember, when you start to worry about how your book might impact me, that I know you Rach. I know you really well. And whatever you need to do or whatever you write is going to be exactly right for you. I think that's what I'm trending towards, you know? Just that ultimately, we all have to and get to do whatever is right for us."

I closed my eyes and pictured him there in front of me.

Gently placing each hand on my shoulders and turning me towards him, the way he always would when he wanted me to really hear him.

I'd look up at him, the way I always would, and he'd tilt his head down as if to try and come a little closer to my level—lovingly, earnestly.

The way he always would.

"Rachel?"

"Yes?"

He'd meet my gaze, and with a very serious smile say,

"There is no right way. There is only the way you do it."

acknowledgments

This book would not be possible without the love and support of my mother, the trust and acceptance of my father, the adoration and stability of my brother, the vulnerability and courage of my friends, and the wisdom, persistence, and unwavering faith of my therapist.